HOW TO DO LIFE
A Buddhist Perspective

Books by Traleg Kyabgon

Actuality Of Being: Dzogchen and Tantric Perspectives, Shogam Publications, 2020, 9780648332176.

Vajrayana: An Essential Guide to Practice, Shogam Publications, 2020, 9780648332152.

Desire: Why It Matters, Shogam Publications, 2019, 9780648129318.

Luminous Bliss: Self-realization Through Meditation, Shogam Publications, 2019, 9780980502251.

Integral Buddhism: Developing All Aspects of One's Personhood, Shogam Publications, 2018, 9780648114802.

King Doha: Saraha's Advice to a King, Shogam Publication, 2018, 9780648114864.

Song of Karmapa: The Aspiration of the Mahamudra of True Meaning by Lord Rangjung Dorje, Shogam Publications, 2018, 9780648114864.

Karma: What it is, What it isn't, and Why it matters, Shambhala Publications, 2015.

Four Dharmas of Gampopa, KTD Publications, 2013.

Asanga's Abhidharmasamuccaya, KTD Publications, 2013.

The Essence of Buddhism: An Introduction to Its Philosophy and Practice, Shambhala Publications, 2002 & 2014, 9781590307885.

Ninth Karmapa Wangchuk Dorje's Ocean Of Certainty, KTD Publications, 2011.

Influence of Yogacara on Mahamudra, KTD Publications, 2010.

The Practice of Lojong: Cultivating Compassion through Training the Mind, Shambhala Publications, 2007.

Mind at Ease: Self-Liberation through Mahamudra Meditation, Shambhala Publications, 2004.

Benevolent Mind: A Manual in Mind Training, Zhisil Chokyi Ghatsal, 2003.

Photo facing page: Traleg Kyabgon Rinpoche the Ninth

HOW TO DO LIFE
A Buddhist Perspective

Traleg Kyabgon

Foreword by Ringu Tulku Rinpoche

SHOGAM
PUBLICATIONS
2021

Shogam Publications Pty Ltd
PO Box 239 Ballarat Central
Victoria, Australia, 3353
www.shogam.org
info@shogam.com

First Edition

Edited by Salvatore Celiento

Designed by David Bennett

Library Reference
Kyabgon, Traleg, 1955
How To Do Life: A Buddhist Perspective

Printed book ISBN: 978-0-6486863-4-7
E-book ISBN: 978-0-6486863-5-4

DEDICATION

Dedicated to you, the readers of the teachings of the great Traleg Kyabgon Rinpoche the Ninth.

Contents

Section Four: Happiness

Foreword

During Traleg Kyabgon Rinpoche's life, he taught extensively, not only providing translation and commentary of Tibetan Buddhist texts, but also direct and spontaneous teachings that were very practical, and gave down-to-earth advice on how to do life better. Rinpoche gave advice on how we can review and manage our relationships with ourselves, others, and the world in such a way that can enhance our experience of life generally, and how we can more heroically face the many challenges life presents. *How To Do Life* is a collection of teachings given by the Traleg Kyabgon Rinpoche on topics such as love and relationships, understanding emotions, and working with depression and destructive emotions. Rinpoche provides a fresh approach to reviewing our experience, and explains the Buddhist perspective on building awareness and reducing suffering. It provides insights that can help us all *Do Life* better.

Ringu Tulku Rinpoche

Biography of Author

TRALEG KYABGON RINPOCHE IX

Traleg Kyabgon Rinpoche IX (1955-2012) was born in Nangchen in Kham, eastern Tibet. He was recognized by His Holiness XVI Gyalwang Karmapa as the ninth Traleg tulku and enthroned at the age of two as the supreme abbot of Thrangu Monastery. Rinpoche was taken to Rumtek Monastery in Sikkim at the age of four where he was educated with other young tulkus in exile by His Holiness Karmapa for the next five years.

Rinpoche began his studies under the auspices of His Eminence Kyabje Thuksey Rinpoche at Sangngak Choling in Darjeeling. He also studied with a number of other eminent Tibetan teachers during that time and mastered the many Tibetan teachings with the Kagyu and Nyingma traditions in particular, including the *Havajra Tantra*, *Guhyasamaja Tantra*, and the third Karmapa's *Zabmo Nangdon* (*The Profound Inner Meaning*) under Khenpo Noryang (abbot of Sangngak Choling). Rinpoche studied the *Abhidharmakosha*, *Pramanavarttika*, *Bodhisattvacharyavatara*, *Abhidharmasamuccaya*, *Six Treaties of Nagarjuna*, the *Madhyanta-vibhaga*, and the *Mahayanuttaratantra* with Khenpo Sogyal. He also studied with Khenpo Sodar and was trained in tantric ritual practices by Lama Ganga, who had been specifically sent by His Holiness Karmapa for that purpose.

In 1967 Rinpoche moved to the Institute of Higher Tibetan Studies in Sarnath, and studied extensively for the next five years. He studied Buddhist history, Sanskrit, and Hindi, as well as Longchenpa's *Finding Comfort and Ease* (*Ngalso Korsum*), *Seven Treasuries* (*Longchen Dzod Dun*), *Three Cycles of Liberation* (*Rangdrol Korsum*), and *Longchen Nyingthig* with Khenchen Palden Sherab Rinpoche and Khenpo Tsondru.

When Rinpoche had completed these studies at the age of sixteen, he was sent by His Holiness Karmapa to study under the auspices of the Venerable Khenpo Yesha Chodar at Sanskrit University in Varanasi for three years. Rinpoche was also tutored by khenpos and geshes from all four traditions of Tibetan Buddhism during this time.

Rinpoche was subsequently put in charge of Zangdog Palri Monastery (the glorious copper colored mountain) in Eastern Bhutan and placed under the private tutelage of Dregung Khenpo Ngedon by His Holiness Karmapa to continue his studies of Sutra and Tantra. He ran this monastery for the next three years and began learning English during this time.

From 1977 to 1980, Rinpoche returned to Rumtek in Sikkim to fill the honored position of His Holiness' translator, where he dealt with many English-speaking Western visitors.

Rinpoche moved to Melbourne, Australia in 1980 and commenced studies in comparative religion and philosophy at LaTrobe University. Rinpoche established E-Vam Institute in Melbourne in 1982 and went on to establish further Centers in Australia, America, and New Zealand. For the next 25 years Rinpoche gave weekly teachings, intensive weekend courses, and retreats on classic Kagyu and Nyingma texts. During this time Rinpoche also taught internationally travelling extensively through America, Europe, and South East Asia and was appointed the Spiritual Director of Kamalashila Institute in Germany for five years in the 1980's.

Rinpoche established a retreat center, Maitripa Centre in Healesville, Australia in 1997 where he conducted two public retreats a year. Rinpoche founded E-Vam Buddhist Institute in the U.S in 2000, and Nyima Tashi Buddhist Centre in New Zealand in 2004. In 2010 Rinpoche established a Buddhist college called Shogam Vidhalaya at E-Vam Institute in Australia and instructed students on a weekly basis.

Throughout his life Rinpoche gave extensive teachings on many aspects of Buddhist psychology and philosophy, as well as comparative religion, and Buddhist and Western thought. He was an active writer and has many titles to his name. Titles include: the best selling *Essence of Buddhism; Desire: Why It Matters*; *Vajrayana: An Essential Guide to Practice*; *Moonbeams of Mahamudra*; *Karma What It Is, What It Isn't, and Why It Matters*; *The Practice of Lojong*; and many more. Many of Rinpoche's books are translated into a number of different languages including Chinese, French, German, Korean, and Spanish. Rinpoche's writings are thought provoking, challenging, profound, and highly relevant to today's world and its many challenges.

Rinpoche was active in publishing during the last two decades of his life, beginning with his quarterly magazine *Ordinary Mind*, which ran from 1997 to 2003. Further, Rinpoche founded his own publishing arm Shogam Publications in 2008 and released a number of books on Buddhist history, philosophy, and psychology and left instructions for the continuation of this vision. His vision for Shogam and list of titles can be found at www.shogam.com.

Rinpoche's ecumenical approach can be seen in his other activities aimed at bringing buddhadharma to the West. He established the biannual Buddhism and Psychotherapy Conference (1994 - 2003), and Tibet Here and Now Conference (2005), and the annual Buddhist Summer School (1984 to the present).

Traleg Kyabgon Rinpoche IX passed into parinirvana on 24 July 2012, on Chokhor Duchen, the auspicious day of the Buddha's first teaching. Rinpoche stayed in meditation (*thugdam*) for weeks after his passing. A traditional cremation ceremony was conducted at Maitripa Centre and a stupa was erected on the center's grounds in Rinpoche's honor.

It is a privilege to continue Rinpoche's vision and initiatives, and to continue to make the profound teachings of Traleg Kyabgon Rinpoche IX given in the West for over 30 years available through his Centers' activities and Shogam Publications. Rinpoche's Sangha hope that many will benefit.

Acknowledgements

Thank you very much to the unsurpassed Traleg Kyabgon Rinpoche the Ninth for giving us these precious teachings so that we all may suffer less and learn the nature of true happiness. Thank you very much to Ringu Tulku Rinpoche for the beautiful foreword. Many thanks to Traleg Khandro for her invaluable guidance in editing these teachings and for elucidating the meaning of Traleg Kyabgon Rinpoche's words. Many thanks also to David Bennett for formatting the text and creating the beautiful cover design and thank you to Anthony Kramer for transcribing many of the teachings that make up this book, and to all of the transcribers who do so much important work.

Salvatore Celiento

Editor's Introduction

The power of Traleg Kyabgon Rinpoche's teachings have a profound impact on the spiritual path, everyday life, and relationships of those who have the great fortune to hear, contemplate, and practice meditation with them. Rinpoche's teachings translate misunderstood concepts into clear, current, and relevant language that is appropriate for all students living in the modern world. This profound ability to bring the Buddhist teachings to life with such vibrancy is a great gift to us all, those who seek to lessen suffering, increase happiness, and be of skillful assistance to others.

According to Buddhism, the nature of our relationships and the world is that we are interdependent. We depend on each other for survival, happiness, material needs, and needs for love and affection. In this case, when we benefit others, we also benefit ourselves. According to the teachings of this book, there is also nothing wrong with wishing that in this life, we ourselves experience happiness. In fact, happiness should be one of our major goals. When we benefit ourselves in the proper manner, we are also better able to assist others to suffer less and have greater joy, love, compassion, and fulfillment.

In this book, Rinpoche elucidates the topics of happiness, relationships, suffering, emotions, how to lead a meaningful life, and many other aspects of our worldly and spiritual lives. These profound, direct teachings provide the key to unshackling ourselves from constrictive forms of behavior, thinking patterns, and emotions. If we take the words to heart, Rinpoche's teachings have the ability to liberate us from that which prevents happiness, meaning, and fulfillment.

These teachings are different from the commentaries on classic Buddhist works of literature in that instead of following the outline of a text, they are an outpouring of spontaneity from the heart of one the greatest masters of Tibetan Buddhism of our time. It is classic, authentic Buddhism that is transmitted from heart to heart. I hope that you will take the teachings of this book to heart and apply them to life, meditation, and relationships so that you can enjoy greater meaning and joy.

Salvatore Celiento

HOW TO DO LIFE
A Buddhist Perspective

Section One

Living a Fulfilling Life

Chapter One

Right Vision, Big Vision

From the Buddhist point of view, if we are to think about a fulfilling life, it should include two different goals: the distant goal and the more immediate goal. The distant goal is enlightenment. The immediate goal is to do the best one can to lead a life that has some meaning and significance and to not squander one's opportunities. In order to do that, one also needs to contemplate on the distant goal. In other words, to truly have a fulfilling life, one needs to try to integrate these two different goals. One should be aiming toward enlightenment in an extremely serious manner. We should not think that it is somewhere in the distant future, as if "it is not going to happen to me" or that "it is not real." We should also not think that enlightenment is all there is; thinking that it is all one should be aiming toward. It is not helpful to think that one's daily life experiences, because they happen to be part of our everyday life, are a samsaric delusional state and therefore, do not merit any serious attention. Similarly, it is not helpful to think that our everyday life experiences are trivial, superficial, or illusory, and our ultimate goal, the attaining of enlightenment, is the only thing that really counts.

Generally speaking in Buddhism, we do not simply aim for the ultimate goal without considering our immediate goals. The integration of these two goals allows us to have a meaningful life, one of significance. Integrating the two brings meaning and significance to our life. This is done in order to develop our relationship with ourselves, others, the phenomenal world, and ultimate reality. Throughout this first section, we will follow these themes and elaborate on how we can inject more meaning into our lives.

First, we will speak about the two goals. In order to integrate and sustain the two goals, we need to develop a clear and expansive vision. Having "right vision" is an important part of making an effort to achieve the objective of making our lives more significant. We will not succeed if we have the wrong type of vision or a small vision. Therefore, having the right vision from the beginning is an important part of this. What is the right vision? It can be described in many different ways but fundamentally speaking, from the Buddhist point of view, the right or proper vision means that we need to have a bigger vision. Our vision should not be limited or constricted. We can only think about attaining enlightenment and simultaneously have aspirations of things to achieve on a daily basis if we have a bigger, more inclusive vision. A big vision is extremely important because if we have small vision, whatever actions we perform or tasks we take on are going to be limited by that vision. Therefore, having a big vision is an important part of giving ourselves the proper encouragement and feedback.

As samsaric beings, we are often quite conditioned to have small visions or to approach bigger visions in an unachievable way. We are conditioned by our egoic preoccupations and obsessions that subsequently limit us. With egoic preoccupations and obsessions come negative thoughts, nagging doubts, thoughts of suspicion, and fears and anxieties in terms of one's capacity and what we are aiming for. We may think, "This is not possible. It can't possibly happen. It may not be real. What if it is all illusory? I don't have the capacity to realize that goal. I can't perform this task. I can't do this job." From the Buddhist perspective, we need to learn to break through the walls that we have erected around ourselves due to egoic paranoia. Buddhism says that we have erected many varieties of walls around ourselves and these become a form of entrapment. We create a prison for ourselves.

When we have a big vision, we are already challenging the dominance of our egoic perceptions and obsessions. Our ego can be a very fragile entity according to the Buddhist way of thinking, and it is incapable of having a truly great vision that is realistic. If ego has some kind of big vision, it is a counterfeit one—fanciful and fabricated. Because ego is a fragile entity, it is easily disappointed, hurt, and wounded. This may then interfere with our efforts to succeed in all of our endeavors, including our spiritual practices. Time and time again, the Buddhist masters have reminded us that ego interferes with our spiritual endeavors because the ego sees what we are doing from a particular perspective—some sense of a fixed, sometimes insecure and brittle, highly conditional self-identity. If things are not working out in the way that ego demands, the ego becomes threatened and may even disintegrate, often described as an identity crisis that may be mild or severe.

From the perspective of Buddhism, if we truly want to have real vision, we do not put our complete and total trust in our egoic identity, but rather, we develop trust in the ground of our own being, our authentic being.[1] The egoic entity/identity is a superficial "everyday life" form of identity that we may inadvertently cling on to. In reality, our identity lacks any real stability. Therefore, from the Buddhist view, the reason we can feel so frustrated with some of our activities and the outcomes we experience, why we may feel like a failure, is because it is in ego's nature to see things in that fashion. From the Buddhist point of view, we cannot have a big vision if we are looking from a fixated egoic viewpoint. To have a big vision, one has to develop trust in one's authentic state of being. In that way, we can be on more stable ground so that if there are fluctuations or difficulties and we fail sometimes, we are not traumatized or wounded by the failure. Outcomes can be experienced within a broader perspective and not taken so personally, thus providing greater opportunities for personal growth and an accumulation of better understanding, appreciation, and wisdom.

Ego makes many unrealistic demands on us. We may try to meet those demands but the ego is rarely fully satisfied. Therefore, no matter what we do, even when we achieve a goal and succeed at a task or venture, our ego may remain dissatisfied and discontent. We may never feel good enough, rich enough, or whatever the case may be. We may always feel that we could have done better or that external circumstances are against us. There is always some variety of subconscious activity informing us that we have done a bad job, are not trying hard enough, could have done better, or deserve more.

The fundamental and vital starting point is that our big vision should be seen from our own expansive and authentic state of being's point of view and not from the limited, egoic perspective. From the standpoint of the ego, the view changes from moment to moment, day to day, month to month, and year to year. Therefore, it is unreliable and may create instability. This is not to say that ego has no function at all. In Buddhism, we do recognize that ego has a function. Presenting ourselves, our identity, in a fairly consistent manner to others helps in all kinds of communication and interactions. Our egoic identity can help others to know who they are dealing with. It helps to have a consistency and to be reliable.

In that way, one can demonstrate one's strengths and how one can be useful, helpful, and relied upon, et cetera. It is important for the ego to function well, but it should not define us. Identity is an aspect of us but it should not be given total and complete control over our lives. As samsaric beings, we are normally looking at ourselves from the standpoint of seeing our ego or identity as all or most of what and who we are.

One of the fundamental points is recognizing the limitations of the ego. The other is to become cognizant that there is so much more. We need to develop trust in our original, authentic state of being, our buddha nature. Using a Buddhist analogy, we make an effort to plant white seeds, positive thoughts and emotions. In other words, ego is accustomed to thinking in an extremely negative manner. All of the negative thoughts and emotions arise due to ego's struggle with paranoia, insecurity, and demands. To counter that, we need to teach ourselves to think more about positive things. This is the case whether it is in relation to engaging in our daily activities or our spiritual activities such as meditation practices. We need to approach our thinking about our lives in a more positive manner. Learning to inculcate positive thoughts and emotions—the planting of white seeds in the psyche—is important in developing our ability to sustain the bigger vision by developing trust in our authentic, genuine state of being. Further, engendering positive thoughts and emotions provides perspectives that also help progress our more immediate goals.

I have seen it said, even in certain Buddhist literature, that we should not, for example, aspire to achieve certain levels of perfections as they are not real, and because they are not real, we will be disappointed when they do not come true. This is suggesting that if we do not have high aspirations, we will not be disappointed. If we are not disappointed, we will be happier and our life will seem fulfilling. However, it may seem that way, but in reality, we cannot find real fulfillment if we have not reached or aspired to reach our full potential. From the Buddhist point of view, the idea that any discomfort or unpleasantness is necessarily bad for one's psyche or mental well-being is completely misguided. Whether one aims high or low, as long as our mind has not learned to reorient itself, it will only think of defeat, failure, and mediocrity. It will not think in positive terms because ego is accustomed to thinking in negative terms. If we aim very low, even if we say, "There is no such thing as success and it is all the same," this does not mean that we are going to avoid feeling like a failure or totally defeated by various obstacles, situations, circumstances, and other people.

Therefore, in Buddhism, our expectations need to be great. At the same time, one must have an idea about one's capability at that given moment, which is not to say that this is the only capability that one possesses. Capabilities, capacities, can be cultivated and they are capable of growing. It is mistaken to believe that if we have high expectations and limited capacity, then the gap between the expectation and the capacity is such that it can never be bridged. It is not helpful to make that assumption. We need to rethink, reorientate, and recognize that our capacity can build and change. Even if the gap is not completely bridged, one may still experience growth. That is far better than never having tried to lift oneself above one's normal functioning capacity. Just like the body that we can train to have greater capacity for endurance in terms of strength or oxygenation, in a similar manner, we can train other areas of our lives. We can have a clear and definite picture of the expectation that we have for ourselves and in terms of the goals that we want to achieve. If we have established that, then as we progress, we can sustain the bigger long-term vision that we set for ourselves. In this way, we can overcome constraining negative tendencies and habits of mind and body.

From the Buddhist point of view, too much emphasis is often

placed on our life circumstances. For example, it can often be said that one cannot aspire for great things if one is raised by difficult parents, brought up in trying economic circumstances, or has limited education. From a Buddhist perspective, such circumstances have some influence because everything that we experience is dependent on varieties of causes and conditions. Some of these factors would have played a role in shaping the mental attitudes that we have developed. Capabilities may have also been shaped by some of these factors. However, according to Buddhism, it does not need to define us.

Even if an individual's parent struggled with alcohol use or had other issues to contend with, this does not mean that this person is any less capable of becoming something that they wish to become. If the circumstances and situations have not been so favorable, it does not automatically follow that the person's capacity is going to be limited for the rest of their life. Let us look at this from another perspective and picture a person who has come from a very prosperous family background, attended the best college and had a good education, and whose parents showered them with love and all the material things that they could wish for. Even in seemingly fortunate situations such as this, many people have not reached their potential. Under such circumstances, their capacity may not have been tested and they could remain underdeveloped. The environment within which we are born and grow up in will never be entirely conducive to reaching our full potential. Our personal circumstances, upbringing, and environment are not everything. What counts even more is the individual's determination, having focus and aiming high, having great expectation and big vision. All of these qualities can inspire us to want to do more than we are already doing. This is an important part of the notion of bridging the gap between expectation and capacity. As I mentioned, capacity is something elastic. It is not fixed. We do not come into this world with a fixed quantum of capacity. Our capacities could diminish as we get older or they may increase, depending on how we are living our life. This would depend on whether we were living a fulfilling life, or alternatively, not living a fulfilling life.

The other point that we need to contemplate if we are to sustain our big vision is dealing with our past, in other words, not allowing our past experiences to spoil our present and future possibilities. As Buddhist teachings keep reminding us, the past is past. It happened and it is gone. It is no more but the present and the future on the other hand, are not a closed book like the past, but rather, pregnant with possibilities. When we allow ourselves to become victimized by our past, then every day, we would be failing to take advantage of the many opportunities that come our way. It can be difficult to see new opportunities if we are focused on making negative evaluations and assessments about ourselves, our life generally, and how we see the state of the world. We may be carrying negative assessments regarding many aspects of our lives, such as things we may have done and our relationship with our parents, friends, work colleagues, other people, et cetera. It is difficult to see a meaningful and positive way forward with such a mindset. We can carry around our past as a very heavy burden.

From the Buddhist point of view, if we want to live our life more fully, we need to deal with our past and just let that go of that so that we can take full advantage of the present. Otherwise, we allow the past to color all of the present situations and experiences, our relationships, job situations, and our perception of the world. When we do not see things with any kind of freshness, everything can be colored by how we have seen and experienced things in the past over many years. We continue to see these things in the same manner. This is part of the burden that we carry. We must get that burden off our backs.

Letting go of the past enables us to more easily recognize the good fortunes that do come our way, things that we normally may not see. Due to our egoic habitual preoccupation of always harping on the negative, even when good things happen, we may not recognize them. So often, it is only in hindsight that we realize how good things were. Therefore, along with letting go of the past, we need to truly recognize and acknowledge when good things are happening. We can otherwise be too busy dwelling on and reliving bad memories and experiences, past hurt, slights, and denigrations. When we are less burdened by our negative mind and can see that there are good things happening, we may be surprised how these occurrences can be quite frequent. In fact, on a daily basis, there are more good things happening in our lives than bad ones, but when bad things happen, even if only occasionally, we immediately latch on to them. If good things happen, we ordinarily take them for granted. We can feel that we are entitled to have these good things happening.

From the Buddhist point of view, taking things for granted is not a helpful attitude. It is a negative attitude that in itself, generates more negativity. Taking things for granted ensures that our painful experiences become more painful and our good experiences go largely unappreciated. The pleasure and enjoyment that we may have received from having these experiences would then have been radically reduced. When we lack appreciation, we lessen the pleasure we can experience from good things happening and experience more pain from bad or painful circumstances. From the Buddhist viewpoint, it is better not to think that when good things happen, "I deserve it. This is how it should be. I am entitled to it." When bad things happen, we should avoid becoming completely enraged and incensed as if such things should never happen to us. According to Buddhism, change, upheavals, and the unexpected cannot be helped or avoided. That is how things are in the world and in life; they are impermanent and insubstantial, as the Buddhist literature constantly reminds us.

Taking things for granted may also exacerbate our sense of failure, depression, and feeling of inadequacy because a life can lack enjoyment. Therefore, having gratitude for all the blessings that we have received is an important part of living a good life. To lead a good life according to Buddhism is to have that sense of gratitude. When we feel gratitude, when we feel, "I'm blessed to have this wonderful experience," the joy is then increased so that one's life becomes more enriched. In that way, the attitudes that we cultivate determine whether we are having a fulfilling life or not. According to Buddhism, it is not just what a person was given at the time of birth in terms of physical attributes, intelligence, or socioeconomic background, but whether the individual has the resolve to want to make a difference and make an effort to better themselves—to set certain goals for oneself and then make the effort to work toward and attain those goals. Accommodating upheavals without seeing oneself as a victim means that whatever we encounter does not need to disturb or diminish our resolve.

In Buddhism, in relation to progressing on the spiritual path, one has two different types of goals, the immediate goal of leading a fulfilling life and the distant goal of enlightenment. In immediate terms, we need to learn to integrate spirituality with everyday life experiences. If we do that, we are already on our way to attaining the distant goal. Without attending to the immediate life experiences, we cannot do anything about the distant goal of enlightenment. Consequently, it is only from increasing a genuine sense of goodness in oneself that one becomes transformed. If one becomes transformed in a positive way, both psychologically and spiritually, one becomes that much closer to attaining the distant goal of enlightenment. These two goals therefore, are not separated. Sometimes people think that enlightenment has to be pursued at the expense of everyday life experiences and should be seen in total isolation. I would like to emphasize that these two goals are not mutually exclusive. In fact, proper application toward achieving one's immediate goals done in an effective manner also leads us to enlightenment.

Both goals have to be seen as something real. It is easy and I suggest, often encouraged, for us not to have too much trust or faith in anything, even if it is simply an idea. According to Buddhism, this is self-defeating because underlying skepticism or cynicism could end up being at the root of most of our experience. Feelings such as despair and depression may become a pervasive attitude if we do not fundamentally believe in ourselves or anything else. If everything is treated in relation to its pragmatic value and use, and nothing is treated as having an intrinsic value or value in itself, we might think we can use other people, certain ideas, or anything at all, only for their use value.[2] We may even lose respect for ourselves and our own existence. That is not how one finds fulfillment in life. If we do not believe in anything, we would have nothing to genuinely nourish and nurture ourselves. However, if we have lofty ideals and these are truly good within themselves, they have the power to infuse our own lives and those of others with joy, affirmation, and a sense of positivity. We would then be less given to despair and depression. Such experiences of meaninglessness and despair can come from extreme skepticism, cynicism, doubt, and the tendency to look at everything critically. Thinking like this can remove enjoyment and pleasure even from simple things such as reading a good book or watching a nice movie. We could end up seeing everything with the "crooked eye" of criticism and cynicism.

The Buddhist view of developing a more positive attitude helps us to believe more in our own ideals and goals that we wish to attain, allowing our life to have greater meaning and fulfillment. We would also be in a position to be more generous and giving to others. Alternatively, we only have ego to rely on and ego is not a good guide. Egocentric insecurities are capable of leading us down the path of misery, despair, and catastrophe. One needs to develop a genuine sense of trust in oneself, in the authentic state of being, and in the distant goal of enlightenment. There must be some trust that enlightenment is real and not fabricated, trust that we can progress in this life, both on the mundane and the supermundane levels, and trust that this is real. Human beings can progress and attain and actualize higher and higher levels of their potentialities. This is all real. This is all possible. It is not made up. From Buddhist perspective, that is the way to begin on the spiritual path.

Such an approach provides a solid foundation from which to proceed. If we proceed in a tentative manner, any step that we take will be wobbly and those steps will not take us so easily to the destination because we are not sure-footed on the path. So to take confident steps on the path, one has to be standing on solid ground and that comes from a real belief in oneself. When we say "self," this does not mean one's egoic persona but belief in one's genuine state of being and a genuine trust in all of the ideals that we wish to realize. We cannot realize those ideals if we ourselves hardly have the confidence to believe in them. I see this as the basic starting point of the spiritual path and having a fulfilling life. In the next three chapters, we will be following this theme of one's relationship with oneself, with the world, with others, and one's relationship with ultimate reality. This is where we start—with oneself—having some idea that all of these things that we want to do and realize are real and important and something that we can put our trust in.

Sometimes people are afraid to say such things fearing being branded a dogmatist or fanatic. But a dogmatist or fanatic is not someone who believes what they believe in a very strong manner, but rather, someone who wants to push their agenda onto others or prove them wrong. That is a different situation to what we are discussing here. I see no necessary relationship between having firm belief in certain things and being intolerant and disrespectful of others who have a different view.

Chapter Two

Relationship with Oneself and Positive Self-Image

There are four important themes that we will discuss over the next few chapters—one's relationship with oneself, with the world and with others, and one's relationship with ultimate reality. First, to reiterate briefly, in Buddhism, right from the beginning, we have to see the importance of having trust in one's authentic state of being, which is also often called the ground of being or in some Zen and Tibetan literature, the original dwelling place. To lead a fulfilling life, we have to have a vision for our life. Without vision, it is difficult for us to actually go anywhere. It guides us. We also have to think in terms of a starting point. In this instance, we think of it in terms of our original, authentic state, our genuineness, and state of authenticity and not only in relation to our ego or normal everyday self. This is where we make our beginning. We approach our vision based on the original state of being. This also has to be seen as a way of overcoming egoic influences. Following this, all of our possibilities and potentialities can open up. The more that we rely on the limited view of our ego to save us, the more it does the opposite; it can let us down and we end up feeling like a failure, frustrated, and discontented. Our egoic perspective can go on in this way and life becomes an ongoing struggle. Rather than developing a sense of ease, there may be a sense of dis-ease as a continual companion in the course of our lives. Therefore, we need to recognize this limitation and instead adopt a better attitude toward our past and current life and do this on a daily basis. We are capable of freeing ourselves from past, unresolved issues. For one, we can avoid relying too much on our past circumstances and external influences to define us, including those from our parents. This is an important part of ensuring that we are free to redefine ourselves and not caught in a static and excessive focus on the ego.

Taking this into account, it is important that we develop a positive image of ourselves. Based on the idea that we have to start the journey, guided by our goals, we need to work toward our many goals, spiritual and mundane, and our job is to integrate the two aspiration fields. With regard to mundane goals, as long as they are worthwhile pursuing, we should pursue whatever it is that we want. The fundamental point is that whatever mundane goals we wish to pursue should be in synch with our pursuit of spiritual goals. There must be harmony rather than tension between the two. Some believe that what is worldly and what is spiritual must always be in conflict or separated. However, in actuality, there is no contradiction. Of course, they can be in conflict if we are pursuing the wrong kind of objectives in our life; they may then come in conflict with our spiritual pursuits, especially if a pursuit is guided by egoic preoccupations and obsessions.

In the previous chapter, I spoke about the negative influences that we experience, arising not only from external sources, but also from the negative thoughts and emotions that we continuously indulge in. These may create a very poor image of ourselves in the mirror of our mind and that of others and the world. How we see ourselves is very important. If we want to do something, first we have to look at ourselves and clearly see the answer to the question, "How do I see myself?" According to Buddhism, due to our egoic entanglements and all of the emotional complexities and confusions that we have generated, we have an extremely poor image of ourselves, or at least, a very distorted one. Whatever image we have of ourselves would then come through in terms of what we think and say and how we interact with others. Contemplating how we see ourselves and the influence that this view has on our quality of life is important in relation to our ability to lead a fulfilling life. What we see in ourselves, how we see ourselves, and whether or not we think of ourselves as somebody of worth and with value, makes a difference. If we hold on to and indulge in varieties of distorted views about ourselves, such as thinking, "I'm unattractive, unintelligent, and insignificant," it creates an image of ourselves that we end up really believing in. This ends up coloring every aspect of our interactions and relationships with the world, others, and ourselves. Buddhism does not say that one should not be concerned about developing a healthy sense of self. Developing a healthy sense of self is an important part of Buddhist practice.

Rather, Buddhism says that the more we are caught up in our egoic fantasies, dreams, and aspirations, the harder it is to establish a proper, healthy self-image. This may be contrary to what many people believe that Buddhism is saying. It is often assumed that Buddhism says we should let go of, transcend, go beyond, or at least, ignore the ego. That is not what is intended in Buddhism. If we try and get rid of the ego, we may create a huge problem, especially if one is already grappling with some sense of low self-esteem. From a Buddhist perspective, low self-esteem and egoic preoccupation go hand-in-hand. They are not separate. From a Buddhist standpoint, it would be a self-defeating exercise to prop up a sense of ego in order to overcome low self-esteem because low self-esteem is a direct result of egoic preoccupation. It can be seen as a type of self-obsession. The more we constantly compare and contrast ourselves with others, the more our self-esteem may be negatively affected: "Am I attractive enough? Am I intelligent? Am I this? Am I that? Am I making as much money as the next person? Am I good enough? Am I as good as somebody else at work?"

Whatever it might be, this constant distraction of comparing ourselves with others can gradually erode our self-esteem. Our ego preoccupation can become more entrenched and our self-esteem more brittle in response to our assessment of ourselves in relation to others. It may also be a distraction in terms of what we personally believe to be important goals in our lives. Our sense of self can be too highly dependent on our circumstances and what others may value, rather than our own values.

From the Buddhist point of view, it does not help to try to reinforce one's sense of ego. This does not make our ego stronger, even though generally speaking, this is what we normally do as samsaric beings. A healthy self-image comes from feeding ourselves positive thoughts and emotions, thinking of ourselves in a more positive light. Even if we think of ourselves as being a certain way, still, we can be flexible rather than fixed in terms of our capacities and abilities. We can always become more and become something new. The future is open. It is not a closed book. This is one of the main reasons working on letting go of the past is vitally important. Otherwise, we are trapped within a fixed self-image. If we try and solidify our life story, if we see ourselves as a particular person who suffered in a particular way at the hands of a particular person or people, et cetera, we may become unable to move forward. One has to envision, visualize, and imagine oneself becoming the person that one wants to become. We need to allow ourselves this freedom. Doing this helps instill a positive self-image. If we are convinced that we are burdened with the past—with past guilt, regret, disappointment, sense of failure, feeling unloved, unappreciated, and disrespected, or even afraid to make similar errors, et cetera, we can try picturing ourselves differently, free of such shackles. We can allow ourselves to see ourselves freshly, more like the person we want to be. The past is capable of entrenching us in such a way that we can find no respite from our past sadness and disappointment.

The more we feel like this, the more our self-esteem is negatively affected. As it is said in Buddhism, the self-image that we wish to develop has to be pictured, envisioned, and visualized. We have to see ourselves as becoming anew. We then need to inject a good dose of conviction into this. We want to avoid thinking, "I'm just imagining that. Imagining it won't make any difference." Everything that we do, we first imagine, and then we can move toward making it happen. There is nothing of any significance that we do where we have not first imagined it. Why should it be any different when it comes to our sense of self and self-image? If we imagine a greater and stronger sense of self, it will be to our betterment.

Buddhism speaks about self-power and other-power. When we have a sense of power, we are happy. When we are enslaved by others, of course, we are not happy because we must do the other's bidding. When we are tied down in that fashion with someone else holding the reins, it is difficult to be happy. This notion of self-power and other-power occurs even within oneself and this is where Buddhism is quite different. Everyone recognizes that to be enslaved, to be in servitude, is not good and to be free, to have a sense of self-empowerment, is good. According to Buddhism, when the ego is reigning supreme, we are not free, we have handed our freedom over to our ego. This then reduces our sense of self-worth. Ego can be seen as an extremely unhappy creature and it is never happy no matter what we do to satisfy it. Shantideva has said this about being unable to satisfy the ego on many occasions.[3] We can try to do everything that ego says we should do, but then ego becomes dissatisfied again for one reason or another. Sometimes it does not even know why it is unhappy, but it just becomes unhappy. For example, we start meditating and in the beginning, everything is going well and then suddenly, for no reason, aversion to meditation arises. Meditation is seen as a burden, obligation, or duty as if something has been forced upon us. It is as if meditation itself is some form of imprisonment, a prison for the ego. In that way, Buddhism says that we need to free ourselves from the excessive influences of our ego. To do that, we need a proper self-image.

If we develop a proper sense of self-image, our despair, depression, fears, and anxieties can reduce and diminish because we are replenishing ourselves with positivity, good thoughts and feelings, and a positive sense of oneself, but in a different way to how the ego normally works. There is a vast difference between building up one's sense of self-worth in this way and the egoic manner of working. If we have a healthy sense of self-image, whatever we are doing in life on a worldly or spiritual level, we will have an "I can do it" attitude. We can experience a sense of possibility and spaciousness around our ideas and endeavors. It is simply being in a better state of mind to be able to galvanize all of one's resources and use them to help realize one's goals. If one approaches it in this manner, there is a sense of stability without stagnation, whereas the egoic way is tumultuous. From egoistic perspective, the obsession comes from a different place. We can be thinking, "I'll prove that I'm the best," or "I'm so great. I'll show the world how great I am." There can be vibrancy but at the same time, it is stagnant. It is like still water in a bubbly pond. It is not going anywhere. It is simply a lot of activity but nothing is happening.

If there is a steady flow and the stream is directed toward a particular destination, there is movement but still, there is stability. It is not tumultuous. One is not being thrown about, pushed this way and pulled that way, causing a tremendous sense of confusion and uncertainty. Galvanizing one's resources that are based on all of the positive thoughts and emotions that one has been cultivating can be utilized. One then has the sense of, "I can do this. I can achieve that," and one can picture oneself becoming a particular person, somebody one may have earlier thought one could never possibly be. If one can picture new possibilities—it is possible to be a writer, an artist, a businessperson, or a good parent, et cetera—one can more easily see avenues and pathways toward that goal. Sometimes people feel that they do not have it in them. It is extremely good for one to picture oneself being whatever it is that one wants to become. It should not be forgotten that doing this is part of spiritual practice. It is not simply a psychological exercise but spiritual training that then helps us marry our spiritual aspirations with our mundane pursuits at a daily level. Of course, we are referring to positive aspirations. We cannot marry spiritual pursuits and envision mundane, harmful intent, wishing to become something like a harmful dictator. The point is that the positive use of imagination and aspiration aids in our immediate goals of a better, more meaningful life, and the long-term goal of enlightenment.

This sense of self-worth is not based simply on all of the good qualities and attributes that we may gradually come to embody, but it is based on our true nature. This is because we dwell in our ground of being and that is the greatest treasure. This is how it is described in Buddhist literature. The biggest treasure we have is our true nature, true state of being, or state of authenticity. All of the goodness comes from this. Having confidence in that fundamental authentic state of being helps support a positive self-image that we can construct for ourselves. You may ask, "Why should I believe in an authentic state of being? First I want to have some experience of it, then I will believe in it." I believe such positioning may create unnecessary difficulties, because if we have experience of something, we do not need to believe it, we have experienced it. Similar to our many undiscovered potentials, we can believe that one day we will be able to play the piano, for example, before we have any proof or experience of that ability. We need to believe in something that we have not yet experienced in order to progress. Believing in it will then lead to direct experience and experience will confirm what we have believed all along. This is the order in which we have to approach self-belief and building self-worth. It does not make any sense to say that first we must have the experience and then we can believe, despite sayings such as "seeing is believing." If I see a table in front of me, I do not have to believe that the table is there. I can see it. In a similar way, with things that are not visible to the senses but nevertheless not outside the range of our own experience, actual or potential, in this case potential, then believing can also lead to experience. This type of approach, to believe one has greater potential than one has seen or discovered thus far, provides us with the necessary environment for growth.

This notion of ground of being, our state of authenticity, is also not something remote and abstract that we cannot access. If we have done varieties of meditations, we would have had some experience of being at ease with all of the thoughts and emotions arising, where disturbances or confusions do not arise in us. We have experienced a sense of being totally present. This can happen when the ego is not dominating our experience, even if we have these experiences of being totally present only for a moment or brief period. It is possible to have a glimpse of what it is like to be operating from a state of authenticity, from one's ground of being. From the Buddhist point of view, it is practically impossible and also unnecessary to get rid of the ego altogether. The point is not to rely solely on our egoic identity to provide us with what we feel we need in life to be fulfilled. We want to do more than merely exist. Many living things exist, but to live properly is different. To do that, as much as possible, we need to reduce the ego and its obsessive entanglements, the tentacles of egoic influences, upon our sense of self. We can then try to use our sense of self in relation to our ego for our betterment. Both a healthy sense of self and the ego can be used to lead us to experiencing our true nature. It is possible when we have conviction in our greatest potential, our ground of being, that experiencing our true nature, our ground of being will follow from conviction.

Some people believe that the more spiritual we are, the more critical we have to become in terms of who and what we are as a human being, as if there is something fundamentally wrong, deficient, defective, or faulty in us. From the Buddhist point of view, the idea of being fundamentally flawed comes from our habituated way of seeing the world from an egoic point of view, which so often leads to self and other criticism, guilt, and self-condemnation. Such inner conflict, where different sides or aspects of us come into conflict can create inner division. We can become self-divided. Such arising inner tension creates restlessness, agitation, and mental and physical disturbance. There is nothing healthy or spiritual about that.

From a Buddhist perspective, healthy self-image is accommodating. It is forgiving. It permits and allows. It does not demand perfection from us; perfection is something that we aspire to. As I mentioned, some contemporary Buddhists say that we should not aspire to perfection; perfection is not real so why demand it of ourselves? I disagree with this line of thinking because there is no contradiction in aspiring for perfection while at the same time, being gentle with oneself for not being perfect. It is being gentle with oneself, warts and all, accepting all aspects of oneself, forgiving one's failures and defects and accepting that we can sometimes make mistakes and fail. However, having failed at certain things once, twice, three times, or whatever the case may be does not make us a failure as a person. By thinking like this, having that big vision and positive self-image, one can then accommodate all aspects of oneself and still continue to strive for one's own betterment. That is the beauty of this perspective. The egoic view only produces more tension, anxiety, and a split within oneself; one wants to be perfect but recognizes that one has many faults and defects so one can feel defeated by one's imperfections. We can be thrown into guilt, remorse, and be torn up inside. This is not the spiritual way.

The spiritual way is of kindness, to have a healthy self-image, which is accommodating, and aspiring to attain greater and greater levels of perfection. There is nothing wrong, in fact, there is everything right in wanting to aspire to higher levels of perfection. There is no contradiction between wanting to aspire to achieve perfections and being able to accept one's imperfections, faults, defects, and failings. To have this is to have a healthy attitude. We can replenish ourselves with positive thoughts and attitudes. This will automatically go toward boosting our self-worth and sense of self-confidence. Building a healthy self-image is crucial on a spiritual path. When difficulties arise, they need to be dealt with. Our life does not have to be totally free of difficulties for it to be fulfilling and spiritually rich. Allowing our spiritual aspirations to be vitiated by our egoic preoccupations can lead to further inner conflict and we can fuel an ongoing struggle. We can stop struggling so much and deal with difficulties in a different manner. We can make our life fuller and more enjoyable in a true, most basic, fundamental sense. Otherwise, we run the risk of stunting our progress. Our life would then not be fully lived.

In that way, we can see that conviction and "believing" is an important part of making our life work. If we do not believe in something that we want to do or believe in ourselves and our potentialities, we are going to be tentative, hesitant, and overly cautious. Our commitment becomes absent and there is little energy or vibrancy in what we are doing. When we feel good, we can find ways to achieve, find a way to move forward and navigate our difficulties. When we do not feel much sense of inner richness, we may feel powerless and become sidetracked or distracted. If we have conviction and truly believe in what we are striving for and believe in ourselves, this is very strong. It is extremely powerful if we believe in our sense of self-worth, believe in the goals that we want to attain, and believe in our vision. This will then generate a tremendous sense of energy in itself that will propel us forward. It will consequently become an antidote to the continual experience of disillusionment, despair, struggle, disappointment, and all that comes with the egoic struggle. When difficulties arise in our lives—with our finances, health, relationships, or our business is suffering and our children are using drugs—whatever the difficulties might be, we will have better tools to deal with these life crises and not give in to despair.

By highlighting the positive aspects of our life, even in difficult times, and focusing on the range of things that we are capable of doing, and further, stop mulling over all the things that we cannot do or could have done but did not do, we can remain undistracted from our main goals and projects at hand. It is good to focus on all of the things that we can be doing about ourselves—how to make ourselves better human beings, transform ourselves, and do everything possible to boost our self-image and sense of self-worth, while at the same time, being alert toward not falling into egoism. We can build up our sense of self-worth without being egotistical, arrogant, or haughty. These are agents of the ego. If we do that, we will not have to settle for mediocrity or less than what we can become. We do not have to settle for a quarter when we can have, if not the whole, at least three-quarters. The point is that we do not have to settle, thinking, "This is all I can do. This is all it's meant to be. It's written in my karma to only get this far and no further." Buddhism does not say that, even about our karmic history. One's karmic history may have put us here but it does not determine our present and future experiences. It does not reach that far. We can create our own way and our own future. It is not predetermined. Otherwise, there would be no point in doing any meditation practice. There would be no point in developing the bigger spiritual vision and aspirations.

We need to have conviction in ourselves, that we can become a better person, businessperson, painter, or writer, et cetera. It is possible to become a bodhisattva and a buddha.[4] It is powerful to think that exceptional things are possible, they can be realized and not that the only things that are possible are those that one is familiar with or has experienced. What we believe in will become real to us. It will become an experience one way or another. Most of our life experiences are based on belief in something and they are subsequently proven to be true or untrue. Whatever the case might be is fine. The belief can propel us forward. This is a key point.

When we approach life in this way, believing in our aspirations and replenishing ourselves with positivity, we are transported from a place of loneliness to a state of aloneness. Under the influence of excessive egoism, there is nothing but loneliness and a sense of isolation. Even if people are friendly and caring, we can be suspicious of their sincerity and may not feel particularly loved or wanted. We may be in a crowd but still feel lonely. Similarly, you sit at a table looking at your partner and children, conversing, and you are in despair because you believe that they do not understand you. This is life. There can be great pain, as the Buddha said. One can have an underlying feeling of being unloved, unappreciated, taken for granted, lonely, et cetera. So we need to build positive skills to replenish, rebuild, and find our resilience.

The state of aloneness allows us to be more open to others, and intimacy in fact becomes surprisingly more possible, rather than coming from the space of being lonely. When we feel loneliness, we may also feel desperate and afraid and want companionship, which sometimes leads us to making the wrong decisions. Egoic preoccupation and self-absorption only intensify our sense of loneliness. Through a more open and positive approach, learning to look at ourselves in a fresh way and developing a true sense of healthy self-image and self-worth allows us to be alone. It is being able to dwell in our dwelling place, also called our original home. Being alone is a pleasant state to be in. It is not fearful like loneliness. This state makes it possible for love and compassion to arise.

Chapter Three

The Importance of Positive Thoughts

In the previous chapter, I spoke about the importance of cultivating a positive self-image. My main point was that contrary to what many believe, it is not the case that all forms of self-image are necessarily tied up with some form of egoic identity. It is possible to cultivate a positive self-image that is not egocentric but rather, healthy and further, something that we need. To begin our journey, we need to be able to picture and envision ourselves with some clarity and with some sense of power, both on the mundane and spiritual level. On the spiritual level, we have to think of ourselves as being capable of becoming a bodhisattva or buddha.

From a Buddhist viewpoint, this is something that we need to think about if we are to enrich our lives. As part of enriching our lives, we need to have greater appreciation of our self-worth that is not fabricated by our egoic delusions. Otherwise, we swing back and forth from low self-esteem, not feeling at all good about oneself, to being arrogant and self-centered. Most of us swing back and forth between these two. Sometimes we feel terrible and worthless and at other times, it goes to our head, we feel like someone special, something great.

The point is that we cannot do without self-image. Whether we like it or not, we are always going to have a form of self-perception, the kind of image that we have formed about ourselves. This being the case, it makes sense to try to develop a self-image that is healthy and based on reality rather than fanciful thoughts from a delusional mind. If we have a strong sense of self, we can move from loneliness to aloneness. This means that we can be alone with ourselves. Fundamentally, aloneness is related to being able to be with oneself because there is sense of "ease-ness." One can be alone and that means that one is not desperate for companionship. Loneliness only accentuates the hunger for the companionship of others and their approval, love, and appreciation. Aloneness means that one's sense of oneself is not determined by whether one finds approval from others or not, feels judged in a favorable light, or is put down, made fun of, or denigrated. If we have a healthy sense of self-image, a need for the approval of others will be lessened. If it comes our way, that is good, but if it does not, we are not disappointed and feeling dejected, rejected, and lonely. We do not feel abandoned, having nobody to rely on, comfort us, or take refuge in. When we feel more at ease with ourselves, the sense of loneliness exacerbated by conflicting emotions and delusional states of mind diminishes. We can have a greater sense of clarity in ourselves, which then allows us to be able to establish some form of relationship with the world and others.

When we are caught up in our egoic dramas and engulfed in loneliness, desperation, and despair, little thought is given to a genuine sense of communication, friendship, and connection with others and the rest of the world. In order to be able to communicate properly and to be at ease with oneself, in Buddhism, it is said that we should contemplate on our thoughts, language, and action. These are the ways in which we communicate with others, with the rest of the world.

Thoughts are extremely important. According to the Buddhist view, they basically create who we are. Our thoughts give rise to our sense of self, our self-image. They tell us what sort of world we are living in, and about other people; whether they are friendly or unfriendly, nice or not nice, attractive or unattractive. Everything that we experience, we experience because we have thoughts. We are thinking beings. These thoughts in turn impact and fuel our feelings and emotions. Our thoughts are not related purely to the cognitive aspect of our mind. How we think, what we think, and how we use reason is closely tied up with our emotional repertoire. The range of emotions that we feel is largely determined by our thoughts and thought patterns. Our thoughts and the stories that we build with these thoughts generate experiences and ignite emotional responses relevant to those thoughts and stories.

Therefore, thoughts affect our emotions and feelings. How we feel, whether we feel depressed or elated, is determined by our thoughts. As soon as we have a positive thought, we feel uplifted. If we feel that somebody has said something nice, we also immediately feel uplifted. As soon as we feel that someone has said something bad about us, we can instantly feel depressed or angry. This is important to consider because, according to Buddhism, it shows that it is not so much what others are saying about us that determines our mood and emotional experiences as much as what we think and how we interpret what has been said. For example, when we feel judged by our actions, what has been said is seen as less important than what we think has been said about us. Our judgments on what others have said, or thoughts we have about ourselves, be they something positive or negative, can affect us deeply. Thoughts are not like ripples on the surface of a pond or waves on the surface of the ocean but they go deep and often, they take root. Thoughts have a tendency to latch on to certain things—attitudes, feelings, beliefs, et cetera. We can get fixated on an idea, person, or object, whatever it might be. Once our mind is focused on that and gets fixated, a lot of thought energy is poured into it. The energy generated around such thoughts shapes our experiences. These experiences in turn shape our attitudes and views and impact the kind of individual that we become, shaping our personality, predilections, tastes, likes, dislikes, and so on.

This is why in Buddhism, we are taught to pay attention to our thoughts because they do not simply come and go without leaving an imprint. Even a seemingly fleeting thought can nevertheless be very persistent and if unchecked, take root in our psyche. Buddhism takes this term, "taking root" very seriously. Once negative thoughts take root, they can turn into our developing a negative disposition, becoming a negative type of person. If unchecked, we can see everything around us and ourselves in a negative light. According to Buddhism however, this has nothing to do with reality, how things actually are. In Buddhism, this is also the reason why it is said that mind is so powerful. Mind is not so powerful due to psychic or other worldly powers or something like that, mind is extremely powerful precisely because it can shape who we become and how we see ourselves and the world. According to Buddhism, we can learn a great deal from observing our mental activity and its effect on us. Simply seeing the effect of this mental activity on our well-being and sense of self can empower us. Attaining that which Buddhism focuses on, it is a way of self-empowering, helping to create the state of aloneness that is self-sufficiency and self-reliance. As we will see in the next chapter, this notion of self-reliance does not lead to the idea that others are not needed or that we do not need to be part of humanity. On the contrary, one begins to develop a sense of sympathy and empathy with all beings.

This form of self-reliance is important and it comes from realizing that we can empower ourselves. If the things that are said or done to us by others were more significant than what is going on in our own mind, our power to change would be very limited. We do not necessarily have the power to change the opinions that others hold regarding us. We can try to persuade them, we may even try to coerce them, but ultimately, it is not up to us. If, as Buddhism says, what is going on in our own mind is more important than what has happened or is happening externally, that means that we have the power to create and recreate ourselves. We do not need to hand that power over to others. So when we feel bitter, resentful, and do not want to forgive others, even though our egoic mind has taught us to think that by doing so, we are protecting ourselves, we are in actuality not protecting ourselves at all. We are victimizing ourselves and doing so repeatedly. If it is true that someone has done a terrible thing, on top of that, we punish ourselves by becoming bitter, resentful, and going over it again and again, reliving the painful experience in our minds. This is how we victimize ourselves beyond what has actually happened to us. Due to egoic delusions, we think that this is the way to shield ourselves from others harming us. In fact, we become more vulnerable because if we hand over the power related to how we are going to feel to others, we leave ourselves open to their abuse. Who determines how we are feeling and what we are going to experience? If we think someone is saying something nice and we then become elated or they say something horrible and we immediately feel down and depressed, we have given our power to others. Strengthening our own sense of self provides greater equanimity within all our experiences and interactions with others.

In Buddhism, we need to consider this and learn to empower ourselves so that when we interact with others, it is more genuine and authentic. We need to maintain and build our own strong sense of self or selfhood. Our fears and anxieties about others can then begin to diminish because ultimately, we are going to be less affected by the actions and words of others, which is not to say that we ignore them. That is the opposite of what Buddhism teaches. The more we let these things get to us, the less happy we will be and the more brittle we become. Our self-esteem and sense of self-worth will be affected by many external influences. This is one aspect of self-identity and the use of thoughts, language, and action.

The other aspect is that instead of waiting for others to shower praise and say positive words about us, if we are more conditioned to positivity, telling ourselves positive things, we become enriched. We are not so dependent on hearing the encouraging words of others. If we receive them, this is good, but even if we do not, we can teach ourselves to say encouraging things to ourselves rather than negativity and negative feedback. In other words, we do not have to be at the mercy of others, waiting for someone to say a few encouraging words in order to feel good. We can do this ourselves, thinking good thoughts and saying encouraging words to ourselves. Such positivity can affect how we behave, our actions. Our behavior and interactions with others can be influenced by the feedback we give ourselves. As it is said in the teachings, a more positive mental environment manifests even in our physical demeanor, how we hold ourselves and physically present ourselves. If we rely on others, the perspectives and view will vary enormously and will be unpredictable. We may hear some good things and we may often hear negative things. Even if an individual is not saying bad things to us, if we are conditioned to greater negativity, this is most likely what we will hear. We may be suspicious of compliments or meet positivity with cynicism. Building awareness in our own self-talk and how we hear the words of others can be an extremely powerful tool in Buddhist practice. Lojong practices are an extension and important part of this positive feedback.[5] Even if one is not saying things to oneself out loud, nevertheless, one can give oneself positive feedback. Negative feedback is capable of becoming quite pervasive and ingrained. When we observe our thoughts, we may be surprised how regularly and consistently we give ourselves negative feedback; "You are not good enough. You are too fat, too tall, and not attractive enough." Such mental impressions can leave us feeling terrible.

When Buddhism refers to using the power of the mind, this is what is being spoken about. It is not referring to psychic or other such abilities. Buddhism acknowledges that such abilities may exist, but these are not seen as real mind power. Real mind power is when we can work with the mind to transform ourselves. From the Buddhist perspective, what is going on in our mind can impact and determine how much energy we have, for example, our level of enthusiasm, vitality, and vigor. Do we have vitality or not? Of course, the physical aspect plays a role in this, but it is the mind that truly determines whether one is enthusiastic and energetic or feels depleted, wearied, burnt-out, and burdened. If we wish to live a fulfilling life, the best way to become more enriched is through the use of mental power to generate positive thought. It is not simply through pacifying the mind and entering into a meditative state. That is one important way to work with the mind, but the most effective tool relates to the use of the power of positive thoughts and words. From a Buddhist point of view, if we do that, we can gradually learn to also use that in relation to others.

According to Mahayana Buddhism, thinking well of others and a variety of circumstances et cetera is the key to living a good life.[6] However, if we have not learned to utilize these tools in relation to ourselves, it is difficult to utilize them in relation to others. We may often approach it back to front. One may wish to have good thoughts about others such as compassion and love but one has not actually utilized the positive thoughts and emotions in order to help oneself. This can be quite depleting. For example, after doing meditation on compassion, we may feel that all of our compassion has been used up and we may feel depleted and de-energized. One may even become frustrated and depressed knowing that there is so much suffering yet one has very little capacity to do anything. However, if we replenish ourselves with positive feedback, we can become energized. It then becomes easier to have good thoughts about others and use language that avoids directing negativity toward them. We can make people feel good about themselves and avoid words that can be intimidating, demeaning, and so forth. Shantideva has said that most people's response to us will correspond to how we have behaved and communicated with them. Kind words and thoughts are like magnets, they draw out people's positivities and we have the capacity to bring out the best in them. This also applies in relation to oneself. If we are constantly coming from a negative mental space, others will respond in kind.

From the Buddhist viewpoint, positive thoughts and words that we use in relation to ourselves should also be used in relation to others. If we can do this, we can begin to develop a genuine sense of communication. Real communication takes place first because one is more self-sufficient, not completely dependent on the assessments or judgments of others and secondly, because one has been able to realize the power of the mind itself. The use of one's mental power is sufficient to determine our moods, levels of happiness or unhappiness, and capacity to communicate with others in a more effective manner. They are all interconnected in that way.

Thoughts and words are connected with action. Often, we tend to isolate action from thoughts and words. We may think that actions are more important than thoughts and words and therefore, we do not give them much attention. We may believe that as long as someone is not acting on them, one can have the most atrocious thoughts and that is okay. All manner of things may be said and we also think that this is okay as long as these words are not translated into action. However, from the Buddhist perspective, we cannot isolate these three aspects of ourselves. They are interconnected. Sooner or later, what we think and say will come out in our behavior. Even if we are not acting it out with full force, nevertheless, something of it will seep through.

From the Buddhist point of view, it is the thoughts and words that we should be paying more attention to rather than the actions that we perform because real transformation comes not from changing our behavior, but from changing our mind. If we change our mind, we do not have to bother about changing our behavior. That will naturally follow. However, if we try to change our behavior but have not changed our mind, nothing would change in the end because that same behavioral pattern, even though not repeated in exactly the same way or context, will be repeated in some other context with similar outcomes. While not exactly the same, as an example, it is similar to transferring one form of addiction for another. If we pay attention to and change our mind and thought patterns discernibly, behavior change will follow. How we communicate and relate to others, what we listen to and read, and how we choose to spend our time can enable us to take power back and empower ourselves.

When we do not pay attention in this manner, our self-determination and self-control may be weak. If we cannot find a positive outlook in the face of difficulties, it can be difficult to improve our behavior, as our will can be weak. We may wish we could reduce a bad habit or bad behavior and feel guilty when we repeat such actions. We may even chastise ourselves. Some kind of vicious circle is created. If we can skillfully learn to handle positive thoughts and positive reinforcement to ourselves, we become empowered and the potential for our actions to bear fruit increases. Enabling ourselves to live life more fully in this way is a sign of integration within oneself.

Under the influence of ego, we are fragmented, dispersed, and our energies go in every direction because our thoughts are scattered. Our words come out spontaneously like disembodied entities that just spew out of our mouth and go in all directions but nevertheless, have an impact on others and our state of well-being. How we live and behave becomes compromised. We have only a diminished life and are unable to live fully.

We are not cultivating positive thoughts for moralistic reasons, believing we must have good thoughts, and that if we have bad thoughts, we will go to hell or that if we have good thoughts, we will go to heaven. We are talking about thinking in terms of self-empowerment and developing the ability to enrich and recreate ourselves. "Self-transformation" in Buddhism means recreation of oneself. In other words, whether we like it or not, as soon as we are born, we are constantly changing. Even though we are changing, it may not be for the better. On some level, self-transformation is always going on. We need to seize the opportunity to transform ourselves in a fundamental way and recreate ourselves in such a manner that there is improvement and betterment and how we think about ourselves, the world, and other people has been changed. We would then have discovered a way to increase happiness and reduce suffering and work toward enriching others, our environment, and ourselves.

In Buddhism, the key to self-transformation therefore, is in thought. If we were thinking in the right way, our capacity would increase. We would feel that we could do all we need to do because we would feel self-empowered. This is because we would have been thinking all the right things and thinking in the right fashion. If we think in the wrong way like we ordinarily do, we know the consequence of that. In order to develop conviction in the efficacy of this self-empowering technique of the cultivation of positive thoughts, all that we need to do is pay attention to what is taking place in our minds now, with all the negativities going through our mind, and the effect that this is having on us. If negative thoughts have that effect, why would the positive thoughts not have an effect on us? Buddhism says that the positive thoughts have more power and bear more fruit than the negative thoughts, emotions, and feelings. This is because once these things are generated, they will keep on flourishing and to support this, there are things that we can think about to make them flourish even more. Therefore, in that way, when Buddhism speaks about the importance of thoughts, this means that thoughts have the capacity to transform us. Thoughts keep us imprisoned but thoughts also have the capacity to free us.

There is a notion often held about Buddhism that one should aim toward a state of thoughtlessness or that all thoughts are somehow bad. Many instructions are given about observing and managing thoughts during meditation, especially in relation to *shamatha*[7] or tranquility meditation. In analytical meditation, *vipashyana*,[8] one has to also deal with thoughts. Generally, in Buddhism, far from ignoring thoughts, they are taken extremely seriously. As Buddha said in the *Dhammapada*, "Our actions follow thoughts like the imprint left behind by the revolving wheel of a chariot." Thoughts leave imprints; they do not simply pop into our head only to vanish without a trace. On the contrary, our thoughts are responsible for our karma, traces or imprints, disposition, and character. They very much create who we are. It is our thoughts that have left karmic imprints, in particular those that are repeated and habitually arise in the mind. Our thoughts can develop attitudes and dispositions that become very deeply seated, and create the kind of human beings that we become. In this way, we can see how powerful a thought is. Contemplating the significance of thoughts in this way gives us the power to change ourselves. Realizing that one's thoughts are capable of being transformative is very powerful and liberating knowledge to have. No matter how powerful certain individuals may be or what trying circumstances we may be placed in, if we are using our thoughts in the right way to help maintain a healthy perspective, outlook, and attitude, we can always find a good way to deal with any circumstance, situation, and difficulty. This is the key and how we become empowered.

Leading a fulfilling life in Buddhism does not mean life without difficulties but one without struggle. Struggle is the main characteristic of how an egoic mind copes with difficulties. With struggle, one becomes depleted of energy. Longchenpa's trilogy called *Kindly Bent to Ease Us*, literally translated as, "Finding comfort and ease," explains that under the influence of ego, we are always in a struggle with something.[9] The ego is always grappling with some form of dilemma or bewilderment, even spiritual struggles. Gradually, as we begin to transform and empower ourselves, life's difficulties do not necessarily go away. We may still get sick and old and there may be people who wish to harm us. We may be faced with so many difficulties that cannot always be prevented. Nevertheless, how we deal with and cope with difficulties can be totally different and this is what is important. This is also what determines whether one has a fulfilling life or not. A fulfilling life is not one without difficulties or problems. We can have a fulfilling life with difficulties if we have the right attitude and are approaching everything life presents us in a proper manner, where we integrate the mundane with the spiritual. We have a fulfilling life when we conduct ourselves on a daily basis in a way that is in tune with our spiritual ideals. Paying attention to thoughts and attitudes in this way is not only spiritual, many Mahayana Buddhist masters have said that paying attention to thoughts is important for practical living because we come to better understand how our mind operates. Transforming our mind will have an impact in relation to all aspects of our life, not solely spiritual, but even the mundane. As a result, we become a better human being and whatever we do will be done better, be it parent, writer, artist, et cetera. How we deal with others would also improve.

From the Buddhist viewpoint, we do not have to completely rely on our egoic mind and identity to see us through on a daily level in terms of survival. There is an alternative way of living that is much more enriching, enjoyable, and empowering. Certain pains and unpleasantness may be experienced from time to time but the deep sense of despair and depression characteristic of the ordinary samsaric mindset will diminish. This is what takes the light and luster from our life and existence. Therefore, it is better to not be so committed to having a negative slant or perspective, but rather, to being able to see things in a much more positive light. This is not to say that one is in a delusory, manic state, seeing everything in a fantastic light despite the circumstances. In a very fundamental sense, there is some form of underlying goodness, a type of beauty, that is all-pervasive. The samsaric mindset does not allow us to see that normally, it is excellent at highlighting the negative. Whenever something goes wrong, even if it is not a big deal, it is made into a big deal. Even if what has happened is not so very bad, we think of it as terribly bad. That is the samsaric mind at work.

Therefore, paying attention to thoughts, language, and action helps us to avoid being caught in the extremes of either coating every experience with negation or creating an unreal "love and light" revelry. In a grounded way, we can see that there is goodness in oneself, in others, and the world. There is a fundamental trust in spite of all the bad things that are happening on the surface. This is the Buddhist view, that on the surface, many bad things are happening, but fundamentally, we have to see some kind of goodness in all things as an underlying reality; a cushioning agency that is all-pervasive and supports all things.

Chapter Four

Relationship with Others and a Meaningful Life

In this section, as I mentioned, we are approaching the subject of a meaningful life in relation to three aspects: in relation to oneself, the world and other people, and in relation to ultimate reality. In the previous chapter, I spoke about the importance of paying attention to our thoughts, words, and deeds. According to Buddhism, we are the product of our thoughts. We become what we think. It is not simply the case that we pay attention to what we do and we will be alright no matter what we think. For example, we may think, "It's only a thought anyway. It doesn't matter. It's just a thought." In Buddhism, more weight is put on thoughts than deeds because deeds follow thoughts. Thought does not normally follow deeds. Even if we try to do something good, if our intention is unclear, diluted, or impure, that deed, even though it has the appearance of being good and wholesome, is in fact not complete. It is only partially or somewhat good but may not be essentially good. If the thought behind the action is pure and sincere, even if the action has unintended consequences such as our meaning well but the actions end up having the opposite effect, still, that is not as bad as our doing things with dubious motives, hidden agendas, for selfish reasons, or with unclear, impure intentions. We enrich ourselves and our motivation and actions by trying to cultivate certain varieties of wholesome and positive thoughts.

According to Mahayana Buddhism, poverty of the mind is worse than material poverty. We may have riches but if, as Chögyam Trungpa Rinpoche has said, we have a poverty-stricken mentality, we will lead a fundamentally impoverished life. However, if we start to fill ourselves with good attitudes, open and positive and ways of looking at things, and develop wholesome emotions, we can become more enriched within. This helps us overcome loneliness. We would not be feeling so lonely, isolated, and have a desperate need for the affection or approval of others. This does not mean that if we follow the Buddhist Mahayana path we should not care about whether people shower us with love and affection. If it happens, then it is good. On the other hand, the greater the desperate need, the less we can attract from others. If we create enrichment within ourselves, that deep void to fill is not there. We can be alone instead of wallowing in our own loneliness and desperation. A poverty-stricken mentality will diminish as we develop a greater and more comprehensive experience of enrichment.

In Buddhism, it is believed that we have to begin with ourselves. We do not start from something external, like a god or reality. One starts with oneself and needs to go from there. We begin working on ourselves first and then we can approach understanding the nature of reality, which I will discuss in the next chapter. Of course, what others are doing is important and we should not be oblivious to what is going on around us with regard to other people and their lives and actions, and so on. In Buddhism, instead of constantly judging others in terms of how they appear to us, judging others as greedy, domineering, self-centered, et cetera, we should spend time on ourselves and try to deal with our own greed, neediness, and tendency to wish to dominate, subjugate, enslave, or terrorize others.

In Buddhism, working with ourselves in this way is not done purely as an exercise in morality, but is an exercise in self-education and self-enrichment. For example, it is not only that we try to avoid being greedy because it is morally wrong, even though that may be true. It may be more important to consider that miserliness can wear us down and close us off from others. We can become isolated, wearied, lonely, frustrated, and plunged into despair. As it is said in Buddhism, this is why we need to plant good seeds of self-enrichment. If we plant good seeds, they will bear good fruit and we will feel enriched. We subsequently would not feel so incomplete, as if we need someone or something else, another car, house, or something to make our lives fuller, to complete our lives. This does not mean that we should not buy another house if we can afford it, but it means not thinking that it is a solution that will complete our lives. Of course we can strive for what we want and need. According to Buddhism, seeking enrichment from external things, thinking that another car, house, or person is going to complete our lives, is approaching it in the wrong manner.

The better and more sustainable way is to put all manner of things into ourselves through our own effort, on one's own, and find within what we often seek from without. If we develop this ability, we will always be in a position to be able help ourselves and especially during times of difficulty, we would have developed inner resources and riches to navigate our way through. When we have to excessively rely on other people, it can be totally up to others how we fare in life. Sometimes people may be nice and show love and affection and at other times, they may not. They may be having problems and be preoccupied with their own lives. It can be problematic if we are too reliant on others. If we more capable of attending to our own needs, we become more self-sufficient. As I mentioned, we can subsequently be alone in a psychological and spiritual sense, not only in the physical sense. This is the way in which we try and work with ourselves. If we can do this, we are then in a much better position to work with others and for their benefit.

Our capacity to interact with others increases from an enriched mental space. The communication or communion becomes more authentic, genuine, and real. When we are not coming from a deep sense of need, a hankering, or deep longing, there is a genuine sense of openness. When we are able to do this, we gain more benefit by interacting with others than ever before because normally, all of our emotional entanglements—constantly seeking attention, or excessive need for companionship, affection, et cetera—prevent us from truly benefiting and being able to interact with others.

Normally, we may want others to clean up their act and be perfect for us. We can think that others should be a certain way toward us and be responsible for taking the first step to improve. From a Buddhist perspective, we should take the first step. We do not wait for others to clean up their acts and become our version of a great person; we should make the effort to improve and open ourselves up. We pursue sharing, participation, communication, and communion with that form of intention and attitude. In that way, extending ourselves to others starts with the sense of giving and sharing. Locking ourselves up in a prison of egoic preoccupation does not allow any space. Developing a sense of space and openness from our side is what allows us to come out of that prison. If we have a greater sense of openness, we can genuinely extend ourselves to others. If there is no sense of openness or space, there is no room to extend and we can become extremely hesitant, suspicious, and uncertain. We will develop confidence through the cultivation of positive emotions and can then extend ourselves with a more giving and generous outlook.

As more positive emotions are generated, they become more pervasive and bonded and the negative emotions become spasmodic and separated. Negative emotions almost always cause friction and conflict. If the negative emotion is overwhelming and has taken over our mind, heart, and being, it is difficult to heal the inner rift and build bridges. A more pervasive positive emotional environment cultivated based on a sense of spaciousness and openness allows us to have sympathy for and empathy with other living beings. Almost all of the positive emotions have this quality. For example, in the Buddhist literature on psychology, non-resentment and similar experiences are also listed as emotions. Non-resentment and the positive emotions are extremely helpful because not only do they propel us to engage in positive actions but they also allow us to more easily bond with human beings and other sentient creatures. If one has that sense, one does not normally need to see others as such a threat. Jean-Paul Sartre[10] supposedly said, "Hell is other people," but it does not have to be like that. Rather, we can realize that one of the great benefits of positive emotions is bringing sentient beings closer together. Therefore, positive emotions such as love and compassion are seen as the foundation to building bridges between oneself and others. If we have some form of love and compassion for others, all of the other positive emotions will follow.

Ordinarily, when we speak about love, it is described as a strong, powerful emotion. That is precisely why generating a powerful emotion such as love can be so helpful particularly when we are instructed to show love and compassion to all beings. When we show love, affection, or even compassion toward just one or two people that we have dealings with, these emotions can be overpowering because love, in many instances, is mixed with many other emotions, including unsavory emotions. Love is often accompanied by such emotions as fear, confusion, suspicion, doubt, hesitation, and so on. All of these different experiences may become intermingled with our experience of love. We can be thrown about, indicated by the expression "falling in love," with the word "falling" suggesting that it is like plunging into the unknown.

When we cultivate love and compassion in this context, it is helpful because we subsequently learn to extend ourselves beyond a few people to many others—human beings, living creatures, animals, and the organic world, the environment. In this way, we can understand emotion in a more intimate fashion. When we are thrown about by strong emotions, we do not have a chance to fully experience them without some sense of being overwhelmed. By extending our love and compassion to all different kinds of beings, the love that we feel is less likely to be mixed with other strong emotions, especially negative ones like jealousy, rage, and so on. We can become so enraged by the object of our love that our jealousy disturbs our stability and clarity of mind to the extent that we behave irrationally and in other unhelpful or even harmful ways.

For these reasons, it is helpful to try to experience love in another manner and context. In actuality, this may have a healing effect on the love that we feel for our spouse, parents, children, relatives, and friends. It may clarify aspects of what we are feeling. We do not have sufficient space to truly see what is going on when emotions are churned up and we are agitated. Things are not clear at all. If we have the experience of love and compassion in the proper fashion, this completes us as a human being. When we have the capacity to feel for others, it defines us as a human being. We are not defined simply by having rational capacity, although that is important. As human beings, we are capable of reason and the use of language. Our thinking capacity is incomparable. As far as we know, no other animal has developed a sophisticated language to the extent that we have. What truly makes us human is our capacity to care for all things and all beings. This may be something that other beings lack even though they care for their young and seem to show signs of feelings of affection. Even though we often behave like an animal, nevertheless, we are also capable of having very refined emotions that extend to all living things and beings. According to Buddhism, this is very noble; to have these forms of emotions ennobles us.

Using our intelligence only to rationalize does not ennoble us. Caring for others is what truly ennobles us. Even rationalizing love in a relationship can become similar to a business deal; "If I do this for you, I expect you to do this and that for me. If I scratch your back, you scratch mine." Sometimes relationships can literally be reduced to this. When we are able to give for the sake of giving, extending oneself and one's love and compassion to all ennobles us. In itself, this is rewarding because it lifts us up. When managed and understood properly, such all-encompassing kindness brings tremendous joy and excitement into our lives. It is not exciting or joyful to have to wait around for somebody to give us love, affection, and compassion. It is not joyful at all. It is very painful. However, if we take the first step and extend ourselves in this way, that is the reward. It is extremely rewarding, ennobling, joyful, and it completes us a human being. When we have a caring attitude toward all living things, we have climbed the ladder in terms of human development.

In Buddhism, we do not think of life as a straight line between birth and death. We see life as similar to climbing a hill. In other words, we need to climb up and aim toward attaining something higher, elevating ourselves. That is seen as the goal and purpose of living. Instead of going on foot and becoming tired and exhausted, if we generate love and compassion, it is like having a vehicle that we can use to climb that hill. The spiritual path, the journey, and our life become easier and enriched when we have real love and compassion. The sense of inner emptiness that we feel becomes filled. No one or anything external can ever fill that emptiness. We can keep shopping and buying things or forever try to find the right person, and so on, but that sense of incompleteness and "It's all for nothing" feeling will still be there despite a lifetime of achievements. Even if one has been successful at different pursuits and has a loving family, this does not fill it. However, if love and compassion are born inside oneself, that vacuum becomes filled and this is what makes one feel enriched. One begins to feel that one has something to share. Otherwise, one feels that one has nothing to share. One is only thinking about receiving from others. One can feel so incomplete and undernourished that one has to find nourishment from others. The more that love and compassion develops in our heart, the more we feel nourished.

In this way, one needs to recognize that by being useful to others, one is truly useful. When we feel emptiness inside ourselves, we may feel useless, worthless, helpless, and hopeless. When we feel love and compassion, we do not feel useless. Rather, we feel our worth, good qualities, and we also feel enriched. We are capable of becoming more self-assured and confident in ourselves when we know that we care for others. We develop a fundamental understanding of ourselves as useful and worthwhile knowing that we are willing to do something for others, even something seemingly insignificant.

As the great Tibetan master Patrul Rinpoche and many others have so often said, we should not ignore the little gestures that we are able to perform.[11] It all mounts up, accumulates, and amalgamates. Patrul Rinpoche used the example of water dripping into a bucket; one drop at a time, the bucket will quickly become full. Therefore, little things that we do will accumulate and in that way, we become enriched. We do not have to think, "I have to do something really dramatic otherwise I am not making any difference or being useful." It is not about burning oneself out, giving everything until we are exhausted. According to Mahayana teachings, this is the wrong approach. Rather, we build a positive and spacious inner environment with the accumulation of positive thoughts amalgamating into positive attitudes and actions. Understanding the power of thoughts to transform, building such inner richness, is very self-sustaining. We become more able to generate and regenerate love and compassion. Doing little things as much and as many times as possible is what ennobles us. This is what makes us become rich inside. In that way, we do not have to think about receiving gratitude from others. If people are grateful for what we have done, that is fantastic, but if they are not grateful, we have already been rewarded. This is how one should think rather than thinking, "I did so much for that person but they show no appreciation whatsoever." This is our egoic mind interfering. We have to see things in a new light.

There is nothing more rewarding than doing something beneficial for others. Similarly, nothing makes us feel more useful than doing something useful for others. Getting another haircut, buying a new pair of shoes, and pampering ourselves make us feel good only for a short time. If we do something for someone however, the warm feeling we gain will last an extremely long time. This will then also boost our sense of self-worth because we think, "I have done something that is good. I helped somebody and this is a good thing." This form of pride is healthy and helps us feel good about ourselves. If we do not show any loving-kindness and become withdrawn, always thinking, "I must have love and compassion. I need to have others showing it to me," we will not feel enriched. We will forever remain impoverished. In that way, we aim toward peaking, attaining our full human potential, through love and compassion. According to Mahayana Buddhism, when we care and open up, so many other possibilities become actualities. If we have developed insight into the human condition, we can open up more confidently and our love and compassion can begin to flow; all the other hidden creative energies and positive qualities inside us can also begin to find their expression.

With regard to strong negative emotions like rage for example, if we are feeling enraged much of the time, this will unleash or unlock many other forms of negative emotions and feelings and cause them to become manifest. The same also happens with positive emotions. Here, we are discussing the importance of generating and using love and compassion to draw out all of that which is good in ourselves, to have that become more active rather than such qualities remaining dormant. According to Buddhism, if we believe in rebirth, we have been around for a long time and there are all forms of seeds or potentialities inside us, both good and bad. It depends on how we are dealing with our feelings, emotions, and attitudes. If we have the healthier kinds of feelings and emotions, all the positive seeds will mature and become manifest. Love and compassion find their full expression when we are interacting, communing, and communicating with others.

An additional virtue of love and compassion is the finding of self-transcendence. When we do not have love and compassion or care, when we believe that we are in love but are doing it as some form of barter or exchange, we do not find self-transcendence. If we show real love and compassion however, we find self-transcendence. We know what it is like to be able to function without having the egoic identity ruling our life. Through this, when we can show sympathy for and empathy with others through love and compassion, we become a real human. When we care, we are living a full life. According to Buddhism, it is not a full life if we do not care.

It can sometimes be easier to show love and compassion to strangers and people in far away places. This is important and in Buddhism, when we do meditation on loving-kindness, we do visualizations where we include all sentient beings. However, the fundamental practice of loving-kindness has to be done with people that we have contact with and then extend out from there. This giving, sharing, and mutual care that we are trying to generate becomes a spiritual concern. It is the ultimate goal of living as a

Buddhist. If we have this, whatever we may be doing as a person in terms of vocation, interests, hobbies, and spiritual practices will turn out right. The Buddhist view is that if we have loving-kindness, everything that we do will turn out right. If we do not have loving-kindness, whatever we do in terms of vocation, family, personal and public life, interests, hobbies, or whatever the case may be, will not turn out so well because we would not be coming from a good place. Many Mahayana masters say that if we have loving-kindness, we will feel that we are in charge of our life and that it is not out of control. If we do not have this, it will always seem that we do not quite have a handle on our lives; we feel lost and do not know where we are or are going. Loving-kindness has a way of illuminating our mind and heart and if we have a genuine sense of loving-kindness, that in itself would shed light on our life. We can feel less like we are wandering in the dark, lost and confused.

Any feelings of hurt, rejection, and dejection that we have felt in the past will also begin to melt. We would realize that their significance has been greatly reduced in our lives. The wounds that we have had to contend with can become healed. Therefore, there is no better medicine or antidote to any of our afflictions than loving-kindness. Of course, thinking clearly and rationally is not a contradiction in terms of the generation of loving-kindness. Problems often arise in life because we have not been thinking clearly or paying attention to our thoughts. Coupled with a caring attitude, we can resolve many problems in life. If we truly care and feel for others, this is the most powerful healing. In that way, when we give, we are receiving. Whether others return the favor or reciprocate is not the issue. We have already given something back to ourselves as soon as we have given to others. It is important to repeatedly remind ourselves of this. It is easy to become discouraged and slide back into our old thinking habits that say, "I'm always giving. I'm always trying to do the best I can but nobody does anything for me. Nobody cares. I don't feel appreciated or needed. I could disappear tomorrow and nobody would notice." We should not entertain these negative forms of self-talk. If we believe in karma, karmically speaking, when we give, we have already received. We do not have to wait for the other person to return anything to us. If they do, that is fantastic. According to Buddhism, it does matter what people do but it does not matter as much as we believe. If they withhold their appreciation, we do not need to feel bad about it. Often, others show their appreciation but if we are not looking with eyes of compassion, we may not see it. It is like a child, for example, that does not see the love and compassion that they have received from their parents for many years and still feels uncared for. My point here is simply that because we may feel unappreciated sometimes does not necessarily mean that people are not showing appreciation. This is worth thinking about.

Sometimes good things happen to bad people and bad things happen to good people but this should not disproportionately concern us. According to Buddhism, bad people are already suffering even if externally, some good fortune has come their way. Even if good things happen in a nasty person's life, such as winning a million dollar jackpot or being promoted at work, from the Buddhist perspective, we should not look solely at the obvious, thinking that a bad person has been rewarded or escaped scot-free. Bad things may happen to good people, but good things are also happening to them. Good people are rewarding themselves with who they are. Despite the fact that externally, something may have been taken from them such as illness, death in the family, or bankruptcy, whatever it might be, nevertheless, good people are still rich inside. Conversely, bad people may have the outward appearance of having good fortune come to them, but in reality, they still have the poverty-stricken mentality. "Bad people" are usually called "bad" because they have no control over their negative emotions. They are excessively aggressive, arrogant, ruthless, and cruel and therefore, they are suffering from these afflictions. Due to their aggression or other negative afflictions, they may experience constant discord and inner turmoil of one type or another. They may live in fear of a destroyed reputation, loss of status, being broadly disliked, and so on. When we look at it in this manner, bad people are not getting away with anything. Good people on the other hand, are still living a fulfilling life injected with meaning.

This is the Mahayana view, and if we look at it in this light with the right attitude, we are capable of living a truly fulfilling life. Otherwise, these thoughts will distract us; "Maybe this path is not really right because there are people who do terrible things and they seem to have a good time. I am trying to do my best, to care for others, and I don't feel appreciated. I don't feel needed. Nobody seems to care for me." These thoughts will diminish us instead of ennoble us. Since we have the opportunity to enrich ourselves despite what happens externally due to a death in the family, erroneous financial decisions, unexpected divorce, or whatever it might be, we would still feel rich inside if we had that magnanimous, generous spirit that does not allow the thoughts of impoverishment to enter and corrupt the real goodness that is already present in us. As Trungpa Rinpoche said, basic goodness is present in everyone.

Interacting with and caring for others are worthwhile pursuits and make our life more fulfilling. We do it not purely for the sake of others but also for ourselves. When we are dying and review our life, we can say, "I did not waste my life. At least I did some good things. I helped some people." We would then feel that, "I lived quite well." If we leave this world without having cared for anyone, even if we leave millions behind, when we die, we die as a poor person. This is the Buddhist view. If one dies with the heart and mind filled with positive attitudes, love, and compassion, one dies a rich person. These riches are not left behind like millions of dollars but rather, one carries them into the next life. There is no reason why we should not believe in rebirth. These riches are not left at the gates of death like the money that we have to leave behind. We cannot carry those forms of riches but we can carry the amassment of what we call merit (Tib. *bsod nams*). We carry those riches with us into the next life. For example, if someone moved from one country to another with so much wealth that they could set themselves up quickly, in a similar way, you would go into the next life and set yourself up with all of the inner riches. Everything is good and you live your new life with ease and without anxiety and worries.

Chapter Five

Relationship with Reality

In the previous chapter, I spoke about the benefit and importance of extending ourselves to others as a way of enhancing our psychological and spiritual development. The second benefit that I mentioned was the cultivation of positive emotions and how they not only lead to good actions, but also enrich and inject meaning into our lives. Further, if we develop positive emotions, they have a natural attraction; positive emotions cause people to bond whereas the negative emotions interfere with people's relationships and their capacity to bond with each other. Negative emotions come between children and parents, partners, friends, and even different groups of people. Negative emotions almost always lead to friction, conflict, and strife. Positive emotions on the other hand, bring about a sense of harmony between oneself and others and a space is then created so that one can communicate with others more easily.

The third benefit is that positive emotions have a healing effect. Often, we may carry or nurse some form of hurt, a slight that we have suffered at the hands of someone or an unpleasant childhood experience. When positive emotions begin to flourish in our hearts, all of these hurts naturally begin to recede without deliberately trying to overcome them. In that way, the positive emotions are also extremely helpful in providing an opportunity for us to be able to heal and more openly and confidently connect and bond with others.

Further, the primary positive emotions of love and compassion create an environment that would be conducive to automatically bringing the other positive emotions into being. In the same way, the primary negative emotions of excessive desire and anger bring out in us other negativities such as resentment, jealousy, bitterness, et cetera. Therefore, if we give birth to love and compassion, all of the other positive emotions come into being. It is enriching. We do not need to wait for someone to give us love or show a caring attitude. Rather, we can produce it ourselves. The beauty of positive emotions is that we can bring these into existence by ourselves; we do not have to receive them from others in order for them to manifest. We can produce them within ourselves at any time or place.

Thinking in this manner, one extends oneself to others and sees that working for the benefit of others is one of the most beneficial ways of also being useful to oneself. We truly experience self-worth when we have done something significant and there is nothing more significant than doing something for others who are in need of help. This ranges from giving small gifts to sharing encouraging words and generating good thoughts. All of this helps. We are not only helping the object or recipient of our goodwill, but we also benefit. Therefore, we do not have to wait for a reward because the gesture itself enriches our inner state of being. It is its own reward. We need nothing more than that because when we do something good, we also feel good, enabled, and self-sufficient. There is nothing bad about it. All aspects of that form of gesture have positive qualities attached to it.

This is how we can overcome cynicism and darker moods such as the experience of despair. It is only when we do not connect well or properly that we become vulnerable to dark moods and emotions. If we concern ourselves with the well-being of others and seek to alleviate the suffering of others in a connected way, it becomes a joyful act for oneself. From the Buddhist point of view, we create joy when we are able to be encouraging of others and help alleviate some of their pain and suffering, even if only in a small way. For example, if someone is feeling lonely and unattractive, by helping to make them feel differently about themselves and injecting a sense of self-confidence in them, one has done a tremendous job. That is the reward. Seeing someone happy makes us happy or at least, seeing them feeling a little better than minutes earlier gives us inspiration and encouragement. We begin to see what the teachings are saying about caring for others. Therefore, we extend ourselves to others not only because it is praiseworthy, ethically sound, and the right action to perform, it is all of these things, but also because of the many other benefits that one gains from such actions. Building such motives and perspective not only creates a solid ethical framework from which to guide our conduct, but it also includes many other psychological and spiritual benefits when orienting ourselves toward the world and to others.

The final point I wish to discuss on how to lead a fulfilling life from a Buddhist perspective has to do with how we relate to ultimate reality. This is extremely important because how we relate to others will be dependent on how we view reality, what we think reality is. Whether we acknowledge or are conscious of it or not, we all have our own personal philosophy, some notion about what is real, what is not real, whether there is something called ultimate or absolute reality, or whether the only reality is what we see, hear, smell, taste, and touch—what we know about the external world through the senses. We all have a fundamental philosophy of life. What we do or think, how we relate to other people, and so on, is determined by that personally developed philosophy. This cannot be escaped or overridden easily. That being the case, from the Buddhist point of view, we have to be clear about what we think reality is because what we do in relation to ourselves and others is dependent on that.

Contemplating and trying to understand reality helps to develop wisdom. Extending ourselves to others and developing positive emotions, filling ourselves with goodness, is extremely important, as we have been discussing. To lead our lives in this manner, properly and sustainably, requires us to also develop greater wisdom. It is more than very likely that from a Buddhist perspective, we do not yet have sufficient wisdom to experience ultimate reality. Embarking on the path, practicing contemplations and meditation, and approaching life as we have been discussing would allow us to develop such wisdom. More particularly, wisdom comes from contemplating on what is real, what is not real, what is ultimately real, what is relatively real, and so on. From the Buddhist point of view, this is not seen solely as an intellectual exercise because whatever we think reality is will determine how we live our life. Everyone has opinions about such matters and one lives by these beliefs. For example, believing that God exists or that there is no God may have a tremendous influence on how we live our lives.

From a Buddhist perspective, to develop wisdom, we must first cultivate insight. When insight matures, it becomes transformed into wisdom. Insight is developed from looking at life; first looking at what we see, hear, smell, taste, and touch and then looking at the world in terms of what we cannot see, hear, smell, taste, or touch. With the first, according to the Buddha and subsequent Buddhist masters, when we look at the world through our senses, if we are observant, we see constant change everywhere. We see that things are in a constant state of flux. Nothing is abiding. According to Buddhism, there is a tremendous lesson to be learned here but we rarely fully appreciate the psychological relationship that develops in terms of what we experience through the senses—what we see, smell, hear, taste, and touch—how the apprehension of the world through our senses can shape our character, personal preferences, likes and dislikes, and the impact that this has on the quality of our lives and how we experience the world.

How we cognize and respond to our sensory input has a tremendous influence on shaping a range of fixations and obsessions. Because of these fixations and obsessions, our vision has become not only unclear and blurred, but also narrowed or blinkered. When we become fixated on different things, often, the only thing visible to us is the object of our fixation. Nothing or very little else is included within our field of experience. Other things tend to fade into the background. Whether the fixation is on money, food, fame, or good looks, we are capable of being motivated to pursue it to no end. If we become obsessed with something, everything else can pale into insignificance. For example, one may even stop caring about friends, parents, or siblings because, as we know, obsessions can take over. While we may not often go to that extreme, according to Buddhism, every sentient creature has degrees of all kinds of fixation and obsessions. Being fixated on money, body image, fame, or whatever it might be, may become all that counts and nothing else. It can blind us even to some of our greatest achievements and joys.

Such distortions stop us from properly and fully experiencing the world in which we live. We may think that what we are experiencing is the real world but according to Buddhism, we are not immersed in the real world. The world that we live in is obscured by our fixations and obsessions and is thus a somewhat make-believe world. We live in a world colored by our distortions and fantasies. Fixations and obsessions have their grounding in delusion or ignorance (Skt. *avidyā*) and therefore, a lack of insight into the nature of reality is evident. From the Buddhist viewpoint, we need to begin taking notice of the world, what we see, smell, taste, hear, and touch within our meditation while we are hopefully in a better position to keep our obsessions at bay. We can learn to calm the mind at least temporarily and through using the power of mindfulness and awareness, we can look at the world more completely and with less distortion. We can then better see what is going on. This will tell us a great deal about how the world is when it is free of our fixations and obsessions.

According to Buddhism, when we do this, we will see that the world is in a constant state of flux. Ordinarily, our mind does not allow us to deal with the world in that manner; it prefers to latch on to something and hesitates to let go. We seek to sustain our view of reality even though it is largely based on our own fixations and obsessions. Subsequently, it is as if we wish to keep everything the same, in freeze-frame, as if there is no movement. As I mentioned, the samsaric mindset is such that there is much turbulence but no movement, like bubbly water in a pond. In a similar manner, there is a lot of agitation in the mind but it can take tremendous effort on the part of the individual to shift gear. Tremendous effort may be needed for the mind to shift even a small amount. Once the mind gets settled into its own version of reality, it can become set like concrete, becoming harder and harder over time. Our thoughts and emotions attach themselves to an object or belief, and the fixation and obsession starts its solidification process. It begins to settle in and can then be hard to budge.

If we can truly see the world properly, even momentarily through arresting our fixations and obsessions for a time, a shift in our mental structure can gradually take place. Our mind would begin to loosen, freshen, and become more inclusive. This is because if we observe the world properly, we will gain more insight into the world than what we immediately see and experience. We are not referring to ultimate reality at this point, but the reality that we perceive on a daily basis.

According to Buddhism, it is not the case that how we experience what we see, hear, smell, taste, and touch exists as we experience it, in reality. This is not seen as direct experience of the real world. On the contrary, what we see, hear, smell, taste, and touch has more to do with our mind than the reality "out there," such as the object of smell, the object of taste, or the object of touch. Because our mind is so selective and choosy, it settles only on certain things due to either our attraction or aversion to things. That then becomes our version of reality. Reality becomes whatever one believes it is. For a money loving person, money is the ultimate reality, the most real thing. For a romantic, romance is the ultimate thing and little else may matter. Even if one cannot find enough to eat, if one can chase after an object of one's dream, this becomes the ultimate. If we can see our mind working in this way to distort reality, we begin to gain insight into reality. We can then see that there is a discrepancy between what is going on inside of ourselves and what is going on outside of ourselves.

The Buddhist view is that what is going on inside does not abide even for a moment without changing. Some changes are subtler than others and are almost undetectable. Our emotional responses to things can be quite habitual but nonetheless, while they may be similar, they are never exactly the same. Our memory can change, our love can change, and our abilities can increase or diminish. Our blinkered solidification of the world happens within our minds, not outside our minds. If we look at a wooden table, for example, we do not see it changing from day to day, but if we saw a wooden table two years ago and then see it today, we may more easily observe the differences. It will not be the same. Everything has subtle forms of change that are happening in this manner. Many more objects are changing even faster than a table, such as clouds passing in the sky, as Buddhist teachings say. Clouds do not sit still when they gather; they are always on the move and do not hover around or sit still even for a brief period. Everything about life and the world is like that. In Buddhism, this insight is seen as extremely profound, even though initially it may not appear to be so very profound. How we experience the world rarely fully corresponds with how the world is. Rather, it corresponds with what is in our own mind and makeup—our prejudices and preferences, what is acceptable to us and what is not, our obsessions and fixations. If we truly think about it, it is enormously profound because it reaches all corners of our lives, mental, physical, intellectual, emotional—everything.

If we recognize this strong habitual tendency, it is then possible not to get too fixated on certain things. If we do not get too fixated, our ability to enjoy life would greatly increase. If we are fixated on eating hamburgers and mashed potatoes every day and we do not wish to eat anything else, if we look at it more objectively, the level of enjoyment is limited and highly conditional. If this person becomes less fixated on that specific type of food and becomes more open, the ability to enjoy food greatly increases. Food is one example, but it also applies to everything in terms of our range of experiences. Even if we believe that we are often being open minded, some deep variety of fixation can always be located. There are many different forms of fixation. If we can sometimes relax our fixations, we directly connect with the world more panoramically, recognizing its fluctuation, complexities, and movement instead of resisting seeing endless change and trying to freeze-frame our experience. We would see the world much more clearly. We would see the movement. Otherwise, we can only see a static reality, which is not reality at all. From the Buddhist point of view, this is the starting point to understanding not only relative reality but also ultimate reality. To fully see reality, first we have to see this. Otherwise, it is difficult to begin this journey.

Everything within and without is in a state of motion and there are a whole host of causes and conditions involved in producing this reality. There is not solely one thing that gives rise to something else. This is not only true of the world but it is also true within ourselves. It is not true only of the physical reality that we perceive through our senses. If we direct our attention inward, we see the same complexity of causes and conditions happening in our mind. The mind is also in a state of constant flux. The same pattern is being repeated in the mind as outside the mind, with different causes and conditions giving rise to anger, jealousy, hope, fear, despair, ecstasy, or whatever the case may be. Therefore, we see that what arises in the mind is very similar to how physical things come into being and pass away, arise and dissipate.

Buddhists say that this shows us that things are not substantial. We have to understand the Buddhist definition of certain words and when Buddhists say that things are not substantial, they mean that things are produced. If something is substantial, by definition, it would not be a product, it would have existed right from the beginning. When we say that things are non-substantial, to reiterate, this means that things are produced, meaning one thing needs something else or otherwise, it would not come into being. Therefore, everything is dependent on causes and conditions. All things that come into being are dependent on causes and conditions. A substantial thing, according to the Buddhist definition, has to be non-dependent. If something has substance or essence, it must be self-existing. Non-substantial does not mean nonexistent but rather, that things do not exist by themselves.

From the Buddhist viewpoint, insubstantiality or lack of permanency should not be seen solely as an intellectual exercise. It has a direct bearing on how we perceive reality and ourselves and how we deal with our emotions, feelings, and thoughts. This is because our thoughts, feelings, and emotions are not separate and are self-generated. They have a cause and certain conditions, when present, may be the catalyst for thoughts, feelings, and emotions to arise. The same insight we gain into the nature of our mind, emotions, and thoughts also applies to the external physical or material world. If we see it in this manner, we can become less fixated and obsessed. There would be more movement in our mind and ability to harness and encourage positive emotions. Our experience of life would be enhanced. Otherwise, we can feel stuck and powerless to change anything internally or externally. When we feel like we are engulfed in deep despair or other such strong emotions, we can feel caught and find no exit strategy or way to improve our situation or state of mind. We can feel helpless. From the Buddhist point of view, if we try to understand the reality of what is happening, it will help to free all this up because all of our misconceptions could be challenged and dispelled and our fixations and obsessions reduced. This insight is extremely helpful. It has important practical value.

We can then go further and see that since everything is a product of causes and conditions, this implies that everything is devoid of an enduring, unchanging essence. There is no underlying reality or permanent state, meaning that there is an absence of underlying reality to the world of phenomena that we perceive through our senses. In other words, we do not experience the world directly as it truly is, we experience the world through our senses. How we interpret what we experience is therefore dependent not only on the capacity of each sense—eyes, ears, et cetera— but on our beliefs and general conceptual frameworks. It is not just dependent on the world outside us. This is the Buddhist view called "emptiness." In brief, emptiness means that things are devoid of essence or substance. It does not mean they do not exist. It simply means that things do not have any form of enduring essence and everything is dependently produced.

From the Buddhist perspective, this insight is helpful on the spiritual path because we can then make sense of bondage or samsara and also liberation. When we are unenlightened, we are in a state of bondage and when we become enlightened, we are liberated. How do we move from a state of bondage to liberation?

Due to the nature of things being emptiness, it is possible for one to be in a state of ignorance or bondage and also become enlightened or liberated. If reality were something different, permanent or substantial, such transformation would be impossible. Without a fundamental reality of insubstantiality or emptiness, if one is deluded, confused, and living in samsara, that would be the true reality so that even if one could conceive of liberation or enlightenment, it would not be possible. It would only be a dream that could not become a reality. Enlightenment would not be possible because reality would be the state that one is already in. In the ultimate sense, one cannot have two realities. We cannot have two ultimate realities because the whole notion of "ultimate" would be made redundant. If the samsaric condition represents reality, enlightenment or liberation would only be a dream. As Mahayana teachings say, samsara and nirvana are possible due to reality being what it is; empty, insubstantial, uncaused. This is why ignorance and bondage are possible and why liberation and enlightenment are also possible, due to ultimate reality being what it is. As Nagarjuna said, "Because of emptiness, everything is possible. If emptiness were not true, nothing would be possible."

It is important to remember that according to the Buddhist way of defining reality, that which is completely real and free of distortions such as exaggerations and embellishments, does not change. Buddhism believes that our lives are pregnant with possibility due to emptiness. This means that everything has the capacity for transformation and everything, even if not detected by us, is always changing. When understood in this way, emptiness can be seen in a very positive light. Negative interpretation sometimes foisted upon the concept of emptiness is generally misrepresentation or misinterpretation. As I said, the notion of emptiness in Buddhism does not say that we and the world around us do not exist, but rather, that everything changes. Thus, we as individuals can change and transform. We do not have to feel so caught. As Nagarjuna said, otherwise, nothing would be possible. If emptiness were not true or real, everything would not be in a state of flux and nothing would be possible. Everything contains possibility due to the reality of emptiness or insubstantiality. Therefore, it is positive.

To use an analogy, it is also said that the sky is nothing but without sky, there would be no mountains, stones, wood, or earth. We would not be able to make bricks, fashion pillars and beams, and therefore, build houses and so on. The sky provides the space for us to carry out all of these activities. In a similar manner, emptiness itself is not a thing. Reality is all-encompassing yet we cannot grasp at it as another entity amongst other entities. Nevertheless, without emptiness, there are no potentialities or possibilities, nothing could be done or achieved. Similarly, unless there is space, we cannot fashion anything with material objects. If it is soil, we can dig it up and create a mound or build a mud brick wall and create a garden in order to grow food. We can do whatever we wish with the soil and the space. This is first main point.

The other point that I wish to make is that as we begin to progress and deepen our understanding of reality, insight into the nature of things is transformed into wisdom. As this occurs, our ordinary mind or consciousness becomes transformed into wisdom mind or wisdom consciousness. Purely for conceptual clarification, we can look at ultimate reality from a subjective or objective point of view. Subjectively, there is wisdom, objectively, there is emptiness and both wisdom and emptiness are ultimately real. Wisdom/subjective reality can be seen as a counterbalance to emptiness/objective reality.

Even though it is called "wisdom mind," it is not seen as representation of purely cognitive activities of the mind. It does not simply mean that Buddha knows many different things, even though that is true. It also means that wisdom mind has the aspect of compassion, which represents the best of all the positive emotions. When we say compassion or Buddha's compassion, we are using compassion as a generic term to cover the whole gamut of creatively expressed powerful positive emotions supported by wisdom. Buddha's wisdom mind has these two aspects.

To truly see reality properly, one needs to see the non-duality of what we perceive through the senses, the everyday life reality and its nature, which is emptiness, as not separable. In Buddhism, we do not want to split reality into two—one reality that we can dispense with saying that it is illusory, and the other "real" reality thinking that we should try to attain its true realization. Buddhism does not say that. Buddhism speaks about the unity of appearance and reality, "appearance" meaning what we perceive on a daily basis, and reality, which is emptiness. We need wisdom consciousness to perceive this unity properly. Such pure perception is developed over time. We first develop and cultivate insight so that we can grasp this notion of non-duality. According to Buddhism, if we make the effort to understand non-duality and the nature of reality, we will experience tremendous change; in how we see others, express our emotions, and how we conceptualize and experience ourselves, others, and the world. We would be building an understanding of how the world is and how we interact and engage within it. We would develop an understanding of what is truly happening. This would be in contrast to how we normally decide what is going on in the world. We are normally speculating about what is happening from a narrow, blinkered, egoic, highly personalized perspective. When we gain more insight, we become transformed, open, and inclusive through gaining insight into reality.

It is important not to think of this as an intellectual exercise but rather, as being extremely practical. Whatever we believe is real will impact on what we think we are and how we see and experience the world. If we believe God has created us, we would think and go about relating to the world in a particular way that in some way corresponded to our beliefs. If we think of reality in the Buddhist manner, it would also have an impact on our daily life, how we deal with our emotions and feelings, and how we relate to other people and situations generally. It would also impact the relationship that we have with others and the world through our senses; what we see, smell, taste, touch, and so on.

From the Buddhist viewpoint, seeing ultimate reality is vital and everything else must be founded on that—how we relate to others and how we relate to ourselves—because if we understand reality, we will see that "subject and object" or "myself and other," is also a dependent concept. Self is there because of the other. As it is expressed, there cannot be a single, free floating, self-existing, isolated ego. All of the individuals, the selves of the world, are interconnected. One is either the subject or object in relation to the other. From the Buddhist point of view, in this sense, "self" should be seen a relational concept rather than a label for a form of self-existing entity, an ego. A "self" is a self one moment and an object in another. In a different context, self becomes object and in yet another context, self is the self. It depends on the perspective and point of view. There is the agent, act, and object acted upon. For example, if I help an individual, there is the relationship of being a helper and a helpee. In Buddhism, this is not seen as simply an intellectual exercise, but if one thinks about it deeply, it will transform how one thinks about oneself and others.

The same happens with the natural physical world that we inhabit. In Buddhist language, the relationship is called "container and content." All the sentient beings and other things that inhabit the natural world are called "content" and the natural world is called the "container." There is a relationship between the container and the content. A container without content would not be a container. A container by definition means "something that contains things." Content, on the other hand, suggests "the content of something," therefore, it implies a container. In Buddhism, this is called *pratityasamutpada* or interdependent arising.

When we look at it in this manner, showing positive emotions to others becomes natural. If there is the interconnectedness of everything, it makes sense that the showing of positive feelings and emotions, bonding of human beings and humans to other sentient creatures and our environment should be natural. It is important to see love and compassion as natural emotions that with an interconnected and inclusive perspective, would naturally arise. In fact, it is unnatural to have an absence of love and compassion. If everything is interconnected, to have emotions that make us feel cut off from one another, seeing everything and everybody as discrete, individual entities, self-sufficiently existing, self-enclosed egos, means that there is no proper room for the notion of communication, communion, or bonding. Reality demands that we come to the realization of the interdependent nature of all things, and therefore, the interdependence of all living beings.

This is a brief introduction to the notion of ultimate reality, as it relates to the topic of leading a fulfilling life. Leading a fulfilling life ultimately has to come from understanding interconnectedness and the interdependent nature of all things. If we recognize this, we will then feel a sense of belongingness. Otherwise, we can feel uprooted and disconnected, as if we do not belong, and are cut off, not connected to anyone. When we feel this way, loneliness and despair become our companions and the quality of our life diminishes. However, if we are better able to relate to others and ourselves and make peace with ourselves, we can have less anxiety, suspicion, and paranoia about others. This can bring us much more of a feeling of ease. Even if we cannot make peace with everyone, still, this approach and perspective of connection with others and interdependence would automatically contribute to improving the quality of our life.

As I also discussed, one of the keys to leading a fulfilling life is knowing how to enrich oneself by oneself, so that we are not too dependent on others. Not expecting others to make our lives fulfilled is important because they may not be able to do that for us. Having such expectations can lead to tremendous disappointment. We cannot depend on that outcome. If we gain love from others and if they pay attention to us and are grateful for the things we do, of course, that is a wonderful bonus in life. But if we can learn to enrich and replenish ourselves, we do not need to burden others with all of our expectations of how they should be for us. We can enjoy our life whether we find support and love from others or not. By being more self-sustaining, we are better able to receive more from others and give more to others without the burden of too many expectations. If we do not enrich ourselves, even if others show love or affection, we may not see or appreciate it. We may not even believe it and be in a state of mind to be able to receive it. We may think that we do not deserve such love. All sorts of things can go around in our minds. There could be so much negativity in our mind that we are not able to fully benefit from what we do receive. When we feel unfulfilled, our minds can cook up all kinds of things and we do not know what is what and which is which. We may not be able to see what is actually going on. If we are thinking all manner of things from many different angles, creating so many illusions and fantasies about what is going on, what we want may elude us. If we can enrich ourselves, we also have more to give. When we are receiving gifts of love and acknowledgement from others, we know what we are receiving.

If we truly want to try to live our life following the Buddhist path, we need to replenish ourselves through generating positive thoughts and emotions and reflect on our interconnection and interdependence with others and the world. We need to reflect on the nature of reality, building insight, wisdom, love, and compassion. We must have conviction in what we are doing because without conviction, we cannot progress.

Buddhism is a very reasonable form of religion or spirituality but I do not think people become transformed simply by knowing that Buddhism is rational, insightful, and makes sense. We become transformed if we believe in what we are doing and pursuing. In this instance, we are referring to belief in Buddha's teachings. It is important to believe in what you do and then exercise your mind and examine, analyze, think, reflect, and contemplate. Progress is dependent on and based on commitment. In this instance, we are also referring to commitment to the Buddha's teachings. No one becomes transformed simply by knowing something. Otherwise, physics professors and many other intellectuals and deep thinkers would have become enlightened already. We become transformed when we have some form of passion and conviction without turning into a fanatic. To have strong beliefs provides catalysts for progress, change, and transformation. So if we definitely believe that Buddha's teachings are not only helpful but true and we have conviction in that and do not constantly withdraw, becoming tentative, hesitant, with one foot in the door and one outside it, we can progress without being sidetracked by constant niggles and doubts. It is reasonable to think that the Buddha is believable and was a person that we can put our trust in. There is a big gap between conviction and fanaticism. Conviction propels us forward. If we do not have conviction, it is difficult to move forward with certainty. I believe that Dharma is very beneficial and has so much to offer. When we have the opportunity to practice and study, consider, and contemplate it, it is best done wholeheartedly, as there is much benefit to be gained.

Section Two

Relationships in Everyday Life

Chapter Six

Self-knowledge and Relationships

As far as the idea of relationship in Buddhism is concerned, it is extraordinarily important to be able to understand what the two veils or obscurations mean. The first is the "veil of emotional conflict" and the other is the "veil of conceptual confusion." As long as one is not aware of these two types of confusions and how to work with them, any form of relationship that one might be engaged in would give rise to a degree of complication, misunderstanding, misinterpretation, and misassessment of the situation. From a Buddhist perspective, we need to develop insight and awareness into how we relate and respond to the world, how we formulate our experiences. With additional insight, we can better assess what is necessary to improve our experience and how to go about skillfully responding to a situation in an appropriate, wholesome, and ethical way. Without such clarity regarding how we express our emotions, our conceptualizations, and how we interpret experiences and situations, we can become confused and misguided in any relationship especially in terms of what we seek to establish.

When we begin to look at these two obscurations or veils of

emotional conflict and conceptual confusion, we can see that they are intimately related to our day-to-day experiences. There is an intimate relationship between our emotional experiences and our deep-seated beliefs, opinions, and intellectual processes. It is sometimes assumed that emotions are a matter of the heart, related to one's physicality and therefore instinctive, whereas thoughts and concepts are seen as mental and more intellectually based. So it is seen as a dichotomy between our mental processes and our emotional experiences. Emotional experiences are commonly seen as something that sometimes arises seemingly from nowhere and they can overwhelms us, as if they were entirely different and separate from our ways of thinking or conceptualizing. In Buddhism however, we believe that there is an intimate relationship between how we go about expressing our emotions and the way we think about, interpret, and conceptualize situations and circumstances. Therefore, there is an intimate relationship between emotional conflict and conceptual confusion. We need to develop insight into how these aspects that are in relationship happen and interact.

For instance, we say that we are "falling in love," "overwhelmed by love," and "I had no choice but to fall in love." From the Buddhist perspective, "falling in love" without choice does not exist. "Falling in love" is based on many things and has a strong link to our conceptual interpretations. We place these interpretations on a particular experience. In this sense, it is not an experience of overwhelming physical sensation or feeling alone, but intimately related with how one interprets that situation and experience.

If emotions simply happened to us and we have no choice in the matter, we could not speak about creating good or bad karma. If there is no choice, then how can we support the idea of change, transformation, or progress? From a Buddhist perspective, we are responsible for our actions or experiences, including how we manage our emotions. One cannot be made responsible for something when one has no choice in the matter. Our varieties of emotional experiences, as well as being fuelled by past experiences, the content and quality of our thoughts, and our ethics and beliefs, are also related to outcomes that we wish to achieve. Emotions are more often than not used in a strategic manner. We use our emotions to elicit certain responses and gain certain results from others. They are used to gain specific results within our interactions. Rather than being seen as something that happens to us, emotions are seen as something that we create and invariably use in a strategic manner, even if somewhat unconsciously.

For example, within a couple, if one partner wishes to go to the theatre and the other does not, certain strategic steps may be used through expressing a particular type of emotion so that eventually, they do not end up having to go to the theatre. In the beginning, one person might make certain statements such as complaining about how the partner ironed their shirt or that they do not have the pants that they wanted to wear; in so doing, they create an argument. Afterward, the person may say, "I'm so sorry. I didn't mean it," but they may know deep inside that it is not that they were overcome by anger and had no choice, but rather that they used certain responses in order to achieve the desired result.

Due to this process of creation, we can speak about creating wholesome or unwholesome karma. Much of what determines whether we are creating wholesome or unwholesome karma depends upon the manner in which we express our emotions and react to situations and how we interact with other human beings. If we are using emotions in a strategic manner, we are responsible for our actions. However, we can learn how to become more skilled and adept at expressing our emotions so that the way in which we express them becomes progressively more wholesome, constructive, and less destructive or manipulative in relation to ourselves and others. If it is love that one is experiencing, it can be shaded by a desire for control, resentment, jealousy, and other types of negativity. Then, not only does the negativity harm others, it also has a negative effect on us. If we seek certain things in a relationship that seem good for us but hurt or destroy the other person, we may still believe that our actions were not all bad because we are okay. One might be able genuinely believe that it was okay. When we investigate the way we use our emotions in an unwholesome fashion, we can see that it is also self-destructive; our unskillful way of expressing certain things harms us as well as others.

With this insight, we can see more clearly how emotions arise. We can then also see that we do not have to be stuck with a certain personality trait or character. If one is aggressive or has a jealous trait, one no longer has to feel that, "I am just that kind of a person. I'm stuck with this personality. It's never going to change and I'll never be able to forgive myself." We can begin to see the possibility of being able to change even deep-seated issues that we believe we have. If all of these emotions that we experience are somehow self-constructed through our thoughts, beliefs, opinions, and conceptual processes, there is a way of deconstructing them and reconstructing one's worldview, way of expressing one's emotions, and relating with other people in a more positive and wholesome manner. This is why emotions are neither good nor bad. It is how we are using them to express ourselves and our preferences that determines whether they are wholesome or unwholesome and whether we are creating good or bad karma.

Meditation can be an extremely effective way to develop insight. It is designed so that one can gradually learn how to express one's emotions in a more wholesome fashion and not express emotions that have an inhibiting influence. Emotions can bind us to our samsaric condition and thus have an oppressive and constrictive influence. This can affect our self-esteem and confidence levels. By working with emotions in a wholesome way through recognizing the quality of our motivation and intentions, and by understanding what other mental processes are involved in generating our emotions, we can reduce our suffering. Ultimately, we can become liberated or freed from the samsaric condition. Both of these two processes, one of liberation and the other of bondage to the samsaric condition, are determined by how one goes about working with emotions, emotional conflicts, and conceptual confusions.

There is a common belief that thinking is different from emotions, as if to say that people who think are not emotional and emotional people do not think. In fact, they are intimately related. The more we think, the more emotional we can become, especially if the thought patterns become very repetitive or overly fixated, constantly churning thoughts and ideas over. By doing so, we lose our perspective. When we fixate on one point and continually go over it, it is like playing a song in our heads over and over. No matter what we are doing, it is there. When we experience a lot of fixation and brooding, it can be difficult to meditate as we can find little steadiness or stillness in the mind. These are times when it may be better to be active and clear the head. Once we distract ourselves from these repetitive thoughts and find some mental peace, this can be a good time for meditation and to reflect on the nature and purpose of emotions and consider how they are generated. It is also extremely important to realize that emotions are generated and expressed via the interpretation of different situations and that we use emotions as strategies. One can begin to see one's interpretations and strategies. This type of insight is very revealing and can help us to develop more wholesome, unselfish, and caring motives and recognize the harm that fixation can cause.

It is difficult or impossible to just get rid of a negative emotion. We can, however, change our understanding of and attitude toward our emotions. When we see the emotions as mechanisms, we can begin to make choices to use more positive emotions than destructive ones. Many emotions can be used skillfully and with good intentions and even negative emotions can be transformed with good intentions.

Meditation can provide the opportunity to have some immediacy to remain with and observe what is manifesting in the mind. Staying with an emotion in meditation can defuse its ability to do harm. It can help us avoid turning some negative feelings into actions that we will likely regret. If we are not open or attentive, it is very difficult to know why certain emotions, feelings, and actions are manifesting. Instead of trying to pinpoint a singular cause, our time can be better spent observing the mind and unraveling how we are generating our experiences. In meditation, allowing emotions to arise in the mind, watching the creative display of the mind, can help us build tremendous insight. We can learn from the experience itself by simply letting emotions and other activities of the mind arise in a safe meditative environment so that we can observe and better understand them and how they are generated. These types of meditations are not supposed to be used to create a story about why we are thinking what we are thinking or experiencing what we are experiencing. These types of observations can easily become egocentric and self-indulgent with a sense of self-fixation. Rather than becoming obsessed with ourselves and our stories, we can instead begin to free the mind of these fixations and build knowledge and understanding of how the mind operates. Managing the mind in this way in meditation can provide the greatest opportunity to build insight into the human condition and understand the remedies that can help us reduce our suffering and increase our happiness so that we can be of greater benefit to others and do less harm.

In this way, in our meditation, we do not need to repress or ignore anything. We can realize that there is guilt, resentment, or spite in the mind; as an observer, we can remain with whatever arises undisturbed. If we do not freak out or carry on and become fixated, we can see that it will deescalate and disappear of its own accord. We have an opportunity to recognize the insubstantial and self-destructive nature of such experiences as spite, of being spiteful. We can mistakenly respond with spite or resentment as a way of protecting and defending ourselves from others. However, when we realize the self-destructive nature of these types of emotions, the possibility of letting them go becomes much more realistic. We can subsequently realize that emotions such as resentment do not protect us at all. In fact, it creates varieties of distorted perceptions of reality. For instance, when we are feeling resentful, we become fixated on a particular negative aspect of a person or situation and block our mind to everything else that is present. We build it up so much that we are not at all seeing the situation clearly. That is not good for us and can be detrimental to having healthy self-esteem. We can recognize that these emotions diminish the quality of our lives and our relationship with others.

Another point is that it depends upon what form of emotions we utilize. There is no such thing as resentment and spite simply hovering around in our head as real things. We have created them to deal with different situations so we can make use of them or not. If we stop making use of them, they do not exist. Even falling in love is making a decision and commitment. It is something that we do. For example, love is an emotion that can be used in an extremely positive fashion. It can be the basis of all manner of relationships. We cannot say that love, joy, and so forth are more real than other emotions. In that way, they are all the same.

In some cultures, one is not considered to be in love unless one feels jealous and possessive. Many people feel this way. However, if one looks into it, one may find that it has to do with one's upbringing, cultural values, and ideas that one is inculcated with over a long period of time. If you are feeling jealous, you can meditate on that and let yourself experience jealousy and try to work with it. It is not about simply thinking, "I should not be feeling jealous" or creating a conflict within oneself. In meditation, we can remain with our jealousy and meditate on that because if we allow ourselves to feel jealousy in meditation without judging the feeling, condemning ourselves, rationalizing why it is being experienced, and not interpreting it but simply remaining with it, we have an opportunity to gain some insight into the whole experience.

It can be difficult to work with jealousy in the moment when you are with your partner and in an environment where your jealousy arises. When you are feeling jealous and overwhelmed in relation to someone and are also angry, then it is more difficult. But in contrast, in a meditation environment, you can allow these emotions arise and be with and observe them. One can work with jealousy and all manner of negative emotions through meditation by allowing oneself to experiencing it without judging oneself, and not saying, "I should not be jealous. I hate it." This is because if one responds to jealousy in that fashion, it can consolidate it further.

As long as we do not abuse ourselves, we are using our emotions in the right manner. If anger is not detrimental to you, if it has nothing to do with feelings of superiority, inferiority, or self-condemnation, powerlessness, or isolation, you are making proper use of the emotions. We ordinarily think that by solidifying the ego, we are going to have a proper sense of self-esteem but as long as we have this solid image of the ego, there is always going to be a feeling of lack, a poverty-stricken mentality. As long as we have a static egocentric fixation, it is going to be difficult to make use of emotions properly. If we can loosen this fixation, we have an opportunity to feel good about ourselves without needing to feel superior. There can be a sense of basic comfort in being with oneself.

Our image of ourselves is usually based on competitiveness and comparison; we constantly compare, contrast, and compete. A healthy notion of ourselves is not based upon this. It is much more of an attitude toward oneself that is based on developing inner richness, consideration, and understanding of others.

Interdependency

Interdependency from a Buddhist perspective can be applied to the notion of how the mind works to create experience and how we apprehend the world. We have begun discussing the interrelationship between thoughts, concepts, beliefs, emotions, intentions, and motivations. There may be triggers, deeply held beliefs, and many thoughts and concepts that create the conditions for a particular emotional response to arise. There may be many other variables that also impact on our circumstances such as environmental conditions. Some of our thought patterns can be repeated over and over again, entrenching our moral beliefs, opinions, et cetera. In Buddhism, whatever arises does so due to a myriad of causes and conditions, whether it is a personal experience or something that has manifested in the world. What arises will also disintegrate; there is inevitable and constant change. In all things, there are endless causes and conditions. Within this complexity, from a relationship perspective, being aware of the power of our mental and emotional activity to impact how we act toward ourselves and others and how our emotions are used strategically, requires awareness and insight to see which behaviors benefit ourselves and others and which create harm.

In terms of relationship, from a Buddhist point of view, the idea of interdependency is important to understand and develop. By getting caught up in negative states of mind and emotions, we can develop excessive dependency on others or our significant other. If we are able to express emotions in a constructive manner, we can maintain a sense of clarity within a relationship. While some degree of dependency is normal and reasonable in a relationship, our awareness of interdependency and how our intentions and motivations can affect a relationship enables a greater sense of generosity and giving without having to define a specific outcome for one's kindness. In this way, one can express healthy degrees of dependency, need, and autonomy, while at the same time, expressing great appreciation for the other and the relationship. We can develop a greater capability to have a more fulfilling relationship with ourselves and others. In relationships, if one becomes jealous, possessive, and overly attached, in many ways, one subsequently becomes more dependent on the other person and the relationship. Instead of being somewhat clear and straightforward, it can develop complexities and confusion. For example, if we are seeking to get our way too much, seeking power over the other, we could believe that we are being very independent, but in fact, we can enslave ourselves to the person we are seeking to possess or control. It can then potentially become harder to express free choice for all concerned. One invariably becomes bound.

From a Buddhist point of view, it is important to work with others and maintain a sense of relationship that is unselfish. At the same time, this does not mean that one has to sacrifice oneself in a relationship and do everything for the other and forget to look after one's own interests and well-being. In Buddhism, it is believed that to be able to work with and care for others comes from being capable of caring for oneself and one's own interests. We need to work toward maintaining a good balance between regard for others and regard for oneself.

Maintaining awareness of interdependence is an important reminder that we cannot attribute anything to one cause or to just one person. There are so many causes and conditions behind internal and external manifestations of all kinds. It is so beneficial to maintain an understanding of the importance of being connected to ourselves, others, and the world and to assess the quality of our contributions. From the Buddhist perspective, this can be achieved through understanding how our minds function and how we respond to the world. It is important to reflect upon our motivations and intentions that fuel our conduct. Such reflections and considerations can help to maintain perspective. It is important to keep in mind that there is nothing we can attribute solely to ourselves, be it good or bad.

From a Buddhist perspective, it should be noted that there is an enormous difference between excessive dependency or attachment and affection. Being too grasping, fixated, and attached can create so many distortions and discomforts. For example, our outlook and view can become very narrowed, precluding all but that which we are attached to. However, working on our sense of attachment does not preclude having affection for others. We may think that affection for someone is the same as being attached, but through affection, one can give so much to others. It gives us more resources and opportunities to be generous and kind. In contrast, if we feel excessively attached and fixated, we become more and more incapacitated and dependent. In Buddhism, we have the practice of being attentive and mindful as an antidote. In this way, we try to pay attention to how we go about responding and dealing with our relationships generally.

The first level of mindfulness is to become more attentive and acknowledge what is going on within oneself. We need to be honest instead of denying responsibility for who we are, what we think, and how we act. When we discover and acknowledge a shortcoming such as arrogance, selfishness, or other specific attachments, such discoveries can be met with relief, joy, excitement, and increasing curiosity. It is a gift to get to know oneself more intimately than before. A joyous and interested response is much healthier than being shrouded in guilt and feeling bad about oneself. We should try to not give ourselves a hard time because an increase in self-knowledge is not only a great gift, but it also presents a great opportunity. We need to be easy on ourselves as a result of such an acknowledgement. It is easy to become fixated on a weakness we have discovered in a way that becomes self-defeating, as if it cannot be changed. Having discovered something about ourselves, we may be thinking, "How can I be so awful? I am disgusting and hopeless. I'm like that. I can't do anything about it. I've been like this for years and I can't forgive myself." If we approach self-discovery in this way, our issues and weaknesses can become more and more entrenched, as can our self-loathing and sense of giving up on ourselves or aspects of ourselves and our circumstances. His Holiness the Dalai Lama has said, "Never give up." This is tremendous advice. Rather than discovering a weakness and then condemning ourselves for it, we can create the right conditions to begin to change. Being highly critical of oneself and fixating more and more on personal issues or weaknesses is a good way to convince ourselves that they are insurmountable or that we are simply stuck with who we are. We can even become engrossed in our weaknesses and discomforts, as if little else about us exists. We should never give up on ourselves or dwell in some sorry state of self-loathing. We must show some kindness to ourselves. There is great benefit in keeping things in perspective and reminding ourselves of our good qualities. If we become blind to our wonderful qualities, they can also become hidden from others. If we cannot have acceptance of ourselves, it will be hard to give allowances and accept others.

Interdependence requires us to develop self-confidence, confidence in developing our ability to look at ourselves honestly with both a sense of acceptance and a desire for self-improvement. If we approach our own shortcomings and those of others by expressing negative and self-destructive emotions, we can become overly egocentric, self-obsessed, and attached to our own negativity. All manner of negativity can then follow, making it difficult to realize a proper and more stable sense of self-confidence. Developing self-awareness builds self-confidence. This type of realistic self-acceptance is inclusive. That is, one sees one's connection with humanity and our many shared foibles. Thus, we also become capable of accepting others more fully. The relationship that one has with oneself is reflected in the way that one interacts with others. Some psychologists say that if we are unable to deal with ourselves, we project all kinds of things onto others. By accepting oneself fully, accepting one's limitations, shortcomings, and so on, one would develop a healthy attitude toward oneself. As a result, one would be able to develop a healthy attitude toward others. This means that if one observes oneself and sees a negative state of mind, anger or jealousy for example, one should not then say to oneself, "I'm such a terrible person. I have these negativities." If we do that, we are reacting to the negative emotions negatively and perpetuating them further. We can become frustrated and angry at our own aggression, intolerant with our own intolerance, agitated with our own agitation, and so on. We cannot work with negative states of mind by becoming more negative about them. To be effective, we need to develop a far more wholesome and healthy attitude toward ourselves and our many aspects.

So we can see that it is important to simply be self-accepting and have a positive attitude and outlook regarding our negative states of mind to be able to transform them more easily. If we see our negativity in a positive light, we begin to accept ourselves as a whole person and think, "I have some shortcomings but I also have other good qualities." In this way, we can see the benefit of not denying one's attributes or struggling with one's shortcomings. We can avoid creating conflict within ourselves. We ordinarily create inner conflict and division when we become obsessed with our shortcomings. We can forget about all our goodness and begin to see ourselves as worthless. Such inner division can break down our confidence.

We may feel apprehensive about accepting our negativities, thinking that this approach may let our less desirable qualities loose and we may end up behaving badly, worse than before. That type of outcome is more likely if we remain self-divided and continue to develop more and more negativity about our negativities or worse still, not acknowledging our negativities at all and attributing our shortcomings to someone else. We can lose perspective and develop a very distorted sense of self.

Accepting one's limitations as a way of overcoming those limitations may sound counterintuitive. We need to consider the effect that not acknowledging our inadequacies can have on us and the inner conflict it can create. We can have a very narrow approach to dealing with ourselves, what we are willing and not willing to acknowledge about ourselves. If we are able to accept our limitations, our view can become wider and more inclusive. Accepting in this way does not mean giving in. Accepting one's limitations does not mean giving in or developing a defeatist attitude. Accepting one's limitations means being realistic, not putting too many demands on oneself or others. We are all human beings. We are fallible and make mistakes. So we can build the courage to accommodate all aspects of ourselves. Addressing self-improvement from that more positive perspective provides the best opportunity for growth.

Relationships

We can benefit enormously from loving someone and from the act of giving love. I have often been asked, "How can you love anyone if you are not attached?" We can be dependent on someone and still have a successful relationship; there is no problem there. But if we become obsessively attached, all manner of problems are likely to arise in a relationship. For example, one can feel imprisoned, oppressed, or seek to take the other person's freedom or privacy away. Then it has a negative influence on the relationship. This is why it is said that it is important to become aware of our attachment. It is not like a commandment saying, "Thou shall not have attachment," but rather in terms of being mindful and attentive to see how our sense of attachment is working in our relationship. We can ask ourselves, "What is attachment doing to me and the other person?" We can begin to see that being skillful in a relationship is important. We do not need to manage our tendency to become attached out of duty. With mindfulness, we can reduce destructive tendencies and be more responsive when we can see the effect attachment has on a relationship more clearly.

We can sometimes treat inanimate objects in a very humane way and human beings as inanimate objects. We even speak to inanimate objects and begin to fall in love with our motorbike, car, furniture, house, or all manner of technological gadgetry. We attribute human qualities to the objects that we possess but when it comes to human beings, we may try to turn them into an inanimate and unconscious object. The starting point of any relationship is to not treat the other person as one object among many. Not accepting a person's dimensionality can create a progressively more precarious connection.

When we are not excessively possessive, not seeing someone as an object, we give freedom and space to the other and to ourselves. Rather than only wanting freedom for ourselves, it becomes mutual and operates more on the level of interdependence rather than dependence. As a result, we can work through the self-deception and are able to be less conditional regarding what we accept of others. Emotions are skills that are learned rather than something that has been tossed at us. We can learn how to improve that skill and make use of emotions in a much more constructive way. This is the basis of relationship. This is a simple concept but I think it is an extremely important one to remember because as human beings, we are always with others. Since we are always with others, we have to depend on them and vice versa. In a relationship particularly, this is an important concept to remember.

We treat others simply as objects by using all manner of strategies. These strategies that we have developed are based on emotional skills that we have learned from our childhood. We begin to use our emotions in a very skillful way in order to gain what we want. Often, the way in which we use our emotional strategies is a very self-orientated and selfish one. As a result of this, it begins to become very complicated.

Any relationship can be impacted by expectations from both within the partnership and outside it. Having the right attitude and developing the ability to interact properly is where the impact can be experienced most. In a relationship, there must be a great deal of flexibility so that each partner does not take the other for granted. Taking someone for granted is how we can create a solidified version of each other and develop a reluctance to allow for and accommodate change. However, if you give the other a great deal of freedom in the sense that you are not solidifying your image of them, the relationship can become a continuous discovery. If we remain open, we can continuously see new aspects of the other person and by extension, ourselves.

We may have more of an affinity with one particular person as opposed to another. You are able to communicate more with one individual than you can with someone else. You may have nothing against a particular person but find communicating with them difficult. Each person is unique and we can discover this further if we are able to work through our self-deception. This is because ordinarily, we carry a model of ourselves and others within us. We usually hold a somewhat fixated view, seeing ourselves in a very definite and specific way and also seeing others in a particular way. We can let a person reveal themselves to us, rather than projecting varieties of attributes onto them.

Human beings are far too complex to be able to be instantly known. We wish to know a person as we know our pet for example, but individuals are too multifaceted. Sometimes it takes years. Even if you look inside, we know that there are different things that we keep to ourselves. It takes a great deal of time for these good and bad qualities to come out. So if we do this, the relationship is always a dynamic process. However, if we solidify and put labels on the other person, we subsequently make it static. In this case, nothing is moving and we do not even wish to see the different aspects of the person because we have made up our mind about what they are like.

Ego

We often tend to believe that ego is something premade but ego, like emotions, is something that we have constructed because we live in an intersubjective world.[12] We construct the ego in relation to what we feel we are and how we think other people see us. It is not as substantial and real as we believe it to be. This is what Buddhists mean by egolessness. This does not mean that ego does not exist, but rather that it is not as real as we ordinarily assume. The basic sense of insecurity is particularly associated with the ego and it originates from this because it is so unstable and we subsequently feel that we need to continually reconstruct it. If ego were a solid thing, we would not need to repeatedly construct it but we do in fact go through the process of continuous reconstitution to ensure that our identity is certain and secure.

If we can see the ego as a useful construction, we are able to feel that whatever we do is not actually dictated by the ego. Insecurity is such an important aspect of the ego. We can feel that we are on shaky ground if we are not keeping up with the ego's expectations of who we should appear to be. Our sense of identity, ego, always feels a sense of lack. Since our protective mechanism feels a lack, it goes about trying to organize the world in such a way that one can feel secure. Of course, things are never that easy and much of the time we can feel at risk, demeaned, and exposed, so things do not always turn out the way that the ego wants. Therefore, we misinterpret a situation in terms of extreme self-deception. We can see a particular situation completely differently to what is actually happening so that the ego feels quite secure. It is as if it were better to be deceived than to look at the truth. This is why the expression, "The truth hurts" is correct in this specific context. Truth may not always hurt, but it would hurt if the distortion is corrected and the ego is damaged.

Having good self-esteem and confidence is important and wonderful. However, the aspect of us that is referred to as the ego is extremely narcissistic in the way it goes about establishing self-esteem. It creates an inherent weakness. There is nothing wrong with self-esteem but the way in which we often attempt to find it creates tremendous difficulties for both others and ourselves. We may even arrive at the point of self-destruction or self-abuse in order to find this pathological sense of self-esteem.

The ego is a device that we have created as a result of our interaction with other people and therefore, it is constructed in the image of how we think people see us or how we want people to see us and how we want to see our selves. The more we operate from the point of view of our ego, the more we lose touch with ourselves, who we are more genuinely. Ego is simply a social construction, something to deal with the intersubjective situation. We often tend to identify ourselves with the ego, but when we see the ego as a device rather than solid, this allows us to see that we can make use of emotions in a much more constructive way. Here, there is no real conflict.

Emotions are often used to perpetuate and reconstruct the ego, one's self-esteem, and one's notion of who one is. All of these concepts surround the central ego perspective. We can see our emotional expression as defining us. For example, with the expression of anger, our self-esteem may be at risk if we feel diminished. An outburst can leave us and our egocentricity believing that we are worthless and hopeless. At other times, when impressed with ourselves, our sense of self may become inflated and we become unrealistically proud. Even a so-called emotional outburst, in itself, would be acted out in order to reconfirm our situation, our status, and our ego, whether our sense of self is elevated or deflated. Still, we may seek to secure a certain image we have of ourselves. In that respect, we can see that ego is never static and it continuously reconstructs, recreates, and solidifies. When we begin to see how we relate to our sense of self or our ego, we can begin to loosen up and relax the idea of a fixed identity. In a sense, our identity can be seen as something that we have constructed. We are more than an image or identity. With a different view, we can encourage our emotions in a healthier way and use the ego in a positive way.

Let us now unpack how emotionality can affect our self-esteem, identity, and relationships. Resentment and guilt are two examples of egocentric responses that can arise within emotional relationships. Resentment can manifest as an underlying acknowledgment of the impotence that we feel. Realizing our limitations, we make ourselves the judge of others. Through criticism of others, we can justify our actions. By doing so, we are attempting to protect our self-esteem, sense of status, pride, and ego. Resentment expressed in that way can diminish our standing or strength in the eyes of others. Knowing that we have displayed some futility and pettiness can lead to feeling guilty. The criticism can quickly be turned from judging others to criticizing and condemning oneself. It can be seen as a way of reconstituting our sense of self-identity, self-image, and ego, first, with a sense of protection, second, with a sense of deception regarding what may actually have happened, and third, with a desire to reconstruct and reaffirm who we are, both in our eyes and the eyes of others.

When we view it in this way, we can see that the basis of all this maneuvering and angst is a profound sense of insecurity and discomfort regarding how we perceive ourselves and how others perceive us. We are constantly trying to defend our identity and ego by engaging in these types of processes. Self-deception, self-identity, and ego are intimately related.

We can go through so many emotional upheavals and experiences due to our misassessment and inept response to different situations and people. The more we begin to become unstable and insecure, the more we need to look outward and to others to help find and formulate our identity. We can completely ignore what is actually occurring and misinterpret situations and facts to save ourselves from an identity crisis. We can see how this happens in many situations. For instance, a person who is prejudiced against a particular gender or ethnicity may attribute a fixed set of characteristics to that group, ignoring all variations of their generalized model. One's life, reactions, and experiences become organized around that particular set of concepts and tightly held beliefs. Any evidence to the contrary is met with resistance, fear, and even anger. Anything that does not fit the model is completely rejected. There is misinterpretation of the facts, what the situation is, and what the person is like.

We ourselves may have certain traits that we can only see in others as they do not fit with our personal identity structure. Having alienated ourselves from ourselves in many ways, we may even persecute others who display those very same traits. We invariably organize our lives in such a way that we deny knowledge of certain actions and tendencies that we have within us and pretend that they are not occurring. Sometimes there is a great need within us to keep the truth at bay. For instance, we may be in denial regarding a romantic partner, seeing disturbing traits or tendencies, and explaining away their behavior with self-styled stories of what is actually happening. Knowledge may be denied completely in order to continue fostering ideas of love. However, this would never be the case if we did not deceive ourselves. Often we know something in terms of what the person might be up to. It can seem easier and more comfortable to deceive ourselves than it is to acknowledge what the real facts and situation might be. Until we are willing to look at what is really happening, our deceptions can become detailed and entrenched.

When we consider the complexities and complications that can occur in human relationship, the purpose for self-reflection and the importance of understanding the human condition more clearly become paramount to our personal and spiritual growth. Unless we begin to pay more attention to how we are actually experiencing things and constructing our worldview and identity, we will become progressively more involved in this deception. If we continue to operate in this manner, we create barriers between others and ourselves. Due to so many interpretations and emotional constructions, we become distanced from those we love. We cannot be truly intimate and open unless we begin to look into ourselves and see how barriers are being created. We may often think that an individual is not open to us and that we ourselves are very open. It is difficult to make someone open but at least we have the opportunity and capacity to make ourselves open. This is something that we can do but often, we do not. We may expect that from others even if we do not intend to do it ourselves.

To build insight into the human condition, meditation is extremely important because it gives us an opportunity to look into how our mind is operating, how we make use of our emotions and relate to others, and what variety of images we have of ourselves and other people. As I mentioned, the process of self-deception is taking place continuously but meditation gives us the space to observe the processes of the mind almost in slow motion. This is because outside of meditation, our mind is so busy and so often in an agitated and distracted state that it is difficult to observe what is going on in our head. Meditation is different to thinking or brooding over an issue. Constant languishing over an issue does not reveal anything. Rather, it can make us even more caught up in the whole process of self-deception. Through meditation, we try to become the observer of our own minds. It is not to explain away our experiences but to rest with the mind and allowing the processes around self-deception and other delusions to be revealed. Developing such insight and knowledge about how we deceive ourselves can allow us to experience greater freedom and connection with our everyday experiences.

Self-deception and distraction are often related. We can become so carried away or engrossed in what we are doing that we lose touch with what is happening in the mind on another level. Seemingly out of the blue, we may become angry. Due to our distracted mind, we may not be aware of some thoughts that have been circulating in our minds, destabilizing our mood. It is possible to be thinking all manner of things; "I'll do study and I'll take out the garbage," "They promised to help," or "They are so needy or unreliable," et cetera. Despite such thoughts going around and around in our heads, much of the content can be ignored and still continue. It can even begin to fester until some kind of trigger sets off an outburst and one uncommunicatively turns away in frustration or whatever the reaction might be. We may blame others or attribute an outburst to something unrelated or less related. Such upsets can often blow over in a relationship, but sometimes the underlying issue may remain unresolved and thus such agitations may arise again and again. A habitual pattern of blowing up and making up can become established in many relationships. Of course, sometimes clearing the air and expressing oneself can also have benefits. Most importantly, we can improve things for ourselves and others if we are less distracted and become more aware of our thoughts, motives, and self-talk.

From a Buddhist perspective, it is so important to develop the discipline of paying attention to what we experience, conceptualize about, and have repetitive thoughts about. In fact, this type of awareness can do more for a relationship than simply expressing something such as anger or any variety of emotional outbursts. Often, we think that being expressive, such as expressing our anger, is very important. Like some forms of medicine, this may only be addressing the symptoms and not the causes. Expressing anger may give us some relief, to have let off steam, but it may not have resolved a situation. A latent problem that will build up and cause disturbances can easily become a destructive aspect of a relationship. Through reflection, we have an opportunity to see what is happening and are then better placed to make an assessment of what is actually happening. For example, was the anger that was expressed justified or not? Did it arise due to selfish motives? It is easy to hang on to things, impressions of a person, and a set of reasons regarding why one becomes angry, and so on. Sometimes, what we hang on to cannot be justified and may simply be an excuse or exit strategy to escape taking responsibility for our actions. When we develop awareness, the causes of our agitation and motivations behind some of our behaviors become clarified, both in terms of understanding ourselves better and in terms of our relationship. This is because we can then start to operate with more openness and understanding.

Chapter Seven

Love

In many spiritual and religious traditions, it is important to contemplate the ideas of love, sex, and relationships. If we have some weaknesses, vulnerabilities, and preoccupations while also aspiring toward a spiritual or religious goal, we may subsequently find that certain aspects of our lives are in conflict with these specific spiritual goals. In that sense, it is important to look into it.

In the West, there are two dominant influences on our concept of love. In the Christian notion of *agape*, God sends love down and implants it in the human heart. Even our love for each other and for neighbors is divinely injected. Then we have the Greek notion of *eros* rising from the human levels up to the heavens. One is coming down from the transcendental realm to the empirical realm, and the other is rising upward. In both situations, love is tied up with the sense of transcendence. Due to these two influences, we often think that love is something elusive, that cannot be realized, and one is always chasing after love. People feel that true love is never realized and they say, "I thought it was love but it wasn't because it didn't last." This is because love is so often associated with eternity. From a Buddhist perspective, everything is transient and impermanent. If a certain experience did not last, this does not mean that it did not happen or was a delusion and not real. It is important to make peace with love that does not last a lifetime. Not all love will last. So let us look at love from a different point of view.

Here, it is important to clarify what the word "love" might mean, even if we do not eventually find a complete answer. Love, if seen as predominantly an emotional state, is ambiguous. We are taught different things regarding love and it is something that we ordinarily idealize and sometimes, it is an aspiration that cannot be realized. A great deal of the concept that surrounds love can contain some expectations that make it beyond possible human experience, like chasing after one's own shadow. If it is too abstract, it is then difficult to define it as a definite human experience. This can cause us to look at our relationships in an extremely misguided or ungrounded way. Our expectations can be too unrealistic. If we develop too solid an idea of what a person must be to us in order to be able to love them, they have at least in part become an object to us. Love can be dependent on the other being able to fit into our abstract idea of what love should look like. Our expectations can be so lofty and abstract that our perfect "love" can be considered as immutable and divine, as if given to us by God. Together, we become a religious experience. It is as if we are less human because we have not yet found love. Attraction can sometimes be immediate and overwhelming as well as a joyous and treasured experience. If we become fixed rather than open to the process of discovery, allowing both individuals to have room for expression free of fixed ideas of who or what they should be for us, there may be opportunities for growth. However, things can gradually or suddenly deteriorate. Love is not a thing or an object. Change is bound to happen. Incompatibilities can be difficult to overcome and work with.

From the Buddhist point of view, love is not associated with any notion of God or a deity. Love is seen as a human experience and is connected with a variety of our emotional experiences, some positive and some not so positive. We all know that love can be accompanied by such emotions as jealousy, anger, pride, and so on.

Love as an experience is grounded in the human condition rather than love being injected into the human heart by a deity. If love is seen as a human experience and grounded in the human condition, the idea arises that love does not need to be immutable or unchangeable but like all human experiences, subject to change and transformation. Therefore, love is not eternal.

First, we must realize that a love that is so pure and fantastic that it is going to cure all our neuroses and problems does not exist. In part at least, love, like other emotions and experiences, is a human experience and a strategy that we have developed in order to relate to others and give some dimension to our lives. It is incorrect to believe that if we have a taste of the elixir of love, all of a sudden, we are all going to become so happy and have an extremely rosy life. This is not necessarily a good picture of love. We often regard love as a concept that is removed from immediate human experiences. When we begin to look at it, we can realize that love is like any other emotional experience such as for example, jealousy or pride. There is an emotion and as an emotion, it is something that we have constructed and constituted. Therefore, love, joy, anger, jealousy, and so forth are something that we have created. It is a skill that we have developed. We usually do not wish to acknowledge this; we would rather see emotions as completely outside of our control and as simply happening to us. To describe the experience of love in this way is not to degrade it but to ensure that we understand it as integrated into our human experience, as are other experiences. The quality of our love will be influenced by intentions, motivations, and degrees of attachment, prejudice, opinion, and so forth.

Falling out of love can be interpreted as the love not having been real at any point in the relationship. This is not necessarily the case. While it was experienced, it was love. Expectation and romantic ideals of love can create enormous pressure on a person and the relationship. Many cultures are saturated by ideals that are not found in real life. There are many fairytales and mythologies. We may constantly be on the hunt for the unattainable. Why shouldn't love simply be a human experience and something quite ordinary? Love has to do with complimenting each other, mutual respect, and it includes many other attributes. It might not last, but as long as it lasts, it is real. We do not need to have greater expectations than that. To believe that it must go on forever until "death do us part" is not the most important point. If you are together for that long, that is fantastic, but if you are not, it does not mean that what you have experienced was a lie or complete fantasy.

It can be a "cop-out" to look at our emotions as being outside of our control, not wanting to take individual responsibility and blame for how we feel and act. For example, when we have an argument in our relationship, we often say, "I didn't really mean it. I didn't want to do that, but I couldn't help it. It completely overtook me all of a sudden and I had no control at all." However, if we look at it, we may have been seeking an outcome and our emotional responses may have been designed to produce a particular outcome. In terms of the extreme agitated state of mind, we know what we are doing because we know how to target the person's weakest point and how to make them feel insecure. We also choose these moments to attack the person very intelligently and skillfully. That is often part of a "loving relationship" that we all have to navigate.

We are capable of realizing that emotions are not simply animalistic tendencies that we have inherited from our ancestors, but rather an extremely sophisticated way of being and acting in the world. Normally, when we act out our emotions, it is from habit and the same patterns arise repeatedly. Such repetition does not mean that we gain insight into our different emotional states. Emotions are not something that we have to release, such as for example with urination, where we cannot resist the urge and then feel relieved. Emotions are consciously developed. From a Buddhist perspective, emotions are not considered an impulse.

Understanding emotions in this fashion helps us reorient our relationship to ourselves and the other person. Our relationship can develop on an entirely new foundation. From this perspective, we acknowledge more responsibility for our actions and blame less and less on the blindness of emotions, which are supposed to occasionally make us go crazy and then afterward say, "It was stupid of me to do that but I just couldn't help myself." The other person is then supposed to behave as a forgiving person and come to some form of reconciliation. This may even give us some satisfaction. We may go out of our way to cause drama and make up again, as if making up were so fantastic and uplifting that we have to go through drama again only to say once more, "Well, I didn't really mean it."

Realizing our intentionality and the habitual emotional processes that we generate in particular situations can be very helpful. When we say something, it is exactly what we are saying. When we do something, it is precisely what we are doing. It is important to take responsibility for all of these actions if our relationship is to be genuine and sincere. There is no panacea that can be introduced that will solve all of our problems in our relationship. Concepts of romantic and unattainable love that are supposed to instantly demolish any problems in our relationship certainly will not do that.

To reiterate, we organize our worldview in relationship to emotions and often tend to believe that our emotions are external or internal forces that overwhelm us and completely out of our control. It is common for us to express some kind of denial; "I don't know where that came from. That wasn't me." Even if not publicly announced, it is important for us to acknowledge to ourselves that, "That was me. That was a part of me and it came out of my mouth."

Simply acknowledging that we are the person who said and did it provides a better opportunity for us to look into what is going on. This does not have to be a process of beating ourselves up, but rather, staying and not hiding or running away from how we presented in that moment.

Emotions are important and are created so that we are able to relate and establish relationships with other people. When we look at it in this manner, in one sense, it is quite an uplifting experience because we can realize that we are not the victims of our emotions. That is not always a comfortable feeling because it means that we have to take responsibility for whatever we experience and how we act and cannot blame it on others or our emotions. Taking responsibility back onto ourselves gives us much more freedom. Freedom and responsibility are intimately related but often, we want the freedom but not the responsibility. This tension can create tremendous problems because we cannot be free unless we take on responsibilities and we cannot be responsible unless we acknowledge that we are free. There are many problems involved in exercising our freedom because of the way in which we make use of our emotions, including our emotions in terms of organizing our world, our relationship. These problems arise because even though emotions are used for strategic purposes and can be utilized in positive ways, we begin to misuse rather than make use of them. Since we misuse our emotions, we are confronted with a variety of difficulties.

As discussed, this occurs due to our self-deception. In Buddhism, it is often referred to as ignorance but perhaps this is not a good translation because the word "ignorance" suggests that we are completely ignorant of what is happening and therefore, what we do cannot be helped. The notion of self-deception however, makes it clear that we know what we are doing but want to deny this knowledge. Even if we are in denial and confused about what we are doing, we engage in our activities and relationship with others purposefully and make use of emotions in relation to them. Self-deception, like emotions, is used in order to foster our self-image and self-esteem and to shield ourselves from our fears and the infiltration of too much reality. No matter which variety of experience we go through, all of the experiences are in some way orientated to organizing our self-image and concept of the ego. Even though we often do this for our self-esteem, it can turn out to be quite self-destructive. Much of the self-abuse and self-destructive processes that we go through are mistakenly done in order to foster one's image of oneself, one's notion of the ego. It is orientated toward the establishment of one's narcissistic need. In this way, every one of us expresses some degree of narcissism and self-orientation.

Body and Mind

Here, it is important not to see our emotional experiences, love included, as the mind locked in the body and the body being completely separate and different to the mind. We often create a conceptual and relational split between the two and have the idea of bifurcation of the mental dimension and the physical dimension. If we view mind as locked in our body and all of our mental processes are extraordinarily hidden and covert with all of our physical actions outwardly directed and easily perceptible, there is no way of learning how to understand others. This is because all we can do is infer what the other person is feeling, thinking, and experiencing but we can never directly have any experience of what the person is going through.

In Buddhism, body and the mind are not seen as completely dissociated. There is no idea of partition—the mind somehow locked in the body and the body as a form of mechanism that the mind propels into work. Whatever mental experience we may have manifests through our physical acts. Therefore, whether it is thinking, feeling, or experience, these are all constituted in terms of what we say and do. Whether the person is in love or not is not determined by an unperceivable internal process in the mind but rather, as it manifests. Whether the person is in love or not manifests through action and communication.

If a person says terrible things and behaves in a horrible way toward you and you still believe that the person loves you, there is very likely a problem there, at least from the Buddhist viewpoint. If we think carefully, apart from what the person says and does, what is love? We tend to mystify everything by making it abstract and an ideal form, but it can then be difficult to translate the abstraction into everyday human experience. With love, aggression, or violence, everything gets translated into action. It manifests through what we say and do. Therefore, instead of seeing love as a mysterious occurrence in the mind, we can see it as mind and body being in such an intimate relationship that whatever goes on in the mind is perceptible through one's physical actions.

In terms of sex, from the Buddhist point of view, one also cannot dissociate body from mind. In that way, one does not link sex immediately with the body and say that sex originates in the body and is therefore a base or animalistic tendency that is anti-spiritual. Spirituality and sexuality are not at odds. Our sexuality is not something that needs to be removed, discarded, suppressed, or unacknowledged. We cannot say that all bodily feelings are connected with animal instincts and all the higher functions take place on the mental level. This bifurcation does not contribute to understanding sex properly. This does not mean that sex must be glorified or viewed as extraordinarily important but rather, it means that having sexual intercourse is not an act of defiance or connected with an idea of original sin. This is because in Buddhism, we do not have the idea of original sin and therefore, we cannot link the idea of sexuality with that variety of original form.

Anything can become an obsession. From a broader perspective, desire is a great motivator. We can desire enlightenment. Desire can be very positive and is important to help us achieve and progress in life. If desire becomes unchecked and excessive, we can instead become diminished. We can harm both ourselves and others with insatiability. We can become very blinkered in our view of what should be pursued in life. If we become obsessed with sex, it can become a problem and one can become governed by it. It may be used to exploit or manipulate others. One can be enslaved by it without control and this is true of any obsession. If one were able to have a proper understanding of sexuality, one would find a place for it. It can be an intimate expression of loving-kindness. To enhance a relationship, if we ignore or mismanage either love or sex, the relationship will not be properly nurtured.

Having a successful, loving experience is as important as having a successful or good understanding of what sex is. It is not thinking that, "I have become a Buddhist, so I don't need to think about sex or my bodily feelings because I'm trying to tap into my higher faculties and a higher spiritual realization." There can be an extraordinarily dynamic relationship between our secular life and our religious or spiritual life. Therefore, if one can try to understand our secular experience in relation to spiritual ones, the spiritual dimension can pervade every aspect of our so-called ordinary lives.

Monasticism and Laity

In Buddhism, there has always been the monastic tradition but also what is called the Bodhisattva tradition where no distinction is made between the lay practitioner and the monastic except for individual predilection. If certain individuals can practice better as a monastic and others as a householder, this would not come in the way of their spiritual practice. It is not the case in Buddhism that you should approach it either this way or that way—both options are open. If one wishes to become a monastic, that option is there but so is the option of being a householder and incorporating Buddhist practices in that situation. The ideal is to become a bodhisattva working for the benefit of others. It is not said that in order to be a very good practitioner, it is always necessary for one to become a monastic. A lay practitioner may have more complexity such as career, family, and so on and a monastic life also has its challenges but one can direct one's attention in a more focused way. Just because one is living in a monastery does not necessarily mean that one is going to be a great practitioner. There are many options. It is good to keep in mind that not all great religious teachers were celibate. Historically, in the monotheistic religions, the prophets were married. In Buddhism, there are many past and current married teachers.

I will briefly mention tantricism and the use of sexual energy. There are some practices where one uses sexual energy with or without a consort. Rather than reaching orgasm, the practitioner redirects or withdraws the energy. However, this practice does not preclude the lay practitioner from also simply having sex. The Buddhists, Hindus, and Taoists have similar ideas, although the practices may vary. It is not said that sex is bad or should be avoided unless one has taken specific vows of celibacy. It is not seen as a moral issue, but rather, as using techniques to work with the energy. We can work on ourselves in many ways for self-improvement and to broadly aid our spiritual progression. Being a good person, partner, or lover is also extraordinarily helpful. There is a place for this form of practice and awareness even at a very fundamental level.

Need

Needs, dependency, autonomy, and an acknowledgement and understanding of interdependency all have a place within relationships. It can be easy to mistake need for love. We can believe that we love someone, but in fact, it could simply be need. There can be many things that we love about a person. We may begin to love someone because they seem gentle and kind, but then discover another side that does not appear so gentle and kind. We may love a person's intelligence but find out that they are not as intelligent as we first thought. We go through varieties of decisions regarding the qualities or lack of qualities we perceive in a person. Such judgments may be based more on our own personal needs than how the other person in a relationship actually is. We may need to have someone is our lives and base our acceptance of the other purely on how it makes us feel. We may even seek to convince ourselves that we have more love for a person than we actually do in order to make ourselves believe, "I really love somebody," instead of thinking, "I really need somebody around."

Here, we should distinguish between basic need that is almost a necessity and needs that we have extrapolated onto pathological needs. Being human, of course, we have undeniable needs such as food, clothing, and shelter. Basic human needs exist and in relationship, there can be other types of needs vital for the health of the relationship. Extreme one-sided selfishness can distort a relationship, "extreme" in the sense of needs that are self-orientated and self-centered. These blind a person to the needs of others. When we look deeply at our own basic needs more openly, we can also see the need of others. These can vary from person to person. Some people may need a little extra encouragement or time to themselves, intellectual stimulation, physical challenges, or time close to nature. Understanding one's fundamental needs and vulnerabilities allows us to have a more inclusive knowledge that fundamental human and sentient needs may have a greater diversity than we had considered. To be too conclusive about what "need" is can lead to a self-orientated understanding of what life's essentials are. Can we see the other person's needs?

It is valuable to look at need closely because we can gain a better understanding of ourselves and the insatiability of some of our needs, hungers, and the conditionality that we place on what we believe will make us happy. As a result, we can build a greater understanding of the human condition generally and by extension, a more intimate understanding of others and those most significant to our lives. When we understand ourselves more, we can gradually overcome the need to be strongly self-focused, which is the poverty-stricken and demeaning attitude of the ego. We can experience a richer, more satisfying inner life that is more inclusive of others. Having someone in our life will have less to do with possession of someone or seeing them as an object or prop and much more to do with being "other-focused" and being able to be more open and loving.

Suspending Judgment

To be discerning and to make well-considered choices and decisions is important. When it comes to our meditation practice however, we can benefit enormously from suspending our judgment, even if only occasionally. Arresting our judgment in meditation can help us cut through and gain insight into how our interpretations of the world and our experiences perpetuate our own self-estrangement. We normally make a judgment and place our thoughts, actions, concepts, feelings, and moods into categories such as good, bad, acceptable, unacceptable, and so on. We can impose many restrictions on that which we find acceptable and unacceptable within ourselves. It is possible to reject characteristics that can be attributed to us. How much self-acceptance can we bring to our meditation cushion? It can be challenging to relax our filters and see ourselves more completely. As a consequence, accepting ourselves more develops an attitude of also accepting others as I mentioned earlier. If we can learn to tolerate and accept aspects of ourselves that we earlier could only reject and see as abhorrent, we are in a position to change, progress, and improve.

We can address what we can acknowledge about ourselves. Our relationship with ourselves can become more panoramic and inclusive and less conditional. This type of self-acceptance does not mean that we accept ourselves so there is nothing more to do. Rather, by knowing ourselves more intimately, we are in a much better position to see what is needed for self-improvement. From a spiritual perspective, accepting who we are today at this moment in itself is a sign of great progress.

Addressing our weaknesses is essential on the spiritual path. While we may want to put our best foot forward in normal life with our family, friends, and work colleagues, it is our weaknesses that we need to face when we are on the cushion in meditation. This does not mean that when we sit on the cushion, we are there to just beat ourselves up over our weaknesses and imperfections. When we meditate, we need to sit with all of it, the good and the not so good. We should try to not turn away from ourselves. Our weaknesses, those things that need some work or need improving, are then accessible to us. If we are willing to see all of it, that means that we are also willing to not turn away from the wonderful qualities, embracing that which is wholesome, insightful, and generous. We can even be willing to deny some of our wonderful qualities. If we can gradually stay with ourselves more without judging, we can see ourselves with less distortion and segregation. We do not need to waste time with self-denial or self-condemnation. We do not need to decide what we are willing to work with and what we are not willing to work with. We can impose many restraints upon our meditation experience. This can filter into how we view others and the world. We can condemn ourselves for having an unpleasant thought. It is not uncommon to hear that meditators will only meditate under certain circumstances because sitting with themselves can be too uncomfortable or revealing.

This approach of not turning away from oneself in meditation can spill very positively into our daily life. If we cannot overcome some of the distortions, excessive judgmentalism can be injected into our relationship with ourselves and others. For example, as we have discussed, we can set up unattainable criteria for a love partner. When we find someone has certain attributes that we have been looking for, we may think, "I fell in love at first sight." Over time, flaws and defects that we were not aware of may reveal themselves. Can we accept them? We are always looking for certain attributes and that is not necessarily a problem. Discernment is a worthwhile part of making good choices and decisions. But when you are really in love, even the other's flaws and defects compliment the person. One can have acceptance of one's own and others' strengths and weaknesses and be willing to work with them and make adjustments and allowances. We can see the whole gamut of someone as something quite fantastic.

Insight

Often, people tend to see sitting meditation as a way of calming oneself down or being peaceful but sitting meditation has to do with learning how the emotions are generated, how they can affect us, how we relate to them, and so forth. It is incredibly helpful to gain some insight into how our mind and emotions work. In meditation, when we are in a quiet, undisturbed environment, there is nothing immediate that causes us to feel different emotions such as anger, jealousy, or any other experience. Even so, in meditation, we often have experiences of different emotions arising. We may suddenly feel angry. Rather than leaving the meditation at that point, if we remain and look at what is going on, we have an opportunity to gain some insight into our experiences, how they are generated, and their impact on us. It can be very difficult to develop intricate knowledge and insight of the mind without meditation. It can be very difficult to be aware of our anger as it is arising in daily life. We often do not have the time, space, or awareness to be the observer of the creation of an experience and observe the experience itself as it arises. Meditation provides these kinds of opportunities. When one feels different emotions coming up in sitting meditation, they need not be regarded as anathema to the meditative state. Rather, it is what meditation is for. Meditation is designed for us to gain more insight into how our mind is operating; it has nothing to do with stopping the mind from functioning.

When Buddhism refers to the liberation of thoughts, this does not mean that we need to get rid of thought, but rather that we can recognize thoughts as the manifest creativity of the mind. Becoming more aware of how the mind works is to be celebrated. An expectation that can sometimes follow becoming more aware is the idea that our issues and problems should disappear. When we see more of our mind's activities, we may feel overwhelmed; "Now I know how the mind works so why are all these idiosyncratic issues still here? I am more aware but I still have all this stuff in my head annoying me." If we can celebrate the endless mental display for what it is, we can change our attitude and relationship to the mind. This will help to avoid perpetuating our habitual responses with the same intensity or regularity. If we decide to take some time off and meditate for a few days for instance, the meditation could get pretty rough if old things come up again and again in the mind. We can think, "My meditation has deteriorated. These thoughts and feelings are always coming up in my mind." By reacting to these same reoccurring thought patterns and emotional responses differently, we are beginning to change the effect they have on us. We are dismantling the conditions required for those habitual tendencies to arise with the same impact and intensity. Instead of dreading their continuous reemergence, we can accommodate them without the accompanying disturbance.

It is basically about not reacting in the same way but rather, developing a fresh attitude and outlook. Sometimes, when one meditates for a long time, all manner of things come up and experiences may become even more intense. One may then think, "All these years of sitting have done nothing," but in fact, all manner of deeper layers are coming up. This is an important reason to meditate. Only building awareness will not take care of everything that we wish to work on in ourselves. As I mentioned, meditation is important, but it is not done only in order to calm the mind. That is a wonderful part of meditation, but also the insight that one gains into one's neurotic states of mind, mental agitations, and disturbances can help reduce our suffering and build a greater sense of confidence, peace, and equanimity.

In meditation, just letting one's thoughts and emotions arise and not turning away from whatever arises is working with one's condition. Through vipashyana or analytical meditation practice, our focus is on what we are experiencing in terms of emotions and concepts, ideas, and so on. For example, if we have anger arising in our mind, we can concentrate on that. We look at and accommodate and experience that state of anger instead of saying, "I'm meditating. I should not feel angry," and then getting ourselves all worked up and disappointed about our meditation. Instead, we allow the anger to be there and let ourselves experience it and be aware of it. At the same time, we do not elaborate on it or make up stories about it, as we ordinarily do. In our meditation, we do not need to look for reasons or people to blame for our anger. Instead of that, we remain with the anger itself while maintaining a sense of awareness. If one is able to maintain awareness and allow oneself to experience whatever is arising, we are gaining more and more intimate insight into what we are experiencing and not succumbing to distractions. A point to remember is that the direct experience of our emotions lasts only a short time. What perpetuates them is when we indulge in elaboration and judgment of the immediate experience. Elaborating and judging our current experience perpetuates it due to our conceptual constructions. We buy into stories about the experience and that exchange of thought and consideration solidifies, extends, and imbeds the experience.

To reiterate, through the practice of meditation, with the development of mindfulness and awareness, we can gain more insight into how we are reacting to our thoughts and emotions, how our emotional responses are being formed, and how they affect us. We can see how we use our emotions egocentrically. As a result, we can also gradually develop a healthy attitude toward ourselves so that we are able to carry that over into our everyday affairs.

Chapter Eight

Witnessing Our Own Emotions

To recapitulate, emotions, no matter how they manifest, are not something that simply happens to us but rather are something that we create and use strategically for a particular purpose. That is, we use emotions such as anger, jealousy, and guilt for a particular purpose and to create a particular outcome. Often, the purpose is to solidify or reorganize our self-image, our sense of ego in terms of how we wish others to see us and how we see ourselves. This process may be a conscious, partially conscious, or unconscious process, dependent on our level of awareness and attentiveness in relation to our level of self-knowledge. We use self-deception in order to solidify our identity or ego and create a pretense.

The way in which we need to understand our emotions and recognize our self-deception is to observe and witness the experiences as they arise so that we can see the habitual responses that we have established. Even though we use our emotions strategically and for a purpose, we are not necessarily aware of it because in the process, we deceive ourselves. This is how the self-deception tends to develop. To be able to restructure our life, intentions, motivations, and perceptions of the world in order to see through our self-deception, we can use our emotions, still as strategic communication tools, but in a much more helpful, fulfilling, and constructive ways.

With a growth in awareness and wisdom, we can stop using

certain emotions altogether because they do not serve the purpose that we want them to. For example, resentment, guilt, spite, and so forth do not have any worthwhile use at all. We have been deluded into thinking that by fostering and getting fixated on guilt, spite, or resentment, somehow or another, we will create an appropriate outcome and consolidate our self-esteem or self-image. We can start to see the futility of using certain emotions and instead nurture and use more useful, skillful, and positive emotions. We can see that we have the capacity to organize our world using our emotions in a consistent and habitual manner.

Witnessing our emotional experiences does not mean that we have to rationalize or intellectualize about our emotions. Through firsthand experience, simply remaining with ourselves without contrivance, we experience emotions free of interpretations and labels. Over time, we can learn to rest with our mental and emotional activity without adding self-deceptive layers and motives. If we are attempting to remain with the emotions in an uncontrived way, we can instead fall into the trap of rationalizing them and explaining them away. When we do that, we have simply set up a different form of defense that can also help us avoid developing a more intimate understanding of emotions. Such an approach can lead to our disengaging from our emotions almost as if they belong to someone else. In everyday life, this is what we commonly do. We distance ourselves from our emotions and then rationalize, intellectualize, and place labels of all kinds onto them. This pushes them away.

In our meditation practice, we work on developing the capacity to look at what arises, each single emotion or thought as it arises and allow it be present and accommodated. This would help us to see through self-deception in itself. When we are subject to self-deception, it is extremely difficult to see what is going on. For example, we may ask, "What made me angry?" When we feel angry, we ordinarily simply deal with the symptoms and not with the real problem that has made us angry. We distort varieties of situations and experiences through all forms of interpretation.

In the context of relationship, we become more and more in touch with ourselves through witnessing our own experiences. If this happens, there are fewer barriers between ourselves and others. Varieties of self-deceptions cause us to be distanced from ourselves and this creates a distance form others. As long as we are alienated from ourselves, it is difficult to be intimate with others. By becoming progressively more familiar with our emotionality, we become less alienated from ourselves and less caught up in games and manipulations. Our drama becomes more transparent when we can see what is going on inside ourselves. The situation and our perceptions become clearer to us. Being more fluid and less caught up and fixated on different opinions and experiences provides more opportunity to be open and less judgmental of others. This is similar to catching our reflection in a mirror while committing a crime. We have an opportunity to see what we are doing and this provides opportunities to change and build skill.

Emotions are learned skills so it is a matter of learning another type of skill so that we can make better use of our emotions. This may take time but gradually, as we begin to use our emotions more skillfully and become progressively more acquainted with their nature, we can benefit from them rather than being demeaned or restricted by them.

Interestingly, self-condemnation can provide a form of identity. Through misusing our emotions, we are immersed in a process of self-estrangement and some degree of self-destruction, as was previously discussed. We often tolerate tremendous punishment from ourselves to ourselves. This can leave us with little tolerance of others. We may even try to justify our self-destructive behavior, not just emotionally, but also physically. We may hold extremely strong opinions about others but not be able to see ourselves and our own weaknesses and indulgences. We have an explanation for our particular indulgence but we may condemn someone else's indulgences; "My indulgence is not nearly as bad as theirs." With inertia, our self-destructive habits and indulgence can become comfortable and tolerated. We can become desensitized and lack self-knowledge and insight. This is what Buddha meant when stating, "The condition of life is suffering and the suffering comes from craving which exists in one's own mind." The poverty-stricken mentality becomes self-perpetuating.

When we witness our emotions as they arise and are able to let go of them without getting too fixated, we can gain a sense of pliability and ease. Realizing the contingency of our thoughts, emotions, other people, and the world around us can help diminish our wish for things such as that our identity and ego be fixed. In life, a variety of unexpected situations will always arise. Life can be defined in some ways as a series of upheavals. Circumstances and situations come and go. In a relationship, we may be looking for something definite, permanent, and certain. Relationships can become anxiety producing if we desperately seek such predictability. Stability of mind is to be valued, but rigidity is something very different. Our relationship would be so much more fulfilling if we were not predetermining how we want everything to be. We can lose touch with ourselves and our relationship in the process of trying to make something solid and predictable. We can build up a variety of expectations. We can be so busy cocooning and protecting our identity, ego, and how our relationship should look, that we can become immersed in our own heads rather than in the relationship. We have to be prepared for the most unexpected things. Reflecting on impermanence and the changeable nature of people and things can make every moment more enriching and worthwhile. But if we constantly project ourselves into the future, we can forget about the situation itself as it arises in the present time. We may not notice what is happening due to our preoccupation with what might happen in the future.

People often believe that having a relationship is one thing and doing spiritual practice is something else. On the contrary, relationship can be a perfect opportunity for one to be become less narcissistic, self-orientated, and more open. Many possibilities arise once one begins to deconstruct the notion of ego and one's self-deception because one is beginning to gain a clearer picture of one's intentions, motivations, and modus operandi. We can discover that more possibilities arise when our responses are less dictated by habit and there is more spontaneity and freshness. Many of our choices are dictated by our habits. Even in relationships, we can end up repeating the same mistake over and over and continually ending up in the same kind of situation. It is not something happening to us entirely due to external forces. Difficulties can occur due to the kind of choices we make. Choices are often made based on entrenched and habituated patterns. The less habituated we become, the more possibilities arise in terms of what can be experienced and enjoyed and what can be found acceptable.

In a relationship, nothing may have changed but because of our interpretations, expectations, and insecurity, we may project all kinds of things onto a person or a situation. We can create a myriad of projections of the other person instead of seeing the other person more directly. Rather than seeing a person as this or that, we can reflect on how we are projecting. In Greek mythology, Narcissus fell in love with his own reflection in the water. In a similar way, our selfish and self-orientated attitude has nothing to do with the person that we are but rather, it has to do with the image that we have of ourselves. Selfishness is part of creating a self-image rather than seeing what is arising within our minds. Overcoming a strong self-orientation and selfishness can create a more stable basis for any relationship.

Chapter Nine

Intention, Expression, and Fluidity in Relationships

From a samsaric perspective, we believe that our ego or a strong sense of a fixed identity is who we truly are. In order to keep our sense of identity consistent, we continually reaffirm and recreate it. If we can see the non-substantiality of the ego, it can be used more successfully for our own benefit and growth. For example, anger may arise for many reasons. Fundamentally, it can arise as a response to one feeling isolated or powerless and as a consequence, one seeks to express one's power. Expressing anger can be an attempt to develop a modicum of self-esteem.

The idea that one should not express anger at all is misguided. The same goes for many emotions and experiences. For example, one may momentarily experience jealousy or resentment. As human beings, from time to time, it is likely that we will become angry, jealous, resentful, and so on. Some expression is better than total suppression, as this can create other problems. Having no outlet for strong emotions can create a fixation and trivial situations can become exaggerated. However, if we end up expressing momentary anger as it arises, we subsequently do not sit on it. This may make having a proper discussion about what is actually bothering us more possible. Sometimes, there is clearly something wrong but if we turn the emotion or concern inside completely, inner agitation can build up and proper communication can become hampered. The problem may become distorted or exaggerated, causing the issue to escalate. It is better to manage trivial things well. In that way, they have some importance. There is potential for trivialities to be used as an excuse for expressing the anger but not looking at the real situation. Our responses can be used to avoid properly looking into what is happening. These types of patterns can be repeated and become habitual in a relationship.

No individual is liked by everyone. If someone dislikes you, there is no need for a guilt trip. There also may not be a reason to try to make someone like you. One does need to indulge in a guilt trip, which is a way of perpetuating one's construction of the ego. Not always being liked should not be seen as failure. Each individual cannot be a part of everyone's life. Still, in Buddhism, the importance of compassion is emphasized. To become overly enthusiastic in terms of helping others should also be checked because sometimes a person may not need or want our help. Acting in a compassionate manner is a learned skill. Sometimes, our help may be needed but our skill may not be sufficiently refined. It is important not to impose one's desire to be helpful on others. Helping others effectively takes time and includes our needing to develop our skills. The more we understand the human condition more broadly and our own samsaric condition, the more we will know what may be of most assistance. As the Buddha said, "Be on the middle way," meaning, "Do not be too extreme." In relation to compassion, we should find the middle ground of not being overly concerned and not overly selfish. It is important to find a balance between being outwardly directed, without trying to take the burden of the world on our shoulders and only wishing to look inward, becoming so self-orientated that we forget everyone else in our community and beyond. This is the basic criterion that we need to manage and assess whatever situation we are in. It is the same with the emotional expressions—not trying to be cool and disengaged and equally not trying to shoulder and cop excessive amounts of bad behavior from others. It is also not positive to feel that it is okay to be unconstrained around other people, letting our aggression or other bad behaviors sully the environment of others. Being a nuisance is not an enlightened quality, nor is endlessly trying to put up with the bad behavior of others. Being a better person requires consideration and fluidity. We can avoid solidifying our beliefs into the two camps of one thing as entirely good and another as entirely bad. We can relate more fully with our environment and our experiences so that we are in a better position to assess how to be of the most benefit to ourselves and others. Being too fixed on what is acceptable and what is not acceptable disengages us from the many considerations that may need to be made in any given situation. Having a moral code that is too rigid can lead to some people being condemned unnecessarily, and some bad behavior being excused or accepted despite the harm it may cause others and the environment. Further, becoming overly sensitive and taking offence at just about everything can be very tiresome for all involved and is often couched in that same sense of moral solidification and intolerance that can lead to our not understanding the nuances and dimensions of what is really happening.

So when others are causing disturbances, how do we measure the most skillful way to manage the situation? Discussions may or may not work. Instead of defusing the situation, trying to talk things out could exacerbate the problem. Before launching in to solve a problem, convinced that one's opinion will be shared and understood by others, one can first ask oneself a question; "Is my motivation self-cherishing or not?" Others can often quickly detect a selfish attitude, as their needs or consideration may not be included in what one is saying or trying to achieve. We may seek to change other people's behavior because we feel entitled. It always depends on our motivation. In Buddhism, it is said that it is not the action, what you say and do, that is the most important thing. It is more about why we are saying or doing certain things, what sort of intention we have. If our intentions are totally selfish, then the main disturbance may not be out there; it may be within due to our own attitude and thought processes. Nonetheless, being a Buddhist does not mean that one cannot be assertive. There is an enormous difference between being aggressive and being assertive and being able to speak up when it is needed. Being a Buddhist does not mean that we have to lie down and receive whatever others dish out. That does not create wholesome karma or a wholesome situation for anyone.

If we are pursuing a long-term or a short-term relationship, there will be considerations. Whatever type of relationship we pursue, as long as we know that we are making the choices we make and are taking responsibility for our intentions, there is no real problem. With regard to casual or short-term relationships, mutual respect is often the issue, as it can be lacking. The motivation by one or both parties can often be selfish and lack consideration for the other. Casual relationships frequently include treating the other person as an object rather than a conscious person with free will. One may not seek to know or acknowledge the person's dimensions in case such interchange deflects from the single purpose of the encounter. On the other hand, there is no need to not be concerned for the other person, even in short lived relationships. We can be committed to a person and situation on a moment-by-moment basis, however long the connection lasts. One can be fully present and remain concerned for the well-being of oneself and others in short-term and longer-term situations.

If one is seeking or has decided upon a partner for a long-term relationship, then of course, other concerns and considerations will arise. It is important to check our intentions to avoid unnecessarily subverting its longevity. Equally, we can avoid becoming too distressed over the idea that it may not last. Excessive anxiety can create complexity in and of itself. Keeping in mind that people and circumstances change is an important reminder. It is helpful to be fully engaged and fully committed for the length of the relationship. If the relationship breaks up and we have been working well within that relationship, we can gain some respite, knowing that we gave it our best.

We sometime believe that we should be so good that we should be able to handle anybody, change anyone, and be good to everybody, but reality is not like that. We must acknowledge our own limitations. We are not going to be compatible with everybody. We are more compatible with certain people than others. If we begin to see everything as a choice that is being made, things become much more fluid and flexible because we do not feel that some external force has pushed two people together for good or ill. We know that we have chosen to be in that situation.

Relating to each situation as it arises moment by moment is the most important part, even if conflicts arise, as they will. We can simply deal with the situation in that particular moment rather than using it as a strategy. We often accumulate lists regarding what the other person has done so that when we have arguments, these things come up, even after many years. We have these lists and every time something happens, we add something else to the list so that we end up competing with each other in terms of who has the bigger list. We need to stop and consider the future ramifications of some of our current fixations and behaviors. What are we trying to aspire to? What is happening before us in our relationships right now, today? How, at every moment, are we using our emotions? How are we interpreting different situations and the behaviors of others? It has nothing to do with trying to achieve an ideal, utopic loving relationship. Rather, it has to do with basic human interaction. This is not only confined to romantic relationships but also extremely necessary in our general relationships with friends, colleagues, and others.

Love is a powerful human emotion and something that we construct and use. It is not something that strikes us without cause. Love is not like lightning but something that we create. We respond to a situation, a set of circumstances, and the other person. We may set unrealizable goals and expectations and be unable to see the whole person to begin with, allowing ourselves to only see the parts that we most desire. With greater awareness, we can maintain a more realistic assessment of the situation, our motivations, and expectations. With every relationship comes the need to learn new skills. Having less predetermined expectations and being more responsive in the present is also a skill to be learned. It does not happen instantly. Over time, we can gradually learn how to make our experiences and expectations more fluid and not so static and solidified. If we can see that all these emotional experiences that we have, such as anger, jealousy, and love are being created and recreated by ourselves, we can see its fluid aspect more clearly. Rather than having a solid reality that we attach ourselves to, we can gradually see how we are creating our own realities.

Section Three

Emotions

Chapter Ten

Emotions And Fixation

In Buddhism, the role of human emotion is emphasized in the context of our spiritual practices and effort to transform us from a normal "ordinary human being" to an "enlightened being." From the Buddhist viewpoint, we set two different varieties of goals for ourselves. One is the immediate goal of trying to become happier or how to avoid suffering and attain happiness. We also have another goal that is more distant, called "attaining enlightenment." Buddha achieved enlightenment and this is something that we also aim to attain, but it is less likely that we will become a buddha any time soon. It might happen, but to become a buddha is not so easy. Nevertheless, aiming for enlightenment as a distant goal holds so many benefits. These two goals, trying to attain happiness and trying to attain enlightenment, are not in conflict. If we attempt to achieve happiness, we will eventually also attain enlightenment. What we need to do in order to achieve greater happiness will directly go toward helping us to secure enlightenment.

With this in mind, we speak about emotions in Buddhism. Whether we are happy or unhappy is dependent on which forms of emotions we are experiencing and how we express them. In other words, certain emotions will produce the experience of happiness and joy and other forms will produce suffering, dissatisfaction, and pain. Right from the beginning, we have to realize that from the Buddhist point of view, emotions have to be distinguished from feelings. Emotions also do not have to be seen purely in terms of physiological states and processes. Emotions relate to how we appraise situations and ourselves, our own self-conceptions and interpretations of various events, facts, and situations that we encounter on a daily basis. This means that we experience emotions because we encounter different situations. We do not simply become angry, sad, happy, or just fall in love; we fall in love due to someone, we get angry because of something, and we become jealous owing to certain situations and individuals that we come into contact with.

To experience emotions and for them to arise, we often have to be responding to something dualistically, seeing someone as our enemy or friend, lovable or grotesque. This suggests that our experience of emotions is dependent on our perception of various situations and facts and in addition, how we interpret and what we make of these facts. We have the relevant experience of emotions when these facts are something favorable or unfavorable to us, whether we like certain situations or dislike them. From a Buddhist point of view, it is very important to understand this internal process in order to be able to overcome painful and diminishing outcomes that are so often associated with emotional perplexities.

The purpose of meditation is more than calming the mind. When we do meditation and try to calm ourselves, we may begin to feel physically calmer, our breathing pattern changes, and there may be a change that produces a sense of relaxation and tranquility in terms of neurochemical reactions. Under these circumstances, we may have less negative emotions such as depression or anger. We may feel calm and relaxed. This can lead us to believe that this is the goal; "Through doing this kind of meditation, Buddhists are trying to learn to deal with the negative emotions." However, the better way to deal with negative emotions is to understand how they are generated. When we feel physically relaxed, we may experience the negative emotions subsiding. If we do the calming variety of meditations such as shamatha or tranquility meditation for long enough and practice it regularly, we may enter into that sense of stillness and serenity every day. After a while, we may become a more serene person.

Of course, we do meditation in order to feel calmer but we will not overcome negative emotions by only doing this. If we only focus on calming the mind but do not go beyond that and try to understand how negative emotions arise, our efforts would likely have some superficiality and be somewhat of a patch up job. The effect would not be long lasting. Individuals often give up meditation for these reasons. We may have been meditating for a long period and regularly practicing judiciously and consistently and subsequently feel calmer and less reactive. On a day-to-day level, we may have evidence of a shift and become slower to anger and more easily able to bounce back from disappointment et cetera in times of catastrophe or personal tragedy. A deeper understanding can assist us not to lose ground so significantly, but when one's life is thrown into chaos such as with the death of a loved one, breakdown of a relationship, or the onset of an illness, our calmness and tranquility may disappear. One may then question the value and effectiveness of meditation practice.

From the Buddhist perspective, it is essential to do meditation in order to calm ourselves but we cannot overcome our negative emotions or develop spiritually if we do not also try to understand our emotional life. In Buddhism, we do not think of all emotions as being bad nor do we devalue them. This may be a misunderstanding that some of us have, that Buddhism emphasizes tranquility, detachment, renunciation, and so on. This misconception is based on the idea that if we stay detached, uninvolved, and aloof, we are subsequently not going to develop excessively disturbing emotional states and will not have to deal with emotional troubles.

Buddhism does not believe that. Rather, Buddhism says that if we understand our emotional life well, we are able to live a robust and vibrant life. If we do not know how to deal with our emotions, our life will become impoverished and demeaning. The negative forms of emotions that we experience have a way of beating us down and after a while, we can become exhausted, wearied, and be thrown into despair.

In Buddhism therefore, we attempt to do meditational practices. There are many different meditational and other forms of practice that allow us to learn to deal with our emotional life more effectively so that we will have greater contentment, meaning, and fulfillment in our lives. There is a clear correspondence between lack of fulfillment and a pervasive, underlying, and sometimes overwhelming emotional negativity. Lack of fulfillment is disturbing to the mind. There is a whole inventory of negative forms of emotion that we are subject to when feeling disturbed, such as bitterness, anger, resentment, jealousy, envy, and greed. Our life can become a trap where meaning is difficult to find. This can be very demeaning, quite literally. In Buddhism, this is called "gone bad." When we have many types of negative emotional experiences and are not handling them properly, we have "gone bad." We are not living properly. To cultivate our emotions in the proper manner is to learn to enrich our life so that it becomes meaningful.

Our emotions manifest in accordance with our perceptions of ourselves and others. That is, our self-assessment and assessment of others. With regard to self-perception and other-perception, we use an interpretative framework to make sense of what is going on. Whether it is in our favor or not, whether it is something that we like or do not like, is dependent on our interpretive framework. We do not simply become angry or jealous. Our interpretative framework creates a response to a situation or circumstance that has arisen.

From the Buddhist perspective, these forms of reaction are tied to the "primary emotions." In Buddhism, we make a distinction between primary and secondary emotions. Primary emotions consist of desire and anger and these are the two fundamental primary emotions. Between desire and anger, we prioritize desire. According to Buddhism, desire is at work behind all of the emotions. Whether we have positive or negative emotions, desire is in the background. This is also another source of great misunderstanding that we may have in the West, to think of all forms of desire as being negative. Even positive emotions like love or compassion and the desire to have them, are positive desires. This is to be encouraged rather than discouraged. Desire that arises in the form of greed or the desire to do harm that comes from anger is to be discouraged.[13] In any case, behind all of the negative emotions, we have desire. For example, with regard to an experience of sadness, fear, or jealousy, all of these are related to one form or another of desire. These desires are tied to our concept of self and self-perception. Fundamentally, according to Buddhism, it does not matter who it is, everyone's self-perception is distorted. Therefore, our perception of varieties of facts, situations, and people that we encounter is also based on mistaken perceptions.

Buddhism suggests that when we see certain things or encounter specific individuals, our perceptual schemas cause us to see and experience things in a particular manner. Based on how we appraise the situation, we will experience the relevant emotions such as attraction, aversion, and so on. We do not actually have direct, unmediated contact with objectively existing facts, circumstances, situations, and people. We see things in the way that corresponds to our perceptions and interpretive framework. This means that each individual, according to Buddhism, has certain ways they "experience" which are not direct. It is not the object or experience that are the causes of our emotional responses. It is based on the individual perceptual framework that we employ.

In other words, with regard to a person we believe is being disrespectful, we react to that individual with anger or a similar emotion. Even seeing this individual as being something in particular in the first place is based on our delusional mind, to use traditional Buddhist language. Therefore, this is why two people may be in the same situation or dealing with the same person but draw different conclusions and appraise the situation differently. This happens even before one actually begins to think, "I like this person. This person has some very attractive qualities," or "What a horrible, disgusting individual that person is." Before one thinks this and makes the appraisal, one has perceived that individual to be a certain type of person. When we understand this, we are in a better position to improve our emotional life. If this were not the case, we would endlessly be enslaved by our passions, emotions, and circumstances and situations. These types of changes are not outside of our control. As it is said in the teachings, we may not be able to will away the arthritic pain in our joints or make many physical feelings go away, but our emotional states can be redirected, changed, and improved.

Of course, physical feelings do accompany emotions, but there is a distinction being made between feelings and emotions. A pain in the knee, for example, is a feeling but we cannot say that it is good or bad. We cannot appraise it or attribute any moral value to it but we can do so with emotions. With feelings, we can have pleasant and unpleasant feelings but with emotions, we speak about appropriate, inappropriate, healthy, and unhealthy emotions and those that have moral dimensions, implications in terms of moral psychology. Certain positive varieties of emotion are tied to the virtuous qualities that we have to cultivate, such as love, compassion, and so forth. In Sanskrit, feelings are called *vedana*. The Sanskrit term for negative emotions is *klesha*, meaning negative forms of emotion.

When we have emotions, particularly strong emotions, there is of course an undeniable strong feeling component. Many physical reactions can take place. The body may release various chemicals and our breathing patterns may change. When we refer to emotions, we are speaking about experiences such as fear or anger, which are different to feelings. For example, you may wake up in the morning, exit the door, and be ready to unlock your car only to find that the car is missing. You may experience fear, rage, or both. But if you remember that you did not park the car in the usual spot, that fear or rage immediately dissipates. On the other hand, if during your lunch break you went to a coffee shop and drank coffee that made you feel sick, when you go back to work, you feel nauseated and realize, "I drank coffee and that's why I'm feeling like this," but it may not necessarily make the unpleasant feeling disappear. The unpleasant feeling may remain for some time despite your emotional state unless you take an antidote. When we feel rage or fear, the feeling is there, of course, but it is more than just feeling. When we have positive experiences of emotion, we usually have pleasant feelings accompanying them and when we have negative forms of emotion, we have unpleasant feelings translated into bodily sensations.

According to Buddhism, when emotions are aroused in us, they are not directly caused by something external or objective. The real cause of our emotional upheavals is not solely the perceived object, the angry neighbor or the loss of someone close, but the real cause has to do with our mental structure. Therefore, in Buddhism, to deal with our emotional life in a better fashion, we seek to restructure our mind so that we experience things differently and improve our experiences. This can only come through genuine appraisal of oneself and one's perception of things, events, situations, and other people's reactions, emotions, and so on.

According to Buddhism, we do not think of emotions as being simple, not even primary emotions like anger or desire. There is no reducible essential essence that we can call "anger" or "desire." They are not completely fixed entities or essences. With regard to the whole repertoire of emotions, there are many variations and permutations and they express themselves in a multitude of ways. Ordinarily, we just group them together under the main headings of anger, desire, jealousy, and so on. In Buddhism, not understanding this process is the main cause of our emotional afflictions. Our lack of understanding of the real cause of our emotional afflictions comes about because we do not understand the complexity of our emotional life. We usually think in very simple terms; "Somebody mistreated me so therefore I feel sad," or "Somebody has mistreated me so I feel angry." We react differently to the same situation depending on which variety of interpretative framework we are employing at that given moment. These decisions are very much based on our history and how we have responded to things in the past.

Fundamentally, how we experience emotions is not mechanical. However, from a Buddhist perspective, as samsaric beings, we usually reduce our experiences to something simple and mechanical. It is much more complex than something happening to us and then reacting to it with the relevant emotion. The complexity comes from our emotional states being multifaceted and complex; there is not one single emotion manifesting at a time. In Buddhism, we speak about three and five types of primary emotions. Because we see things in a very mechanical fashion, we can be too quick to think of things in a causal, linear way, believing that one incident brought about a specific event.

In Buddhism, we consider everything that we experience to be multifaceted and are encouraged to learn about and contemplate our experiences so that we can understand how our experiences are created. We may often believe that something external elicits an inner response, that what is eliciting the response in us is something external, completely independent of us, and totally objective. But as we have been discussing, according to Buddhism, nothing is perceived objectively in a complete sense. We normally perceive things in line with our habituated ways of perceiving. In addition, due to the complexity of our emotional life, we cannot locate the emotions either externally or internally.

In the West, there are many theories on approaches to explaining our emotions and emotional experiences. For example, there have been many interesting studies seeking to locate emotions in our biological and neurological systems. Other studies have highlighted the relationship of our emotional responsiveness to aspects of societal or social constructions for example, that experiences of jealousy, sadness, or love are not guided by individual perceptions but rather, are dependent on the society that one is living in. In many theories, there are combinations of causes that range from propensity and the biological to the societal. Emotions are often not given an intrapsychic dimension but attributed to other causes.

Buddhism believes that we cannot locate emotion simply in ourselves or in our interaction with others. However, the notion of interacting with others is important because it is through our interaction with others that we experience emotions; emotional learning and responsiveness are not developed in isolation. At the same time, this does not mean that our assessment of the emotional states of ourselves and others is accurate. Many other variables are possible beyond our own beliefs and assessments. According to Buddhism, there is no simple direct line of interaction between subject and object because the individual is embedded in a network of events and varieties of factors.

When we take this into account, we see that the experience of emotions is an experience where a multitude or variety of factors called dharmas come together. The word "dharma" also refers to Buddhist teachings but it means different things depending on the context. In Buddhism, "dharma" is a very important concept and means "various mental and physical factors." This signifies that nothing is simple and that there are no simple entities. The social environment or a subject who is capable of experiencing emotions has a history, past experiences, and impressions. This means that the individual who is experiencing fear, anger, or resentment is not an individual that exists in isolation. Due to the "dharmas" or varieties of factors, we cannot always predict our own behavior or understand why we feel certain things or behave in certain ways. Looking at our experiences in this way can help us to understand why such intensity of emotions may accompany so many experiences and why we can be blindsided or rendered helpless in the face of our own experiences and emotional responses. If our emotional life were very simple and direct, we would more readily be able to predict the reactions of ourselves and others, including comments, gestures, looks, and gazes. But we rarely can. There is constant change or permutation because a direct one-to-one relationship between the subject and the object does not exist.

As I mentioned, as well as the variety of factors or dharmas, part of our appraisal of situations and circumstances is the strategic manner in which emotions are utilized. For example, if we are feeling a little sad, in order to draw sympathy from others, we may exaggerate the sadness or feeling of loss. If we are a little angry, we may pretend that we are angrier than we are if we believe that it would bring about a desired outcome. Further, we may be experiencing intense sadness but we choose to hide it. We may seek to hide other emotions such as envy or pride and sometimes, we may overcompensate by feigning a different response in order to cover up our real feelings.

Developing a deeper and more inclusive understanding of the complexity of emotions can aid our progress in learning how to deal with our emotional life. According to Buddhism, seeing things as complex does not subsequently leave us in a state of confusion. As a matter of fact, it does the opposite. When we are aware of complexity, we have an opportunity to be more open to what is happening. We can see things much more clearly without needing to be reductive or blinkered. A more unconditional and inclusive view can help us to have a better handle on what is happening than when we try to simplify, exclude, and reduce the varieties of factors or dharmas.

According to Buddhism, when we look at everything in a very simplified reductive manner, it encourages mental fixation, another important concept in Buddhism. We can become fixated on the object of our hate, jealousy, love, or any strong emotion and this then causes tremendous blindness and confusion in our mind. We literally exclude or become blinded to other factors. Our attention becomes myopic and we do not see the background or the context in which certain things are happening. We only see what we want to see, that which has drawn our attention, so we become obsessed and fixated. This is the case whether it is a positive or negative emotion.

Fixation, according to Buddhism, causes disturbance in our mind and this is the primary cause of suffering. The emotional disturbances that we experience come from fixation. When we learn that our emotional life can be seen in another way, as we have been discussing, it can free us up and loosen our mental fixations thereby allowing us to see things from a broader perspective. We can then survey and include more within our experiences and situations. In the teachings, the example given is that it is like the difference between looking from a mountaintop and looking at everything from the valley below.

We try to think about our emotional life in this way. We need to work with fixation in order to develop a healthier approach to our emotional life. All of the Buddhist practices are geared toward dismantling fixation and obsession. We use many different kinds of methods but they all agree on this point. When we become less fixated, all of the untapped emotional expressions that we are capable of come to the fore. All of the drudgery, the relentless, mechanical, and repetitious cyclic experiences and turmoil caused by the upsurge of varieties of negative emotions will begin to subside. Under these circumstances, they subside because we have greater understanding of ourselves and how we function in the world.

This develops from wisdom. Wisdom develops when we learn to work with our mental fixations. In Buddhism, mental fixation is the essence of what is called "ignorance." Ignorance, negative emotions, unhappiness, and pain are interconnected and wisdom, healthy emotions, and happiness are interconnected. The word "interconnected" is used because happiness and so on cannot exist in isolation. Whether we are leading a happy life or an unhappy one, we cannot only pursue one single thing such as wisdom without happiness. They are interconnected like cyclic existence or samsara because we repeatedly experience the same form of upheaval, feeling of dissatisfaction, failure, and discontentment.

In Buddhism therefore, understanding what is happening is important, not only attempting to calm our mind so that the disturbances will not arise. To reiterate, detachment, from a Buddhist perspective, does not mean "non-involvement" per se but rather, it means "non-fixation." Fixation or being fixated narrows our experiences down to only that which we are focused or fixated on, often to the exclusion of all else. Fuelled by experiences of attraction and aversion, fixation and obsession cause mental emotional disturbance to varying degrees dependent on its intensity. Lack of emotional disturbance comes from non-fixation. Therefore, when we are practicing meditation, in Buddhism, we are trying to recognize and overcome fixation. Overcoming fixation comes from understanding the impact that the dharmas, the varieties of factors, can have.

To briefly recapitulate, from the Buddhist viewpoint, we think of emotions as complex mental and physical phenomena. Emotions are tied not only to our sense of subjectivity, but also to our interpersonal relationships and the world at large. This is true even of those emotions that do not have a specific object. If we think of dread for instance, we may not dread anything in particular. It is a feeling directed at some amorphous thing, but nevertheless, it has a form of reference point directed toward something. Due to this, our experience of emotions is extremely complex. Despite the complexity, through greater understanding, we can overcome certain varieties of negative emotions because they are based on our perceptions. The fixation that develops from our appraising circumstances and situations in a particular manner is the cause of our torment and suffering. It is the process of appraisal that ignites negative responses more than the actual experience of the emotion itself. In Buddhism, we make a distinction between emotional occurrence, for example, the experiencing of fear, and the fixation that develops from that fear.

These appraisals and perceptions become habitualized and entrenched in our minds, known as "psychophysical dispositions" or *samskaras* in Sanskrit. We become habituated to perceive things in a specified fashion. For example, if something has given us a complete fright, as a response, it is extremely easy to gradually become fearful of any similar circumstance or for the fear to become more pervasive. Similarly, if something has triggered jealousy in us, it is also easy to subsequently more broadly become very jealous. "Samskara" literally means, "gathering of various psychophysical factors brought together because of fixation." The energies are drawn together and channeled into a single focus, whether it is sadness, fear, anger, resentment, or whatever the case may be.

These samskaras go toward cementing our personality structure, dispositions, and character. This then has a direct impact on what we are and what we will become. Buddhism does not believe in the notion of an isolated self, as I mentioned in section two. The self is always embedded in the surrounding circumstances and situations, always in relationship with someone or something else. This understanding can help us to relate to the experience of suffering, how suffering is connected to our emotions, and how emotions are related to our subjectivity and identity.

Existentialists, especially Martin Heidegger, spoke about "being in the world" to emphasize that there are no free-floating egos hovering about. The self is always embodied, always in relationship with something other than itself. This notion also exists in Buddhism and what is meant by "selflessness." Selflessness (Skt. *anatman*) does not mean there is no self but rather, no free-floating self that is not in relationship with others or the external world.

Chapter Eleven

Emotions, Self-Interest, and the Role of Judgment

In Buddhism, we do not think of emotions purely in terms of strong feelings. Nor are they seen purely in terms of the cognitive activities of the mind such as thoughts, conceptualizing, reasoning, and forming judgments. However, at a basic level, judgments always accompany emotions. In Buddhism, the reason we react with anger, jealousy, or any of the other primary or secondary forms of emotion is because our self-interest is at stake. According to Buddhism, all of our experiences are appraised in relation to whether something is seen as pleasurable or not pleasurable for us. If we find something pleasurable, we tend to seek these experiences out or long for them. Equally, non-pleasurable experiences are not sought out and our response to them is met with feelings of aversion and a desire to avoid them. Whatever is non-pleasurable is non-pleasurable to one's own sense of identity or ego.

Therefore, from a Buddhist point of view, everything that we experience is appraised according to its effect on our self-esteem and sense of the self. This could be anything that is seen as a violation of ego's domain, threatens ego's security, or poses a challenge to our belief in a solid self-identity. If something threatens our identity, we respond egocentrically. We may react with anger, bitterness, fear, and so forth. Therefore, there is a fundamental form of judgment that we perform almost continuously. This does not mean that these judgments are articulated or even fully experienced on the conscious level.

From the Buddhist perspective, we experience in terms of our own concept of self or ego (Skt. *atman*), whether it is attraction, aversion, or likes and dislikes. The judgments that we perform are related to this and are associated with our emotional responses, whether they are negative emotions like anger and fear or positive emotions such as joy and happiness. For example, fear arises when we believe a situation is threatening, whether directed at a person, living being, or situation that one construes as threatening. If one interprets the situation or individual to be threatening, there is subsequently fear. On the other hand, if one interprets the situation differently, there may be a lack of a fear response. The presence or absence of fear depends on the judgments that we make.

Buddhism makes the point that the presence of judgment applies to all forms of emotion. What we think and how we think about things have a direct impact on how we experience our emotions. Often, people are more interested in knowing what Buddhism says about how to manage our emotions rather than what it says about how emotions are generated, but the two cannot be separated. Knowing how to work with our emotions has a direct relationship with understanding how our emotions came to be. If we do not have any understanding regarding how we generate emotions, we can look at our emotions endlessly and still remain perplexed and at their mercy. In our meditation, we can watch our thoughts and emotions arise and dissipate. Being able to be an observer of this process can increase our calmness and stability but it may not build very much insight into what is actually going on. If we have more background information, our meditation practice can become different and more insightful. When building awareness and insight into our emotional life, we first need to assess and appraise all of our emotional experiences in terms of whether they uplift or demean us and whether they are for us or against us. We form judgments about ourselves in terms of how situations make us feel.

The second important point is the notion of "object of emotions" and "cause of emotions." David Hume, the British empiricist philosopher, made the distinction between object of emotions and causes of emotions. There have been many debates regarding the similarities and differences between these two. Hume made the distinction between object of emotions and causes of emotions because he saw that the same object of emotions could bring about different emotional reactions. For example, the one person could be both the object of love and the object of hate.

From a Buddhist perspective, we would suggest that the object of emotion and causes of emotion are not completely separate. Nevertheless, they are not absolutely the same. The object of emotion, for example, what we are angry at, is the intentional object of our mind. Our mental orientation or basic attitude and belief system toward the object is that which denotes our response to it. Therefore, when we are angry, we are angry at something or someone—the mind is directed toward that particular object of emotion.

Here, we also need to understand what "object" and the "object of emotion" mean. "Object of emotion" may or may not be a perceptual object. In many cases, we have a perceptual object of emotion when we experience fear, and we interpret the object via other means such as deduction. We may not have seen the object that culminates in a fearful response. For example, if we are out when it is dark, we may hear rustling in the trees and this may trigger a flurry of thoughts and assumptions, a range of possible scenarios. We see or hear something and then have a series of thoughts that culminate in our belief that there is danger. We have physical reactions related to this particular perceptual experience, which can bring about full-blown fear.

We can also experience emotions without a perceptual object. If we imagine a dreadful situation, we can make ourselves ill with worry without a perceptual object, without seeing or hearing anything. This happens simply through active imagination. If our loved one is on a trip and there is a fire in the area and we have not heard from them, we may imagine the worst scenario and become completely fearful and filled with dread. In the absence of perceptual objects, there are still objects because the mind is directed toward a particular object of fear. Nevertheless, the object is not immediately present. We can also experience different emotions in other ways based on what we are thinking about, through the use of imagination.

Another point to make, particularly in relation to fear and anxiety, is that they may also relate to anger. Even when the object of anger is not immediately perceptually present, through active imagination, through expecting the worst and imputing ulterior motives to someone, we can work ourselves into a frenzy. We can become completely angry with somebody who is not around but we may not have even seen them for weeks or years. Similarly, with regard to fear and anxiety on the other hand, if we have fears about not being able to make ends meet, money, and security, the object may not even be there, as the event has not yet occurred. In this situation, the object of our fear, dread, and anxiety exist in the future. We have not encountered it in the present. This is also discussed in Buddhist literature. Therefore, we have this form of situation in regard to the object of our emotions. Not only can the object of emotion change, but also the object of emotion may not be perceptually present.

There are a large variety of physical and mental causes and conditions that produce emotions. The expression "causes and conditions" that is often used in Buddhism refers to varieties of physical and mental factors. With regard to fear, the feelings of a lump in the throat, rise in body temperature, and change in breathing pattern and heart rate combine to produce the physical feelings that accompany fear. A suite of physical responses is associated with all emotions, positive or negative.

In Buddhism, it is considered important to look at the many elements involved in emotions and to more thoroughly understand the complexity of our emotional life. According to Buddhism, this will produce insight. It would be naive of us to believe that we are angry with a person for behaving in a particularly aggressive fashion and this subsequently produced all manner of physical reactions in us, both perceptible and imperceptible. Some of the changes may also be very subtle. We may have experienced anger or fear in this situation and form the belief that there is a straightforward linear reaction that is taking place.

According to Buddhism, this is not the case. This is because other factors like identification, imputation, and expectation also come into being. We may experience anger, embarrassment, or shame for example, not due to our own experiences but because we are identifying ourselves with someone or a group of people. A whole football team may bring shame on oneself. One's friend's actions may bring embarrassment. Equally, if someone has achieved something that we are proud of, we feel elation, joy, and happiness. There is also this element to our emotions. We do not experience all of the emotions purely in terms of what we have done or felt but also due to others.

Imputation is also an important Buddhist concept, how we impute all manner of characteristics, qualities, recriminations, and intentions to others. In terms of emotional experiences, apart from what we actually perceive, we impute certain hidden or ulterior motives to others. Not only do we try to read the person's facial expressions, tone of voice, physical behavior, or language, but we also try to go beyond that. Even if a person is behaving pleasantly, we may impute an ulterior motive. For example, we may believe that the person is not genuinely being nice. We may believe that there is a hidden agenda and read things into that person's behavior. We may despise an individual, everyone within a certain profession, or all members of a particular ethnic group. We are constantly interpreting, imputing, and intimating the world and those we encounter. Also, how we experience emotions and the impact they have on us have to do with our expectations—what we expect from an individual, group, or society. Whether we are expecting the best or worst outcome or something in between, this also determines how uplifted, happy, disappointed, or enraged we become. All of these different causes and conditions combine to produce the emotional reactions that we experience. It is neither linear nor simple.

This is why it is possible, according to Buddhism, for us to educate ourselves so that we can learn to work with and overcome the severity of emotional states that can drag us down. Further, we can use positive emotional experiences to build a better quality of life and qualities such as clarity and confidence. In Buddhism, this is often referred to as "mind training." The mind may be trained precisely for these reasons. In this way, we can become less victimized by our emotional states.

It is important to keep in mind that there is an absence of a strict causal chain involved in the arising of any emotion. For example, seeing something as threatening does not come about in the same way every time that this particular emotion arises. Because of the complexity and the many related physical responses that accompany our emotional states—responses via the sympathetic nervous system, various chemicals in the brain, other neurophysiological processes, and subsequently produced strong feelings—Buddhism recognizes the difficulty in overcoming some states. It can be challenging and sometimes very difficult to regulate, modify, train, or educate our emotional responses.

It is often not easy, but it means that despite the difficulty, we can choose to respond to things differently through a better understanding of how everything works. This is important to remember, that we can begin to change and make our lives better, always. Just like we can choose to keep on smoking cigarettes or quit, not giving up and giving reign to our entrenched habits does not then mean that we do not have the choice or free will to stop smoking. In a similar fashion, many of the emotional habits or experiences that we have in terms of the occurrence of emotions, such as a sudden experience of rage or fear, arise due to our samskaras, which means that we have adapted ourselves into responding to things in a specified way, which in turn, is tied up with the schemas in our mind. Due to our ideas and beliefs, we often have highly rigid and predetermined opinions that ignite emotional responses, sometimes so quickly that we do not even know where our emotions came from. It would be rare for us to be entirely free to respond or not respond to things without our judgments and schemas jumping to attention. If we can see how our mind works, we can learn to do something to improve the situation.

It would be a mistake to believe that in Buddhism, one should not think of self-interest. Buddhism says that our interests are not being served properly because we do not manage our emotions and thoughts very well and we have fallen into the habit of forming varieties of schemas in our mind. These schemas are not so helpful in terms of self-enhancement. They become impairments, like blinders that prohibit us from seeing more clearly. Due to this tendency of developing a fixed set of schemas in the mind, it can be difficult to overcome our emotional conflicts. But because we have created them, they can be changed, dismantled, and recreated. If our schemes and mental processes were not generally mutable, we would have little power to change anything. A very strong causal nexus would bind us and everything would be rigidly predetermined. We would be working like clockwork.

According to Buddhist thought, we have varieties of mental propensities or structures, varieties of experiences and responses to emotional objects. The processes, causes, and conditions are created, but are not fundamentally predetermined. There is not only a single possible way to respond to any situation. For example, if you have a schema that believes that all dogs are vicious and unpredictable, you would respond emotionally whenever you saw a dog. Due to our schemas, our behavioral responses may be predictable but equally, we have a choice. When seeing a dog, we may show aggression, fear, run the other way, or choose to ignore their presence. Nothing about our responses or emotional experiences is completely predetermined.

"Dependent arising" is a Buddhist term that references interdependence. An emotional response arises due to "causes and conditions," a range of interdependent factors arise. We can become rigid about linking all of these causes and conditions, states, and processes together and making a complete picture that universally fits everybody or every situation over a period of time. In fact, the arising of these many elements produces endless configurations and their manifestation and outcomes are varied and unpredictable. This being the case, we can then talk about the equally endless possibilities of being able to transform ourselves and working with our emotional repertoire. We do not have to be enslaved by our passions and emotions. We are able to free ourselves from emotional servitude.

There are many elements and the arising of drama that can be associated with emotional expressions and the witting or unwitting cases of deceptions, self-deceptions, and deceptions aimed at others. It is important to be aware of how we are using our emotions and what our motivations are. We may behave in a certain way in order to encourage someone to have sympathy for us. We may use emotional blackmail and pretend that we are sadder or more hurt and injured than we actually are. Apart from the dramatic and theatrical aspect to these approaches, as discussed in section two, emotional strategies are used in order to gain favorable results for oneself using deceptions, wittingly or unwittingly. For example, if we are feeling jealous of someone's riches, power, or privileges, we may couch our jealousy in all manner of justifications.

Our discussion thus far shows us that we can do something about our emotional life. When we do Buddhist meditation practices, we attempt to address this by looking into the complexity of how emotions are generated and experienced. Understanding things in this fashion is important because according to Buddhism, we have a tendency to focus our mind narrowly on a single object and become fixated on it. This consequently has the propensity to inflame all of our undesirable tendencies and emotional experiences.

Attempting to understand the co-dependent arising or dependent arising is to understand emotions properly. We can see that there is no simple subject or straightforward personal identity or ego. When we have emotional experiences, subject, object, schemas, propensities, judgments—everything is intertwined. What we think of as "object" is not "out there," existing independently, acting on our consciousness and producing certain physical and mental emotional reactions. There is no subject that is somehow impacted upon by what one is experiencing emotionally. The subject is part of the emotional experience and so is the object. Objectively speaking, our social environment, other people, situations, physical things, objects, and so on, all constitute our emotional life—the feelings, thoughts, and attitudes combined with our conscious experiences as a conscious subject, with our own self-awareness as a living conscious being who can say, "I have this experience of that emotion," someone who has a body that generates feelings and physical reactions. All of these things work together to produce what we call an emotional experience. This is what dependent arising or co-dependent arising means. From a Buddhist point of view, this understanding can give us relief from all of that which produces worries, anxieties, fears, and other forms of negative emotion such as extreme hatred, spite, resentment, and so on.

In this chapter, I have presented basic background information on the Buddhist view, not confining it to any particular school. Buddhism has many different schools and they each have said different things about various matters, but they all agree on the points covered in this chapter. In Buddhism, the emotions are not seen purely in terms of the mind or the body. What the body experiences is a part of it, but what it experiences is not the emotion. Bodily feeling and emotion are not identical. Today, there is much emphasis placed on identifying specific emotions in precise parts of the brain. According to Buddhism, even if we find that certain parts of the brain are stimulated when one has certain emotions such as fear, this does not mean that this is all there is to it. For example, when we have fear and a corresponding lump in the throat, we cannot reduce fear to the experience of the lump in the throat as the primary location. Similarly, we cannot reduce an experience of fear to some activity in the brain. Even if there is a form of correlation, we may never fully understand how the correlation works. This would be the Buddhist view.

In Buddhism, there is also the idea of how the body can act on the mind and vice versa because we believe in the dharmas, the many physical and mental elements that I mentioned. With regard to physical and mental elements, the mind, body, and mental activity do not exist as completely separate categories. The various physical and mental elements or activities are degrees of sentience.

With what we regard as physical, some are completely inanimate objects and the others are not inanimate but organic. Therefore, what we call "consciousness" may be more refined manifestations of the varieties of factors or dharmas. Instead of using the dualistic category of "body and mind," how the body can act on the mind or vice versa, from a Buddhist way of thinking, it is the dharmas that are interacting, dharmas again meaning physical and mental elements, the variety of factors.

Chapter Twelve

Omnipresent Mental Factors and the Primary and Secondary Emotions

The reason that it is important to understand emotions in Buddhism is because of the focus on how to deal and work with emotions within the meditative setting and this is done in order to help improve the quality of our lives. Buddhism involves leading a good life, one that is meaningful, complete, satisfying, and fulfilling. In order to lead a fulfilled life, we need to have a grip on our emotional experiences and emotional life. Failing to do so means a diminished sense of meaning and purpose in life. Life takes on a greater quality when we are skilled at regulating, modifying, and dealing with the varieties of disturbing emotional experiences.

When I refer to "emotional disturbances," I am not speaking about emotional disturbances in the Western sense of having psychological problems as such. According to Buddhism, everyone has some form of emotional problem because emotions can have a strong hold over us. The currents of emotion may carry us away and we are capable of becoming completely engulfed by them and in them. As a consequence, in our lives, we may often lose perspective. We may lose focus on what is important and essential. Life moves quickly and we can easily squander our life. These are the fundamental reasons that emotions are taken seriously in Buddhism. As I have mentioned, in Buddhism, we speak about both negative and positive emotions. Contrary to popular belief,

Buddhism does not encourage us to have fewer strong feelings and emotions. Rather, Buddhism says that we should become a little wiser in terms of which types of feelings and emotions dominate our lives. Therefore, it is essential to learn about this.

Even if we do not often experience positive emotions, we need to learn to experience them more often and more completely. This is an ability that we can all benefit from. When we have negative emotions, we should try to work with them so that the hold they have over us gradually diminishes. It is important to overcome being enslaved by negativity, our emotional impulses and entrenched states. We can gradually work toward having less negative emotional experiences with less frequency and intensity. When we subsequently have the experience of anger or jealousy, the associated negative states of mind such as mood swings and experiences of depression can become less frequent or at least, diminish in intensity. This is the Buddhist approach.

First we need to understand how the negative emotions arise and why they persist and then we can discuss how to work with the positive emotions, their benefits, and how to cultivate them. I have already mentioned that in Buddhism, the notion of dharmas, the physical and mental factors, is very important. We do not think only in terms of isolated, unitary items. Rather, we consider the intertwining of varieties of physical and mental factors, dharmas. The *Abhidharma* teachings are often referred to as Buddhist psychology. With regard to the term "Abhidharma," the word "dharma" means mental and physical factors, as mentioned and "abhi" means to make manifest, to make something that is hidden obvious. Therefore "Abhidharma" means teachings that make the hidden mental and physical factors obvious. Abhidharma is a cycle of teachings that discusses the physical and mental factors. One of the most important Abhidharma works of literature is *Abhidharmakosha*, which means "Treasury of Abhidharma."

We all experience these physical and mental factors but they are often unknown to us. However, they become clearer to us when we study or consider Abhidharma teachings. According to Buddhism therefore, simply understanding the physical and mental factors, in itself, is a way of gaining the upper hand as far as the negative states of mind and emotions are concerned. This is because understanding the negative states of mind and negative emotions is a way to subsequently get a handle on them. The reason for this is that emotions are not simply about feelings and experiences. Gaining an understanding of our cognitive and affective states of mind is actually necessary.

The Five Omnipresent Mental Factors

I have alluded to this in the previous two chapters but I will briefly recapitulate in the context of Abhidharma teachings. Abhidharma teachings say that whether we are experiencing positive states of mind and positive emotion or negative states of mind and negative emotions, five mental factors are at work. These five must be present for us to have any form of emotional experience. These are called the "five omnipresent mental factors." In other words, whenever we have any conscious emotional experience, these five elements must be present.

The first of the five omnipresent mental factors is "feeling" or feeling tone. When we have an emotional experience, we have a feeling and this, according to Buddhism, is divided into two. There is physical feeling and mental feeling. There is both a physical and mental component to feelings. These often go together, but sometimes, they may not. We may experience physical pain but at the same time, mental pleasure. Nevertheless, there is the experience of physical pain and physical pleasure and mental pain and mental pleasure. In addition to the experience of pain and pleasure, there is also feeling of what may be called "numbness." According to Buddhism, this is not only a mere absence of feeling of pain or pleasure but a distinct feeling in itself. The feeling of numbness, neither experiencing pain nor experiencing pleasure, is not a state of no feeling but rather, a more neutral feeling. These feelings are often related with our sensory experiences. For example, visually, when we perceive something, if we see something attractive or repulsive, we have experiences of pleasure or pain. Physically, through tactile sense, we experience pain from touching something hot like fire and pleasure from a cool breeze in the summer afternoon. These also constitute a part of our experience of emotions. They are an essential component in order to have an experience of emotion.

The second is "cognition," which has the connotation of recognizing something. It is cognizing the sensory object to be whatever it is. The emphasis here is that one has some form of determination as to what it is that one perceives. For example, if one perceives a human being, one determines whether they are male, female, or whatever the case may be. We perceive details often referred to as "specific characteristics of the sensory presentation."

The third of the five omnipresent mental factors is "intentionality." When we have an emotion, "emotion" is about something. There is always an object but that object does not have to be present in one's visual field. It may be an imagined object. Intentionality must also be present.

The fourth is "rapport." Varieties of mental and physical factors must be present in order to have an experience. Mental and physical factors cannot be running parallel with each other or operating completely independently of each other. If they were operating independently of each other, we would not have experiences. Therefore, they come together in order for us to have an experience, which is called "rapport" or "contact" in English.

The fifth of the five omnipresent mental factors is "ideation," which means that apart from simple cognition involved in perceiving whatever it is that one has perceived, one forms an opinion, an idea about what one has experienced. One forms judgments about it, whether one believes it is a good or bad thing, pleasant or unpleasant, and so on.

Therefore, from the Buddhist perspective, whether we are experiencing a pleasant and positive mental state, an unpleasant and non-positive mental state, or positive or negative emotions, these five factors must be present. This is why they are called "omnipresent." To emphasize and reiterate, in Abhidharma literature, it is considered that these five must be present in order for us to have any positive or negative experience, a complete experience of emotions.

The Primary Negative Emotions

There are six primary or basic emotions, which are excessive desire, anger, pride, doubt, view, and ignorance. In Buddhism, there is no essence of anger, pride, and so on. These are not entities that we can grab hold of. Each primary emotion can be expressed in different ways. We may not ordinarily regard view, doubt, and ignorance as emotions, however in Abhidharma, they are categorized as negative emotions. It is important to remember that the cognitive and affective aspects of mental functions cannot be separated. Whenever we are emotionally aroused, the arousal is accompanied by cognitive mental activity and vice versa.

The first three emotions of unbridled sensual desire, anger or hatred, and pride, when unchecked, are central to our having negative experiences. Here, desire is not any desire but specifically, sensual desire. The presence of sensual desire, anger, and pride is seen as the primary cause of our emotional disturbances. If we have any form of emotional disturbance, we can always trace it back to either one of these three or a combination of them.

Unchecked sensual desire disturbs us because in this particular context, satisfying our sensual needs can lead to all manner of problems and disturbances particularly when one's focus of desire is completely unobtainable. Excessive indulgence would normally lead to pain. We may not have the means to satisfy our desires, which subsequently automatically leads to frustration and possibly resentment, bitterness, feelings of hurt and rejection, and so on. Additionally, even if one has the means to satisfy these particular sensual desires, if one does not exercise moderation, overindulging in any sensual activity such as overeating for example, leads to pain instead of pleasure. These primary or basic emotions are also usually accompanied by the associated secondary negative emotions. For example, overindulgence may lead to a sense of indolence, depression, and similar negative experiences referred to in Abhidharma literature as secondary negative emotions.

Pride

First, it is important to point out that pride must be distinguished from self-esteem. Here, pride does not mean self-esteem. In fact, in Buddhist psychology, pride is seen as anathema to having proper self-esteem. Pride is seen as something that one has manufactured in order to reassure oneself, to present a false image of oneself to others so that they will think well of us, or to intimidate and frighten others. It is not genuine self-esteem. Therefore, it is said that pride can also disturb the mind precisely because problems ensue when we are extremely proud.

"Comparative pride" is pride that comes from always wanting to compare oneself to others. For example, the person may think, "Where do I stand? Am I as intelligent as that person? Am I as good looking as that individual?" In the Abhidharma literature, we do this in three different ways. One way is to compare ourselves in relation to who we believe is in fact a little better than us. We may wish to compete and try to become the better one. The second way is comparing ourselves to our peers, the people with who we believe we are on similar ground. We may be constantly keeping an eye out, making sure that we are not lagging behind, or at least, that we are keeping pace with them. We may also attempt to stay slightly ahead in terms of our work situation, private life, and so forth. It is constantly competing with our peers. The third way in which we show comparative pride is in relation to those that we believe are inferior to us. We may wish to show off, try to impress, show how great we are, or make them feel bad. Such activity is seen as misguided because however we wish to measure ourselves against others, getting ahead, lagging behind, or staying the same, it will only be relative. Situations and circumstances are continuously changing. Our perceived position or status is never going to be fixed or certain. Therefore, such maneuvering will always lead to frustration, disappointment, a sense of lack of fulfillment, self-doubt, anger, and other responses associated with pride.

The second form of pride is "pride of arrogance." This is simply refusing to believe that there is anyone better or superior to oneself. It is believing that one is the best at everything and that one knows best. This is based on completely false premises and notions. It will always lead to frustration and disappointments due to the simple fact that others will not share our view.

The third form of pride is known as "boastful pride," where we are compelled to speak about ourselves all of the time. Boasting about our achievements, we say, "I've done this. I've done that. I've experienced this. I've experienced that. I know this and that." This type of reiteration and trying convince others of one's greatness is very unhelpful and detrimental to healthy self-esteem.

The fourth form of pride is "self-delusional pride." This could be related to any number of experiences that we have where we have a distorted or deluded form of pride, pride based on the wrong reasons. This includes doing something terrible and feeling proud. One may have gained some notoriety and so from that form of recognition, one may then feel proud. However, this is misplaced.

Egoic insecurity is another inverted form of pride where we are constantly putting ourselves down, saying, "I can't do this. I can't do that. I won't be able to achieve this or achieve that. I don't have what it takes to be such and such a person." Constantly putting oneself down is considered to be a form of pride. While self-effacing, it can also be very self-focused and indulgent. The basic point that Abhidharma is making here is that contrary to what we think and believe, what we are doing has the opposite effect to what we desire and the outcome that we are seeking. Instead of lifting our self-esteem, it undermines it. Whether we like ourselves or not becomes conditional and is a form of belittling. From a Buddhist point of view, belittling is seen as a symptom of pride

In this way, these primary forms of emotions provide the materials for the disturbance of the mind to occur. This is encouraged by the following three other forms of basic emotions, called doubt, opinion, and ignorance. These three support the experience of sensual desire, anger, pride, and so on. Whenever we have very strong desires or emotions, we are thrown into confusion. If we cannot make up our mind, we begin to become confused. We do not know what is beneficial or harmful and so we are thrown into a state of doubt.

Opinionatedness

When we have strong desires, strong anger, and strong aversion toward certain things, we become very opinionated, which in turn can make us angry and arouse lust, strong sensual desires, et cetera. This subsequently leads to becoming very fixated with a tunneled focus. This reinforces the same tendencies of opinionatedness about oneself, one's self-image, and image of others. "Who I am and who they are" become fixed and our conviction and emotions become strong. We are constantly thrown between the two extremes of doubt and certainty again and again. Strong doubt and strong conviction support each other. Therefore, sometimes we are completely thrown into a state of confusion and we do not know what is going on. At other times, we are so convinced of what is happening that we are filled with so much self-assurance and belief in ourselves.

Ignorance

When our emotions are rampant, we become negligent. We do not exercise good sense or exercise our awareness, to put it in Buddhist terms. We lack awareness so we therefore become very negligent and forgetful. These secondary negative emotions arise because we become neglectful. Emotions ordinarily get the better of us and we then become negligent and behave in a manner that we would not normally behave due to our emotions. We say things that we would not normally say because our emotions get the better of us. We can become shameless and lose any sense of modesty or shame. We become unchecked, discourteous, and inconsiderate.

The Secondary Negative Emotions in Brief

The secondary negative emotions also perpetuate the cognitive and affective tendencies to construct the world that we live in. From the Buddhist point of view, we do not see the world well. This does not mean that everything that we perceive is completely created by the mind but rather, it means that nevertheless, what we perceive is different from how things exist. We perceive things in the manner that we do because there are many secondary mental factors that are encouraging to the primary negative emotions.

The first secondary emotion related to anger is *rage*, a form of anger that we experience when we really lose control. It is contingent on anger. The second is *resentment*. This is anger that we hang on to and do not let go, when we do not know how to forgive and forget. We let our ill feeling toward others simmer and sometimes grow. This also has a debilitating effect on oneself. In Abhidharma, this subspecies of anger is described as an emotion that makes us excessively sensitive, too easily provoked, and lacking endurance. In this state, we may not express our anger but as it lingers, an imprint is created in our mind. Unchecked, resentment can simmer and over time, we become very intolerant.

The third, *concealment* or *slyness* in this context, refers to being unable to face up to ourselves and reveal what we are like to others. It relates to hiding our defects and shortcomings.

The fourth is *spite*. In the Abhidharma literature, unlike rage or resentment, spite may also manifest in wishing to say some harsh words or take vindictive measures. Vindictiveness is seen as a component of spite. If one is spiteful, one is vindictive, expressed through verbal attack or slander, written and spoken, in order to undermine someone.

The fifth, *jealousy*, is related to the primary emotion of pride according to Abhidharma literature because the idea of gain and loss is involved. When we are jealous, we want to have the things that somebody else has or we feel the absence very intensely and do not wish that the other person had them.

The sixth is *avarice* or *greed* and is associated with the primary emotion of sensual desire. Being avaricious means having insatiable desire for material goods, material comfort, and material wealth. This is a subset of sensual desire.

It is said that the seventh, *deceit*, is linked mainly with sensual desire and ignorance. We become deceitful when we use different strategies in order to procure that which we want. When we cannot obtain it through proper or legitimate channels, we then resort to using deceitful tactics, which perpetuates our sensual desire and ignorance.

The eighth, *dishonesty*, is not a cool and calculated thing that one has chosen to adopt as a way of obtaining certain things that one desires but it is intimately, inextricably bound up with our emotional makeup. In the Abhidharma literature, the prototypical form of dishonesty is pretension, pretending to be somebody that one is not. An example of this is a confidence trickster. The idea is that whether one is using deceit or being dishonest, we may believe that we are being clever, but these maneuverings and tactics are grounded in and contingent on our emotional structure and makeup. They can disturb our equilibrium and inhibit our success.

The ninth, *mental inflation*, refers to only being concerned about one's external appearance and forgetting oneself. Here, one identifies oneself with the appearance that one is projecting to others. In this way, one can become a stranger to oneself. One begins to believe in the inflated image being projected.

Associated with anger, mental inflation, and pride, the tenth, *malice*, is described as the opposite of kindness. A malicious person is a completely unkind person. We can see that there are subtle distinctions between these different forms of anger. Not everyone who is angry is a malicious person. A malicious person is someone who uses anger in a specific way and is very unkind. A person may be kind yet angry, but a malicious person on the other hand, is incapable of love, compassion, or caring for anyone. They only have the intention to hurt, maim, or inflict pain on others. This is another subspecies of the primary emotion of anger.

The eleventh is *shamelessness*. According to Abhidharma literature, some of these secondary emotions are connected to anger, some to sensual desire, some to ignorance, and some to two or three of them. Shamelessness is tied to all three, sensual desire, anger, and ignorance. This means that if someone becomes blinded by greed for example, that person's greed becomes an overwhelming obsession. They may not care about their reputation or who they hurt. If one has been involved in criminal activities, one's partner and children may be brought to shame and may feel hurt but one is incapable of thinking of such consequences due to greed. It is similar with anger or arrogance. If one experiences all-consuming anger, that anger overtakes the person and they become totally reckless and lack a sense either of themselves or others in terms of what they are doing. Sometimes, when one feels slighted or when one's ego has been bruised, this may drive somebody insane and they might do something completely outrageous, like taking life. From this point of view then, shamelessness, if unchecked, becomes a supportive factor of unbridled sensual desire, anger, and egoistic tendencies.

The twelfth is *guilt* or *lack of propriety*, which is difficult to translate accurately but means something like guilt, meaning not wanting to acknowledge other people's needs, welfare, value, and so on. Again, motivated by excessive desire or anger, one is driven to do things that are detrimental to oneself and others.

The thirteenth, *depression*, is discussed in more detail in chapter nineteen. In relation to the Abhidharma literature, depression is mainly related to the primary emotion of ignorance or the misconception or misapprehension of reality—the state of impermanence and a lack of awareness. Part of the awareness that is lacking is failing to see one's own richness, beauty, and potentialities. If depression is left unchecked, anger and frustration will likely arise. One would feel angry with oneself, others, and life and circumstances in general.

The fourteenth is *agitation* and is related to the primary emotions of anger and lust or sensual desires. We become agitated when we want to pursue that which we desire and this then brings about agitations because excessive desire can never be fully satisfied. Therefore, it brings about frustration that inflames our negative emotions.

The fifteenth, *lack of trust*, like depression, is connected with ignorance and lack of awareness. It creates an environment that is conducive to the development of a range of negative emotions. The way it is explained in the Abhidharma is that we need to think of trust in four different ways—we can like somebody and not trust that person, we can trust someone but not like that person, we can like a person and trust that person, and we may neither like nor trust that person. In this instance, if one neither likes nor trusts someone, this puts one in a very disturbed frame of mind. When one is suspicious of others, expecting the worst from someone, and harbors a low opinion of others, all of the other negative emotions can then arise including degrees of paranoia.

Like depression and lacking trust, the sixteenth, *laziness*, is connected with ignorance or the misconception or misapprehension of reality—the state of impermanence. Laziness, according to Buddhism, indicates a lack of alertness that leaves us open to negative states. It can be seen as a type of personal neglect and letting ourselves go that can arouse such negative emotions as anger, frustration, and so on.

The seventeenth, *recklessness*, from a Buddhist perspective, means that the body, speech, and mind are not coordinated. It comes from ignorance. There is no real sense of integration or intimacy with our body, speech, and mind, as if they are divorced. Rather than being attuned to ourselves, we may be pushing agendas and harboring attitudes. We have no connection with how our words affect others. It is a lack of relationship with our physical feelings and needs and physical coordination, being detached from our senses. We have no real sense of what we are doing.

In the Abhidharma, this refers quite specifically to *unregulated emotional arousal* or *forgetfulness*, the eighteenth. If we have not learned to regulate, manage, and educate our emotions, we can be thrown and swayed continuously. Like tunnel vision, strong emotions create monofocal perception. Only one thing is pushed into the center of our consciousness and everything else is pushed to the periphery. So we forget everything except the current, all-consuming emotion. The stronger the emotion, the more forgetful we become of all the other things and especially those things that are conducive to our well-being.

The nineteenth, when we *lack awareness*, is where our mind becomes vulnerable to the insidious corrosive effects of our negative emotions and feelings.

The twentieth is a *scattered mind* and has to do with lack of control over our sensory apparatuses. We just automatically yield to our sensory impressions. What we see, hear, smell, taste, and touch grabs our attention.

Concluding Points

Even though things like doubt, opinionatedness, and ignorance are not emotions in a strict sense, nevertheless, they are seen as forms of emotion from the Abhidharma perspective because emotions accompany doubt and opinionatedness. When we have emotional experiences, there are many different things happening. We may not be aware of everything that is going on. From the Buddhist point of view, this is also very important to understand because there are things that are going on in our mind associated with anger, sensual desire, ignorance, and so forth of which we are usually unaware. According to Abhidharma literature, some of these secondary emotions are connected to anger, sensual desire, or ignorance. Sometimes, they are connected to two or all three.

For example, the secondary emotions related to anger include rage, when we really lose control and resentment, when we unforgivably hang on to our anger, which can be very self-debilitating. Long-held resentment creates other tendencies of one becoming excessively sensitive, easily provoked, and lacking endurance, and lingers as an imprint in our mind. Jealousy is related to pride. Deceit and dishonesty are related to sensual desire and ignorance. Malice is associated with anger, mental inflation, and pride, and is described as the opposite of kindness.

Apart from describing the emotional life of our personal mind and mental states, this presentation also describes our relationship with others. As I mentioned at the beginning of this chapter, it is important to have a comprehensive view of our emotional life, in terms of our physical experiences, feelings, mental attitudes, beliefs, and the factors related to our interpersonal experiences. These are all interconnected and relate to Buddhist moral psychology, meditation, and the pursuit of a good life.

Chapter Thirteen

The Relationship Between Cognitive Activity and Emotional Experiences

According to Buddhism, it is possible for us to reach an elevated state. If a we manage our emotions properly and cultivate the positive emotions and develop positive attitudes and so on, it is said in Buddhism that we will advance, go forward, and become elevated beings, called *arya* in Sanskrit. If we allow our negative emotions and negative states to get the better of us, then the quality of our lives can deteriorate rather than be elevated. If we manage our emotions well, even with a few hiccups along the way, we can cultivate a more positive and uplifted state where we can progress and move forward in a very fulfilling way. How do we procure real happiness and cultivate the more uplifting kinds of emotions? Practicing meditation does not guarantee that we can necessarily bypass negativity. To bring about transformation in ourselves, we need to develop an understanding of our human condition. Understanding the power of the mind to lift us up or drag us down is vitally important, for example, understanding how negative states of mind and associated mental afflictions can affect us when harboring negative attitudes and dwelling in negative states of mind.

In Buddhism, the affective aspect of emotion and associated feelings and the cognitive aspect of mind—thoughts, conceptualization, and other mental events—go hand-in-hand. Any cognitive mental act that we perform is always associated with certain kinds of feelings that are accompanied by our desires; likes and dislikes, acceptance and rejection, attraction and aversion, et cetera. These judgments and considerations then inflame our emotions such as excessive desire, anger, and feelings of strong attachment and fixation. The manner in which we become emotionally inflamed depends on our ideas of what is good or bad, pleasant or unpleasant, and acceptable or unacceptable, and this determines how we emotionally experience and react.

It is very difficult to separate our cognitive activities from our emotional experiences. In Buddhism, we see a clear link between cognitive activities and emotional experiences. The reason we become entangled in all manner of delusory mental states is that our cognitive and affective or emotional and feeling states, are intermingled. Therefore, it is difficult to see things clearly in terms of how and why we experience things the way we do on both the emotional level and the various cognitive levels. According to Buddhism, we are not fully conscious of the layers of cognition and emotionality.

As long as we are caught up in these delusory mental states, experiences of happiness will always be interrupted. It is not just that attaining enlightenment or developing spiritually as a person becomes more distant, even being able to be a happy person in a genuine sense becomes difficult. We can always try to procure happiness through temporary measures. For example, if we are able to satisfy our desire temporarily, then we become happy. If we desire something and are able to have it, we may feel happy, but as we know, it is only temporary. In Buddhism, it is nice to have the happy moments, no matter how temporary, but what we are looking for is more of a lasting happiness. This is not purely associated with simple pleasures but rather, a deeper level of pleasure that comes from inner transformation and an increased capacity to experience our lives more broadly in a much richer and more profound way.

Let us now look at working with the delusory mental states in order to help release the grip that they so often seem to have on us. From a Buddhist point of view, it is essential to understand how delusory mental states are created and perpetuated so that this can help us transform and overcome them.

Delusory mental states are perpetuated largely by our own perception of ourselves and our own self-interest. These play a very significant role in how we experience life generally. From a Buddhist point of view, due to ignorance and well-entrenched mental habits and delusory mental states, et cetera, our self-interest is not being served properly. That is why we suffer. Contrary to what is often believed, Buddhism does not argue that we should not look after our own self-interest. In fact, it is considered very important to look after our own self-interest in an intelligent manner, which is something that we ordinarily fail to do. In our normal ordinary state, we never or rarely see the intricacy and interconnection of the many primary and secondary emotions and the varieties of factors or dharmas that produce our many experiences. We remain entangled and it is difficult to see things clearly in such a state. Thus, our own sense of self-care is also deluded. This is why meditation is necessary for helping us clear up the fog, seeing the entanglement, and then beginning to work with our own situation with more understanding and clarity.

It is like a web; the emotional states are not simple but indeed very complex. Our emotional states are connected to our beliefs, attitudes, feelings, and strong primary emotions such as anger, jealousy, and so on. These are then perpetuated through a combination of different kinds of thoughts, beliefs, attitudes, emotions, and so on. Looking at some of the different types of emotions in the previous chapter, we discovered that they are involved in producing the kinds of experiences that we have and that these are associated with our delusory mental states. A straightforward Buddhist definition of negative emotions and negative states of mind, "kleshas" in Sanskrit, has three aspects. First, there is a "state of mind which has a debilitating and corrupting influence on one's body and mind." The second is that "these negative states of mind have the further effect of causing impediments in terms of successfully carrying out our various activities and projects." In other words, our negative deluded states frustrate all of our efforts. What we wish to do and what we want to achieve, our goals et cetera and all of our effort may be frustrated, at least to some degree. Thirdly, "our negative states or kleshas produce unruliness in one's body and mind," in other words, agitation. So the mind and body can be in a constant state of agitation.

How do the negative emotions arise and what causes them? This is another question that needs to be answered. The Abhidharma literature focuses on revealing the nature of the physical and mental factors or dharmas. According to Abhidharma, there are a number of causes that arouse negative emotions and also produce negative states of mind. The first causes are the psychophysical tendencies, or *vasanas* in Sanskrit, deep-seated imprints that are created in our body/mind complex. As long as the imprints remain, we are bound by them in relation to how we judge and respond to the world.

The second causes are the triggering mechanisms and catalysts that continually direct us to specific types of negative emotional responses and negative states of mind. For example, if one is prone to jealousy and a particular set of circumstances arise, one feels jealous. Depending on the personality structure of each individual, what causes jealousy would vary from individual to individual. For example, if one were jealous of the intellect of others, when somebody intelligent comes along, one would be thrown into feelings of jealousy, envy, and the like. However, that same person may have no feelings of jealousy witnessing flirtatious behavior being directed at their spouse. When the appropriate triggers manifest, jealousy arises. In other words, the potentiality or dispositional tendency needs to be present in the person in order for the resultant negative emotions and negative mental states to arise. A person who is not easily provoked into jealousy may not experience jealousy, even if the normal catalysts for provoking jealousy are present. So to reiterate, first the dispositional psychophysical tendency, the vasanas, have to be present in the individual before the second cause, the triggering devices, are activated.

The third reason we experience negative emotions has to do with how we appraise each situation and set of circumstances. Abhidharma literature refers to "the continuous indulgence in inappropriate ways of thinking." In Buddhism, our emotional responses are intimately tied to how we appraise a given situation. Due to our delusions, deep-seated psychophysical tendencies or vasanas, and triggers, we continuously misread, exaggerate, minimize, or ignore what is presented to us through our sensory apparatuses, imagination, and other mental events. Due to our deep-seated tendencies, triggers, and ways of thinking and responding, it can seem that we are condemned to repeat the same negative patterns over and over. As samsaric beings, we have all developed the tendency to get caught up in negative states of mind. According to the Abhidharma, these are the three causes for the arousal of negative emotions.

The Buddhist theory regarding negative emotions and emotions in general is quite sophisticated. I will now broadly discuss the causes of emotions themselves. The question then, is what causes us to have any type of emotional experience? The Abhidharma literature lists six different causes. The first is called the "objective basis" or the "objective condition," which refers to the object of our desire or our expectations, frustrations, elations, et cetera. The second is the intentionality of the mind. Our mind is always directed toward certain objects; object of fear, desire, envy, and so on. The third cause is the attraction to sensory impressions, what we see, hear, smell, taste, and touch. Sensory impressions are also seen as responsible for producing various forms of emotionality. The fourth cause is in relation to how we communicate, our speech or discourse; what we speak about and how we express our emotions verbally. According to Buddhism, what is said has a direct link to our own mental states and also to our own physical condition. The fifth cause is physical and mental habituation. Because of mental and physical habituation, we become preprogrammed to respond in many quite predictable ways. From a Buddhist point of view, habituation diminishes our ability to express ourselves emotionally in an open, creative, and wholesome way. Shackled by past prejudices and experiences, it is possible for our emotional responses to be dominated by just a few highly predictable habits. The sixth cause is mentation, *manaskara* in Sanskrit, which refers to the types of thoughts we have; what do we think about? Even if we have not said anything or visibly expressed ourselves through such emotions as anger or through other physical means, whether an outlet is found or not, thoughts can play over and over in our head. The combination of all of these six causes culminates in making all manner of emotional experiences manifest.

The causes are grouped in terms of what brings on the emotional responses that we have and why we respond in the ways that we do. That is, what are the actual causes, the real causes, for the persistence of our emotional states and responses? It can be extremely helpful to understand and ponder on the causes for the creation of emotions in general and in particular the creation of negative emotions, how the primary and secondary negative emotions and negative states of mind operate and how they can produce delusions and distortions within the mind.

From a Buddhist perspective, emotions are very complex. Some aspects of our emotions are intrapsychic and some are tied to our body and our physical sensations, changes, and reactions. Other aspects are related to our interpersonal dimension. In Buddhism, the notion of moral psychology is relevant here because our emotions are tied to our sense of well-being and are related to how we interact with each other and conduct ourselves in our social environment. Whether we are happy or not is also determined by that, not simply in terms of what is going on inside our body or in our mind; the interpersonal dimension is almost as important as intrapsychic states and processes, that is, what is going on within the mind of the individual.

In Buddhism, there is clear recognition that even though emotions have a number of causes, they are tied to our beliefs, based on our appraisal of situations and circumstances, result from various cognitive mental activities, and are not just tied to feelings and bodily states and responses. Nevertheless, there is clear recognition that these negative states of mind and emotions are very compelling. It can be difficult to overcome them.

It is important to realize, according to Buddhism, that if we can create negative emotions, then we can also overcome them. Overcoming the hold specific types of emotional experiences have on us is not a question of whether we have the willpower to overcome them. From a Buddhist point of view, as we have discussed, it is more about understanding how negative states are generated so that we can gradually work toward undermining the whole system or edifice, as it were. When we work with the primary and secondary emotions, we need to work with them in a piecemeal fashion. There is no need to take on too much all at once. Because different kinds of mental states are conducive to the arousal of negative emotions, instead of trying to overcome everything to do with a negative state such as jealousy, believing "I have to conquer jealousy through sheer willpower," it is more important to find an intelligent use of our mental resources in order to provide a less daunting task and approach, a piecemeal approach. Willpower alone is not sufficient. If we feel our willpower has failed us, we then experience a sense of failure, guilt, and shame. Such responses, of course, will only help perpetuate our negative states of mind. If we take on too much all at once, we can be overwhelmed and if we do not reach our lofty expectations, we can easily condemn ourselves, unnecessarily believing ourselves to be unfixable; "I have tried everything to overcome it, but I still I get jealous."

To avoid such self-condemnation, we first need to begin to develop a better understanding of how negative emotions and negative states of mind are perpetuated. Rather than seeking to overpower a particular negativity such as rage through the use of sheer willpower, in Buddhism, as well as building our understanding, we also employ meditational techniques, contemplations, and other practices. One traditional example that is often used to illustrate the gradual approach to overcoming our negativities is that during medieval times, if there was a fortress that was to be penetrated by an invading force by an all-out assault yet the people inside the fortress were able to repel the external forces, then what one may do is to gradually create a breach in the wall. By removing one stone at a time, as it is said, one may be able to then create a breach in the wall and subsequently, the invading forces can rush in and take over.

Dealing with this negative state of mind while we are meditating allows us to experience it in a safe environment. We should not excessively concern ourselves with the idea of completely overcoming all of the negative states and emotions. For that to occur, one would have to attain enlightenment. As I was saying right from the beginning of this book, there are two goals that are in harmony—the temporary goal of attaining greater happiness and the distant goal of attaining enlightenment. What we do to attain happiness is completely in keeping with our goal of wanting to attain enlightenment. So we may not be able to become completely free of anger, jealousy, et cetera so quickly, but we can still go a long way toward being less enslaved and feeling less bound by our negative states of mind. Our negative states are often treated as shackles, emotional tentacles that drag us down, constantly inhibiting us from going forward.

Knowing what negative states of mind are at work, what causes them to be there, how they are perpetuated, and how all of this then helps the delusory mental states to continue robbing us of our ability to make full sense of our life, is a massive step forward toward improving our life experiences. From a Buddhist point of view, negative emotions and negative states of mind keep us from knowing ourselves, from knowing our own real experiences. The more negative emotions we experience, the more entangled we become. Our ability to see what we are experiencing and how we can improve our situation can become blurred. This is what Buddhism means by the "delusory mental state."

Meditation and the cultivation of positive mental states is a way to begin dismantling the wall of negativity. If we can learn to generate happiness by developing it from within, it is a happiness that is resilient and lasting. If the happiness that we experience normally is contingent, meaning contingent on something other than what we have within ourselves, due to changing circumstances, our happiness cannot remain stable. If we can find some form of happiness that is not contingent on something other than itself, it then becomes self-perpetuating. We find that a happy frame of mind can accommodate many unpleasant experiences and still not fall victim to despair, frustration, and the like. The happy frame of mind is accommodating. An unhappy frame of mind is unaccommodating, therefore, it cannot be happy for very long.

Chapter Fourteen
Giving Rise to Positive Emotions

Buddhism emphasizes the notion of leading a robust of life that is vibrant, engaged, and energized. It can sometimes be mistakenly believed that Buddhism requires one to be passive and disengaged in order to avoid distraction and disruption to one's life. Buddhism believes that certain kinds of activities can lead to disruptions in life and to emotional disturbances. Some disruptions in life can leave a deep and lasting imprint, so care and awareness is necessary. However, in Buddhism, we believe that we are capable of learning to deal with emotions so that our lives can be active and we can have a sense of vibrancy and resilience. Feeling alive and vibrant helps reduce and overcome any sense of enslavement that we may have in relation to our negative states of mind and negative emotions. In Buddhism, meditation and other practices are used in order to bring about the necessary insights and changes so that we deal with life in a more skillful way.

Should one withdraw from activity and cultivate some form of inner mental equilibrium and thus try to find inner peace and happiness? Alternatively, can one be involved with varieties of activities without withdrawing completely, lead a vibrant and active life, and still have the experience of peace and happiness? Withdrawing from activities and the notion of renunciation may be helpful, but it is important to understand that the main thing that we need to withdraw from engaging in is indulging in negative emotions and negative states of mind. That is the bottom line so to speak. From the Buddhist point of view, it is not necessary to withdraw from all kinds of activities. Peace of mind is not necessarily what we acquire as a result of having withdrawn from life's many activities, mundane or otherwise. Such peace comes from having withdrawn from various states of mind or mental factors, such as indulging in negative emotions and states of mind, the negative mental factors.

Many of the positive states of mind and positive emotions that are listed in Buddhist literature have to do with engagement and with working with others. It is not just a question of individual self-cultivation—how we learn to grow as a person, learning to deal with our negative and positive states of mind, negative and positive emotions, dealing with others more skillfully, and how we engage with the diversity of life experiences. In Buddhism, as with negative emotions, all of the positive emotions can be understood as leading to experiences of peace and happiness. We need to know how to generate the positive mental states through understanding the positive factors that are involved. From a Buddhist viewpoint, trying to look at a negative emotion such as anger in isolation may not produce the results we are hoping for. We may learn how to control and manage it, but we are less likely to work with it in a deep and fundamental manner. This is why the different kinds of mental factors are discussed. In the same way as with negative emotions, positive emotions also have mental states. If we are making an effort to train the mind to have more positive thoughts and also be aware of the types of thoughts that arise, we will be able to give rise to positive emotions. The positive emotions arise when there are favorable mental conditions for them to arise. This will also give rise to more experiences of happiness and joy.

In Abhidharma literature, eleven mental factors that give rise to positive emotions are mentioned. If we cultivate these through our meditation, positive emotions will arise. The first one that is mentioned in terms of what we need to cultivate is *confidence* and *trust*. When suspiciousness and extreme forms of nihilistic skepticism and cynicism get the better of us, it is subsequently very difficult to develop positive emotions. When we become very untrusting and suspicious, it is very difficult to have any form of positive emotion of love or joy because a very nihilistic, cynical attitude is associated with a feeling of depression, a pessimistic outlook on life, a pessimistic expectation. In this case, we have an extremely low expectation of other people and the world generally, so it is extremely difficult to see any good in anything. Even if we wish to have the experience of some positive emotions, due to lack of confidence and lack of trust, it may not arise. In order to develop positive emotions, one first needs to have some trust in oneself. Gradually, we need to learn to distinguish between what is trustworthy and what will let us down. If we have been let down previously, this does not mean that we cannot have trust any longer. In the teachings, it says that we can find trust in those things that will not let us down. Relating to one's own ability to overcome problems and difficulties in life can help us to develop trust in spiritual beliefs, things that one will not be let down by. There are many trustworthy and untrustworthy people and making clearer distinctions allows us to have confidence and develop the arising of positive emotions. Without trust, one can be completely trapped within oneself. Developing trust intelligently is the way of bridging the gap between oneself and the other.

The second one, sometimes translated as *self-respect* or *shame* as opposed to shamelessness, is understood as the practice of one being sufficiently self-aware to behave in any way that has regard and concern for others, where one has concern to avoid hurting or damaging anyone or anything. Being shameless, from a Buddhist point of view, leaves us without the necessary requirement to experience real joy and happiness. Shamelessness inevitably leads to conflict, which gives rise to suffering and pain. It does not give rise to the experience of positive emotions and therefore, one will not experience joy and happiness.

The third, *conscience* or *self-assessment*, means to be witness to our own conduct, to monitor what is going on within ourselves—our intentions, motivations, indulgences, and so on. What sort of emotions and thoughts are we indulging in? What are their implications? From a Buddhist point of view, if we pay attention to such mental activity, we can then create a favorable mental condition to experience more positive emotions. If we do not have a checking system, it will be difficult to prevent the negative states of mind from encroaching and impeding our opportunities to cultivate ourselves through the development of positive emotions.

The fourth, *non-obsessiveness* implies that we have a tendency to latch on to things that we are attracted to. From the Buddhist point of view, if we want to have the experience of positive emotions, we have to learn how to delay our reaction to things, in a manner of speaking. Instead of immediately reacting to something that we desire, lust after, or finding pleasure in and simply losing all control and being completely automatically drawn to these things, if one is able to learn to delay one's reaction to them, this is also another way in which we can create some mental space for ourselves so that we can have the experience of joy and so on.

Here, we have to understand that in Buddhism, a clear link is made between dissatisfaction and our obsessive nature. The more obsessed we get in terms of our object of desire or craving, the greater the dissatisfaction. Therefore, dissatisfaction, of course, always leads to the experience of a feeling of being cheated and let down. One does not feel satisfied. One does not feel content and therefore, it is impossible to experience any variety of positive emotion when we are in that state. This of course, also leads to all forms of addictions, including to various kinds of things like food and other pleasure inducing objects of our desires.

It can be very helpful to work with our obsessions and fixations in meditation. Normally, when we are in our ordinary life, we may see something that we really want such as a nice car and then immediately, one may become disturbed, producing a negative reaction like jealousy, anger, or disappointment. But in meditation, we can use our imagination to recall objects of our obsessions and desires. In this way, we create an opportunity to deal with such desires more skillfully and with more awareness. By working with the images and the associated emotions and feelings in meditation, when we are confronted with similar situations out in the world, we would have developed an ability to manage and deal with our responses and decrease our negative responses.

Non-hatred is the fifth one. The mind can be encouraged to become calmer over time, rather than being geared toward immediate responsiveness such as wanting to attack or run, immediate rejection or acceptance of something despite a lack of scrutiny, et cetera. It is difficult to have and maintain a positive mental outlook when one is easily triggered and has a strong tendency toward judgmentalism. Responsiveness without a sense of space or a pause leaves one open to all forms of negative emotions and negative states of mind to arise. From the Buddhist point of view, if we desire positive emotions, this is another aspect that we need to work on, how not to be excessively aggressive or hostile in our posture. Deciding to be more positive is a tremendous beginning.

The sixth one is *non-deludedness*. In order to make real strides in developing a more positive state of mind, we need to understand the impact that our fundamental delusional state, sense of self, and self-perception about the world and our relationship with it have on our state of mind. Our self-perception makes the negative mental factors and negative emotional states operative. In Buddhism, temporary or secondary delusional states are also spoken of and these are contingent on what we are experiencing at any given moment. Our desire to sustain our delusory state and sense of self fuel a strong samsaric tendency to want to evade certain things. Using evasive tactics such as inattentiveness, negligence, and using emotional detours, deprives us of the opportunity to have the experience of positive emotions.

In Buddhism, the seventh, being *energetically diligent* and resilient with alertness is very important in order to develop a more positive disposition. Being mentally sluggish and lacking alertness makes it extremely easy for negatives states of mind or negative emotions to arise and overwhelm us. Therefore, alertness and resilience are seen as a vital part of cultivating a positive mental state.

The eighth is *awareness*, which is considered an essential quality that we should also bring to our meditation. Lack of awareness also goes hand-in-hand with the arousal of negative emotions.

The ninth is *conscientiousness*, which in Buddhism refers to a type of physical and mental friendliness, generating a positive and friendly attitude toward others in particular.

Another quality that is important in helping generate a more positive state of mind and positive emotion is *equanimity* or a *sense of equilibrium*, the tenth in the list. Without equanimity, we can be emotionally stirred up and tossed around. Buddhism describes the experience of negative emotions as like being knocked about in a small boat surrounded by turbulent waters with little opportunity for successful navigation. The experience of positive emotions comes with distinctive feelings such as feeling uplifted. There are also distinctive physical sensations associated with being ecstatic or joyous. For these experiences to also not produce a turbulent state, from a Buddhist point of view, real experiences of joy, "upliftedness," and other forms of positive emotions need to be accompanied by a feeling or a sense of equilibrium; feelings of being grounded, a sense of underlying stability. Feeling some kind of elation, being lifted up, and being transported into higher and more rarified states of exaltation does not nullify the experience of underlying equanimity. Real equanimity, as Buddhism says, is like a friendly aid for the arising of positive emotions.

The eleventh, positivity and developing the attitude of *non-violence* or *non-harming* is the nullification of any intention to cause harm to self or others. Even if anger is present, the intention to do harm need not be present. From a Buddhist point of view then, non-harming is an essential component because it is difficult to have the experience of positive emotions when our mind is filled with all manner of harmful thoughts directed at others.

These eleven positive mental factors can be used as a counterbalance to the twenty negative mental factors or twenty negative mental states that we have briefly discussed. From a Buddhist point of view, these positive states of mind can be developed when we pay attention. It is not so difficult to learn to be a little bit more attentive than usual, a little more mindful, conscientious, alert, and so on in order to help develop mental confidence and trust. By attempting to develop a little bit of each through our meditation practices and contemplations, we will gradually be able to sow what are called "virtuous seeds" in Buddhism.

If we allow ourselves to wallow in negative states of mind and emotions, because of such states as anger, obsessions, addictions, and so on, we will produce states of mind such as sadness, fear, anxiety, et cetera. These are the side effects of the primary and secondary negative emotions and negative states of mind. Under these circumstances, experiencing lasting joy or happiness is difficult. If we turn that around and gradually develop a more encompassing positive outlook on life, we can experience the conflicting emotions with less intensity and regularity. We can experience more positive emotions by doing little things a bit at a time. This has a cumulative effect. This type of approach in Buddhism is seen as very important. Isolating one aspect of our negative or positive emotional states ignores the interconnected relationship that the arising of primary and secondary emotions have. We should consider a particular positive emotion in terms of its relation to other mental states and factors. In a more inclusive way and with greater understanding of the different elements that make up and fuel our experiences, we can benefit more readily from the experience of positive emotions and develop virtuous qualities.

The virtuous qualities that we want to develop, from a Buddhist point of view, are developed from these mental factors. In other words, the virtues are not to be understood purely in terms of our ethical conduct, in terms of how we behave. Our conduct, whether it is virtuous or not, is important, and this is the case not only because virtuous conduct is a good thing to do in itself. From a Buddhist point of view, it is also that these virtues directly relate to our own states of mind. There is a real link between happiness and virtues and a link between happiness and positive emotions and mental states. It is not purely through mental work that we have the experience of happiness but our behavior also has the potential to produce happiness. The mental states that give rise to the virtuous behavior or virtuous conduct are the same as what gives rise to happiness in terms of our mental life.

In Buddhism, virtues go hand-in-hand with the positive mental factors and emotions. Virtues in this context are understood in five different ways. The first is called *natural virtue*, which means certain things are virtuous in relation to our own mental states, for example, the mental state of non-covetousness being the opposite to stinginess. Non-covetousness is a virtue within itself. There are also *virtues by association* and this means that certain mental states are not virtues in themselves but when certain mental states come into contact with positive mental states and emotions, these mental states also become virtuous. For example, interest, according to Buddhism, is not associated with virtue. If that interest becomes associated with genuine love, distinct from non-genuine love, it then becomes virtuous. Love with interest combined gives rise to some action that is beneficial and becomes virtuous conduct. An example that Tibetan Buddhists are fond of regarding virtue by association is that if you mix milk with water, the water becomes more like milk rather than the other way round. The third virtue is called *virtue by motivation*, meaning certain things become virtuous because of the purpose we have in mind. If the purpose is to do something good, beneficial, or wholesome, that motivation turns or converts the various mental factors and emotional states into virtues. The fourth virtue is called *virtue by subsequent relation*. Sometimes, certain positive mental states arise and rather than just arising and subsequently disappearing, they give rise to subsequent positive mental states. The subsequent mental states inherit the "positiveness" of the previous mental states; the arousal of certain states of mind are determined by what has gone before. In this respect, the subsequent states of mind become virtuous because the previous states of mind have been virtuous. "Virtuous by subsequent relation" relates to what we call "karmic imprints" and "vasanas," karmic propensities. The fifth virtue is called *ultimate virtue*, which in Buddhism, refers to nirvana. All of the virtues that we cultivate are geared toward the attainment of that ultimate virtue, which is nirvana, the ultimate consummation of virtue.

Non-virtue is also described in a similar way and relates to negative states of mind and emotions, such as the emotion of jealousy. Jealousy, according to Buddhism, is negative and there is no ambiguity, it is a *natural non-virtue*. The second is *non-virtue by association*, which means something like feelings. Feelings, as we have discussed, are neither non-virtuous nor related to negative emotions. If feelings are associated with anger, then that feeling becomes non-virtuous; a feeling of wanting to inflict pain on someone then becomes a non-virtue. The third is called *non-virtue by motivation*, and this refers to mental states that can be directed in certain ways depending on what we want to do. It is dictated by the purpose, the goal that we are seeking, in terms of what motivates us. What we do becomes non-virtuous or virtuous dependent on our motivation. Apart from the motivation, it may not be non-virtuous as such. It may not even be a non-virtuous emotional experience but because of the underlying motive and the purpose that one has set in one's mind, it then becomes non-virtue. The fourth is *non-virtue by subsequent relation*, which means that the non-virtues always give rise to additional non-virtue. Just like negative states of mind are more likely to give rise to more negative states of mind and negative emotions give rise to more negative emotions, non-virtue also gives rise to more non-virtue. Therefore, subsequent mental states, dispositions, and behaviors would also inherit that from the previous occurrence of non-virtue. The fifth is the *ultimate non-virtue*, which from the Buddhist point of view is the samsaric condition itself. Our existential condition is ultimately non-virtuous because it is permeated by delusory mental states, conflicting and negative emotions, negative states of mind, non-virtuous thoughts, non-virtuous ethical conduct, and so on. These lead to predominantly self-created suffering, suffering that can be ultimately overcome. In this way, from the Buddhist perspective, we can connect the notion of virtues and non-virtues to our human nature.

Virtues are to be cultivated and non-virtues are not to be cultivated and ideally, avoided. This is done not only because virtuous conduct is beneficial to others, but it also promotes goodness in society and brings happiness to others. Buddhism recognizes that engaging in such ethical conduct is good within itself, that it is sufficient to do something that promotes virtue. From the Buddhist point of view, all of these reasons are important but there is one additional reason that is considered to be even more important; these virtues promote our own happiness. The virtues are related to our own more edifying aspects of our nature. The emotional conflicts that we experience and the delusory mental state that we have become entangled in lead to suffering and are demeaning. They produce all manner of negative states of mind related to our base or unalleviated samsaric nature. From the Buddhist viewpoint, this is also one of the main reasons virtues should be taken seriously.

We should think in terms of positive emotions and mental states in relation to how we conduct ourselves and interact with others. We need to think about virtues and vices because in order to have a meaningful life, we need to have some variety of integrated approach to promoting our own life, to exploit and take advantage of our full potential. From the Buddhist point of view, if we want to promote and experience positive emotions, we need an overall approach.

Buddhism includes taking care of our body, how to relate to our body and mental attitudes, emotions, conduct, behavior, livelihood, and how to live. Every aspect of our lives needs to be addressed in order to achieve a more lasting and profound happiness. Therefore, we cannot simply find happiness by trying to isolate our negative emotions such as jealousy, anger, or feelings of fear and anxiety, et cetera. We can become somewhat defeated or self-condemning when these negative aspects repeatedly reemerge as they do; "I have anger issues that will not budge," or "I have some problem with fear." From the perspective of Buddhism, an overall approach to our physical health and mental well-being are parallel. Real health can be worked on and attained with a comprehensive, integrated approach. If we do something such as relaxation, yoga, watch what we eat, and exercise, all of these things combined may produce a good result. By working with only one aspect of oneself, one may not progress as easily. Often, a negative state of mind or emotion is a symptom of our general condition so a comprehensive approach with the different techniques that are mentioned in Buddhism, can help deal with our general well-being.

We should not just focus on positive emotions, positive sates of mind, and negative emotions, and negative states of mind, but what gives rise to them. If we can deal with what gives rise to the emotions, then gradually, as far as Buddhism is concerned, we can succeed. Gradually, we will develop a more life-affirming, positive attitude. We will then flourish. To do this, we need to have larger aspirations in life, as I have been discussing. A comprehensive approach is geared toward aiming for something that is quite exalted and uplifting.

The idea is that according to Buddhism, if our vision is very tunneled and nearsighted, if we have a nearsighted, limited approach and do not see into the distance or see the summit, then every little thing becomes a cause for tremendous anxiety and we can become overwhelmingly concerned. With a wider vision, everything that we experience and see begins to take on a different color, shape, and texture. Everything that we experience begins to change and this is the idea. If we only go about our lives focusing on the daily experiences, we can become more and more entangled in the emotional complexities of what is happening. With a wider vision and perspective to look more broadly and from somewhat of a distance, such perspectives can be generated through the practice of meditation and other such techniques and practices. We can subsequently have a clearer perspective, less entangled in all the little things that are going on. It can be devastating if the only things that we can see are minor but become exaggerated and blown out of proportion. According to Buddhism, this is the samsaric suffering that we experience.

Chapter Fifteen

The Support Structure of Emotions

Often, many people practice Buddhist meditation but do so without going into the Buddhist teachings. They may use Buddhist meditation mainly for practical purposes, hoping to calm the mind or develop mindfulness, awareness, and so on. There is the understanding that if they do meditation, the emotions will automatically become pacified or if they become mindful, they would be able to gain some insight into the mind, fears, and emotions.

But in this section on emotions, I wished to emphasize the importance of understanding what Buddhists say about emotions—the benefit and harm of the emotions and that not all emotions are bad and lead to disturbances. I also wished to emphasize how important it is to understand the Buddhist view of how emotions arise and if we do so, we can see how Buddhist meditation practices relate to what we have been discussing. There are connections between our experience of suffering, negative emotions, negative thoughts, negative attitudes, and beliefs and the experience of happiness and positive emotions and positive feelings and mental attitudes.

This being the case, from the Buddhist point of view, the reason we are practicing is of course to have the experience of happiness, which comes from having some variety of satisfaction; the experience of satisfaction leads to well-being. When frustration or frustrated desires and a feeling of disappointment, discontentment, and so forth arise, it disturb our minds; we become miserable, depressed, and so forth. From the Buddhist viewpoint, to reiterate, there is a key link between our experience of pain and suffering with the experience of negative emotions. When we suffer, the negative emotions, the conflicting emotions, come to the fore and we become completely caught up. Often, we may not even realize that we are caught up in the "eye of the storm." Life may be in a complete state of turmoil but we may not recognize it. Even if we recognize it and realize that our mind is very disturbed, because we have feelings of such strong negative emotions, we may not realize the support structure that is encouraging the perpetuation of the negative emotions.

Buddhist practice is not only confined to dealing with the experience of negative emotions that arise in the course of our day-to-day living experiences and trying to cultivate the positive emotions and so forth. It is also about gradually removing the support structure for the negative emotions to arise. In Buddhism, there is a clear recognition that it is difficult to just not become jealous, for example, not to experience this uncontrollable feeling of jealousy or envy. It may be difficult to stop it even if one recognizes that it is not healthy and does not cause one to feel good. Even so, it is difficult to overcome and if one practices meditation, even if that experience is somehow pacified for a period of time, if a difficult situation arises that would normally trigger a jealous response, jealousy may again resurface or arise. We need to realize that no matter which form of Buddhist meditation we are doing, it is designed to remove the support structure for these negative emotions to arise and at the same time, to create a support structure for the healthy growth of positive emotions to arise. If we understand this, we will see that the Buddhist meditation of shamatha, loving-kindness, mind training, visualization of deities, insight or analytical meditation, and so forth, begin to make sense. This is because they have a specific job to do in terms of either dismantling or recreating the necessary support system or support structure to be put in place. If we can do this through our practices, gradually, whatever is distracting us would improve and our sense of satisfaction in life would increase. There would be a decrease in our sense of discontentment and so on.

According to Buddhism, our normal condition is characterized by dissatisfaction. The notion of the Sanskrit word *duhkha*, which is the First Noble Truth, is often translated as suffering. The wider connotation is pure and simple suffering because it basically signifies something like the sense of dissatisfaction, nonfulfillment, and discontent. We spend all of life wanting something and even if we get it, we may not feel satisfied or sated. As the Buddhist scriptures say, it is like drinking saltwater; it only inflames thirst. According to Buddhism therefore, if we dismantle the support structure for the negative state of mind and recreate a support system for the positive states of mind, we will subsequently feel a sense of satisfaction. The emotions and feelings that we will experience will be much healthier and therefore, it is automatically going to make us feel good and bring a sense of satiation. We would not feel like we have to strive and struggle, constantly struggling, constantly striving toward something. This is not to say that in Buddhism we should not strive. That is not the point but it relates to how we go about this; striving fuelled by negative emotions, drives, feelings, and attitudes only leads to further frustration.

This is why when I took us through the list of positive and negative states of mind, the point was made to become less hostile, distracted, or resentful and more trusting, open-minded, and flexible. From the Buddhist point of view, if we do all of these things, we will automatically begin to feel better, and that is an important point. The other point, to reiterate, is that Buddhists believe in samskaras or mental imprints. Therefore, in practice, we are trying to work with our mind in such a way that the mind will not leave strong negative imprints in the mind. The other side of the practice is basically geared toward linking the mental structure up in such a manner that it does not become a favorable host environment for the negative emotions to thrive. For instance, if a negative emotion arises, it has arisen, but it does not need to linger and turn into resentment, bitterness, or spite.

In Buddhism, meditation practice is used in that way. It is not simply a question of not having any form of negative experience per se, but rather, even if you have negative experiences, emotions arising in our mind, the practices are designed in such a way that we recognize it and see that. The main thing is to be able to let go, not to linger. This is why in shamatha or meditation of tranquility, for example, one thing that we need to do is to be able to let go so that our mind does not become a favorable or attractive place for the negative thoughts and emotions to thrive. If we have awareness and mindfulness, it becomes unsuitable for the negative emotions and negative thoughts to linger. With mindfulness and awareness, first we have to develop mindfulness and then over time, awareness will naturally arise. Mindfulness is training ourselves to be in the present and not chasing after past experiences or anticipating future experiences. Not entertaining these thoughts but rather learning to be present is already exercising and training concentration. In other words, if we do not have mindfulness, we cannot easily concentrate so very well. Mindfulness is not really about being in the present per se but it is about being able to stick to one thing instead of chasing after this and that. The mind is prolific, all manner of things are produced and it goes after many different kinds of objects. In meditation, instead of doing that, we are trying to stay with one object. It is about learning to be with one thing and therefore, the key to this is to exercise non-forgetfulness.

Where does distraction come from? In Buddhism, inner distraction is part of the factors that support a negative frame of mind. Distraction comes from not being able to focus one's mind, so as an antidote, we practice mindfulness. When we are distracted, we forget. We are constantly chasing after new images, thoughts, sensations, sensory input, and feelings of pleasure, pain, and neutral feelings. To be able to stay with one thing, in Buddhism, we ordinarily use the breath as our focus, but we can also use feelings, sensations, and our own thoughts and mental state in order to anchor our minds so as to remain focused.

If we can do this over a period of time, we will develop awareness. When we have developed awareness, there is a presence of mind naturally. Usually, we continue sitting in meditation and things come to our mind and we automatically get carried away and forget; we forget about mindfulness and awareness. Remembering to stay with the object of meditation allows us to develop awareness. One can then have some experience of presence of mind to sense what is happening. We become more observant and perceptive.

The other component of that is after recognition comes non-fixation. Non-fixation means to not get fixated on what one has cognized, seen, or perceived. This is an extremely important point in Buddhist meditation practice. To be able to see what is going on is crucial, of course, but to not get distracted is also crucial. After recognizing what is going on, one does not dwell on that. One has to let go. This letting go is associated with awareness, which is non-fixation, and has to come from the proper practice of mindfulness. If we anticipate the future less and are not excessively dwelling on our past experiences and can just stay with what is going on in our own mind, then we are already learning the ability to let go. The notion of non-fixation is a more refined form of doing this, but in a less deliberate fashion. Instead of trying to become non-fixated, one gently detaches oneself.

In Buddhism, if we become aware of our negativity, for example, we do not latch on to that in our meditation. In our meditation, we have a degree of disassociation as if it is happening to somebody else. One is not thinking, "Why am I like this? Why do I always think something bad? If I were thinking something good, that wouldn't be half as bad." These thoughts go through our minds; "I wouldn't be wasting my time sitting on this thin cushion. Human beings are not born to sit on cushions in this way." We can become the observer of what is happening in the mind without becoming fixated on it. A real sense of non-fixation develops from this ability to observe. If one is having these thoughts and asking, "Why am I going through this? Why is it that I always have such certain feelings?" that is called fixation. This kind of self-judgment or self-obsession is missing the point. Even if we have some rudimentary recognition of what is going on, if it is quickly followed by elaborations on what is happening in our own head, then we have missed the point. Negativity will then proliferate. We will not be able to contain it.

These are some of the reasons that we do the shamatha or tranquility type of meditation. When it comes to the negative emotions, the negative support structure is built on a distracted mind. It is difficult to concentrate when inattentive, clinging to our thoughts, concepts, and experiences, not being able to let go of things, and fostering a general lack of awareness. If we become hostile to our own negative state of mind during meditation, then even in meditation, we are simply reinforcing this negative support structure. The basic point is to be able to recognize and then let go. In Buddhism, we do not have to do anything more than that in our shamatha meditation. Anything extra is unnecessary. This is very important because we are attempting to basically change our mental habits within the meditative environment. In that way, it is not entirely correct to think that the sole purpose of shamatha meditation is to pacify the mind. This is part of what happens, but also by the process of developing focus and concentration in shamatha meditation, one is helping to overcome the negative support structures.

In *Lojong*[14] or loving-kindness type of meditation, we extend our meditative activity beyond recognizing the negative and positive emotions arising and then simply let them go as we do in shamatha meditation. Once we have stabilized the mind in our meditation session through shamatha, we can then practice loving-kindness. In loving-kindness meditation, we try to generate feelings and emotions that we would not normally automatically generate to that extent. The point is that due to our mental habits, we can automatically veer off into thinking something bad about ourselves or others. It happens automatically but as part of our meditation, we can train our mind to actually have the experience of certain emotions. In these practices, we deliberately give rise to specific emotions.

If we have not experienced certain emotions, it may be more difficult to experience them fully. Even when we have had positive experiences of positive emotions in the past, the positive emotions may have been mixed with other negative mental factors, as I mentioned earlier in the book. In loving-kindness practices, the whole purpose is to gradually and deliberately have the experience of more positive emotions. We can learn to have these experiences during meditation again and again and we have to remember the concept of samskara, that these experiences will then leave mental imprints. We should not think, "I'll do half an hour of loving-kindness type of meditation, get up and get on with whatever I'm going to do for the rest of the day, and then it's finished." It does not work like that. Whatever it is that we experience, if we have positive thoughts and feelings and are attentive, aware, not distracted, not hostile, have more of a loving-kindness attitude, and give rise to positive emotions, these leave imprints in our minds. It is like listening to a song over and over, for a short period of time, we may find ourselves automatically singing that tune. Similarly, even if we are not practicing meditation, unlike in the past where the mind would automatically go in the opposite direction, we may find ourselves automatically having a more positive attitude, feeling good, and having some experience of positive emotion. In this manner, we can begin to dismantle the negative support structure in order to overcome negative emotions. In this way, we are building and strengthening a support structure for the positive mental state to arise and this is why we need shamatha meditation as our foundation. To develop the corresponding positive emotions to go with the positive support structure, we do the Lojong or loving-kindness forms of meditation.

The positive mental factors that we cultivate during meditation should be utilized in order to give rise to positive emotions. In Buddhism, there are only three different kinds of positive emotions mentioned; compassion, love, and joy. These are general labels that encompass varieties of positive emotional experiences. According to Buddhism, if we can generate more compassion, love, and joy, we will then have positive emotions.

From the Buddhist viewpoint, we need to do more than shamatha and Lojong practices to develop a better understanding of how the positive and negative states affect the mind. We build on these practices to increase our understanding through vipashyana meditation, also known as insight or analytical meditation. Vipashyana uses analysis to build insight into how we experience things. This is done in general terms not in terms of what "I am experiencing." In a meditation session, after one has practiced shamatha meditation and has settled the mind in concentration for a time, one can then move on to vipashyana.

When we begin the analysis of experience, we are considering and contemplating the difference between what we experience and reality. That is to say, how things are in actuality, without the self-injected overlays and fabrications, the extrapolations, conjecture, exaggeration, and other distortions we place upon our experiences. With vipashyana, we sit down quietly on the cushion or chair and just simply do some shamatha or concentration and then move on to thinking about what we impose on reality. When we do this, we are doing vipashyana meditation. What it truly boils down to in terms of vipashyana practice is to bring some form of clarification regarding how we experience things, what is actually going on; our experiences versus reality. Here, the main thing is to contemplate on our experiences, not our own experiences but rather our experiences in relation to reality or how things are. If we do this, according to Buddhism, we will see that things are constantly changing and everything is in a state of flux.

According to Buddhism, if we come to this recognition, we can do two things; one is to simply say, "Well, yes. I know that everything changes. That is life," or second, one could look at this in a much more meaningful way and then utilize it in order to let go of things. Ordinarily, in meditation, even when we are doing shamatha practice, our tendency is to grab on to what we are experiencing but we can realize that, "I am experiencing this now, but my experience may be different later on." In other words, through vipashyana or analytical meditation, one may come to realize that it is only "my own grasping tendencies" that have not changed. We realize that as far as the experience itself goes, it is never the same. Even if we believe that we are experiencing the same thing, such as recently experiencing some form of pain over a period of time and we have been reliving it repeatedly, from Buddhist point of view, the only thing that has not changed is our unwillingness or perceived inabilities to let go of that experience.

The experience itself, each time one is having that experience, is a different one. It is never the same and is also experienced differently. By thinking about things in this manner, it will allow us to see our own experiences and attitude toward reality because to see things like this is in conformity with the reality. To not see things like this is not in conformity with the reality and therefore, is the product of what Buddhists call a "delusory mental state." Delusory mental states are delusory because they do not correspond to what is truly happening.

This practice is seen as an extremely important practice and Buddhist masters like Shantideva have devoted chapters to the analytical meditation on anger and so on. We do not have to duplicate the analytical method that Shantideva employed in the context of analytical meditation. We do not need to do exactly the same thing. For example, Shantideva may have said that if you have sexual desire, if you believe that touch sensations give rise to our desires, then he said one should also have that kind of desire arising in relation to a pillow because a pillow is also soft. Whether we regard this as relevant to us or not, the point is thinking about our experiences in relation to reality and realizing how, to a large extent, we construct and fabricate our own experiences. This is seen as an extremely important step toward overcoming dissatisfaction and frustration because frustration and dissatisfaction are caused from living in a fabricated world that we have created for ourselves. It can only be frustrating because it is not in conformity with how other people behave. It is all about what we do or what we want, our subjective experiences based on our own feelings and emotions and the intermingling and blending of all of these factors cause us to have the experiences that we have. From a Buddhist point of view, we see that, and this says something about our own powers to be able to change, how suffering and dissatisfaction can be overcome. This is because it has more to do with how we view ourselves and others. This is more the issue than how the world is.

How the world is, is not truly the source of our main problem. It is still a problem, but it is not the main problem. If we understand this, we will be able to live in a different manner. Therefore, in Buddhism, based on all of these meditation exercises, we have to cultivate the virtues in order to overcome the vices that come from negative emotions, negative state of mind, and negative mental factors. If we cultivate the virtues and live a healthy and wholesome lifestyle that is not based on moralistic judgmentalism but more on a healthy way of conducting oneself in relation to one's own view and that of others, our virtues will then flourish. This is also an essential part of bringing about satisfaction and overcoming dissatisfaction in one's life so that we can have what in Sanskrit is called *sukha*, instead of duhkha. As I mentioned, duhkha means suffering and sukha means real happiness. To have real happiness, based on the meditative exercises and so on, we should cultivate the virtues. In this way, the positive mental support system, the positive emotions, and meditational exercises that one practices then support our virtues.

To use some examples, these virtues then find their expression in our virtuous conduct so that we become kinder, more loving, generous, and so on. We become less intolerant and therefore, we can practice patience. Laziness on the other hand, is one of the negative mental factors that also inflames negative emotions because laziness, as it is said, leads to that sense of complacency and defeatism. Here, one does not have good feelings. One cannot bounce back and is easily hurt, harmed, and feels like a victim of circumstances and of other people's harmful actions. Alternatively, one would be able to be more vigorous, energetic, and alert.

These are extremely important because we know that sometimes virtues do not lead to happiness so you may try to be tolerant and generous, but do not feel happy and satisfied. From the Buddhist point of view, this is because the virtues are not supported by wholesome or positive emotions. They are not nourished by positive emotions and then even if one has some experience of positive emotion such as love, it may be perverted by negative mental factors, the negative support system. That is also a factor. If one does not feel like this is injecting any purpose into one's life, in Buddhism, it is because the whole environment is not in sync. As I have emphasized, all of these factors, the different elements, have to come together. Therefore, if the virtues and the positive emotions are not fully supported by the positive support system and positive thoughts, attitudes, feelings, and so on, we will not feel satisfied. We will more likely feel discontent, depressed, and continue to experience all of the negative emotions that go with the vices.

We need to understand the interconnectedness of all of these different meditation practices and approaches in Buddhism. In other words, we need to do all of these different practices. We cannot only do one or the other, shamatha or vipashyana, et cetera. We have to do the range because each practice works in such a manner that will, in one way or another, undermine our negative tendencies. This is what we need to do, not just gaze at the current mental state, whatever it is that we are experiencing at any given time. Rather, the dispositional tendency we indulge in, some form of negativity, needs to be undermined.

In that way, instead of trying to get rid of negative emotions, for example, if we do loving-kindness type of meditation, then just by developing loving-kindness, the emotions of anger and so forth will be experienced differently. This is the Buddhist view. We will automatically experience it differently. Further, if we try to be more patient and so forth in terms of our conduct, this will also have a corroding effect on how the negative emotions and negative state of mind are experienced.

So far in the current section of this book, we have covered the main aspects of the discussion regarding how the Buddhist practices, the meditational practices, relate directly to our emotions and our states of mind. Buddhism does not look down on emotions per se, but it speaks about how we have to make distinctions between the ill use of emotions and the skillful use of emotions. Therefore, the vibrancy, the sense of energy and feeling of lightness that we associate with emotion is retained while the negative downside of emotional experiences is gradually overcome. This is the main point, that if we know how to utilize our emotions properly, the downside of emotions can be reduced, while the "high" that we associate with emotion is retained, but in a transformed way. This is because normally, if we are driven into a state of the experience of a "high," it is not supported by a proper frame of mind. Therefore, the mind is thrown into a state of imbalance even if one is going through an experience of a "high" because one constantly crashes and the downside of the emotional high becomes apparent. According to Buddhism, if we do our practices and learn to gradually deal with our emotional experiences in a positive way, we can experience that "high" but our mental stability will not be disturbed. It will not be up and down like a yo-yo. We would still feel fluctuations. One may sometimes feel very positive and full of life and at other times, depleted and not full of life, but the point is that there is some form of underlying sense of life-affirming attitude that is present. Against all odds, everything is seen as full of potential and possibilities and therefore, there is an underlying sense of positivity, which is a feeling of "high" called joy.

Joy is a very important concept in Buddhism because there has to be joy; otherwise, the other emotions like love or compassion are not properly supported, and depressive moods, frustration, and anger can follow. A joyful mind is supported by the positive mental factors such as equanimity, mindfulness, et cetera. If we have joy, it will be a joyous kind of love and compassion that we experience in relation to the positive emotions. To reiterate, love and compassion can also be experienced in many different ways, dependent on which mental attitudes and supporting system and mental factors are present. This will determine which variety of love, compassion, joy, et cetera we are feeling. These experiences will then support the virtues, which against all odds, will give rise to more sustainable experiences of happiness and a life-affirming attitude.

From the Buddhist point of view, samsara is not perfect and neither are we. There would be things going wrong, but the main point is not to be thrown into a state of chaos, including not seeking perfection in samsara. This is not to say that samsara must be pain-free but as things become more and more demanding, we ordinarily believe that our life has to be completely pain-free—there has to be a pill that we can take or some variety of psychological advancement that will ease our pain and make life more comfortable. We might also believe that our political system and social environment must be perfect. From the Buddhist perspective, it will never be perfect but that does not mean that we should not attempt to make things better. This is our duty as a responsible human being but to seek perfection in samsara is misguided and will only intensify our frustration. In spite of the fact that the world is imperfect and samsara is imperfect, one can still find something to feel good and positive about. This is the perspective that we should develop through Dharma practice. This is also what meditation practice should do. Not only do these practices make us feel better, but we can also relate to other beings in a better manner. Therefore, whatever impact we have on others should also improve and be something good and more beneficial, and so everybody benefits.

Alternatively, negative states such as rage not only harm ourselves but also other people. It makes sense therefore, that if we are coming from a more positive mental state, when we encounter and interact with others, we will have a different impact. In that sense, we are changing the world and having a good impact on other people's lives. From the Buddhist point of view, a feeling of satisfaction from this should be far greater than the satisfaction we would gain through self-centered emotionality such as unbridled expression of negative emotions with a total disregard for one's own welfare and that of others. Through sheer recklessness, we can bring ruin to ourselves and others.

Chapter Sixteen

The Relationship Between Destructive Emotions and Our Thoughts

In Buddhism, we speak a great deal about the destructive emotions. Much emphasis is placed on the emotional aspect of our being because it relates to the cultivation of spiritual interests and goals. It also relates to the domains of morality and ethics and has bearing on our psychological well-being. The reason for this, as we have been discussing, is that in Buddhism, the main purpose of our life is to reach our ultimate potential. That highest potential is called enlightenment. Enlightenment is equated with the state that is completely free of suffering. Therefore, in Buddhism, we pursue our spiritual practices in order to reach the state of perfection where we no longer experience suffering. That is our ultimate goal.

However, as Buddhists, we also have temporary goals. We have to keep the distinction between these temporary and ultimate goals in mind. Sometimes, when people come to Buddhism, they may not make this distinction. While the ultimate goal is to go beyond suffering, the temporary goal is to reduce suffering in a more immediate sense, in our lives and in those of other beings. It is not just human beings who suffer; all living beings suffer in one way or another. We all suffer and our purpose in life is to lessen that suffering. To suffer is terrible. When there is excessive suffering, particularly suffering that we have inadvertently created ourselves, our life can be rendered meaningless, as if it were snatched and stolen from us. The more afflictions that we experience in life, the less leisure or opportunity we have to address the important things. Intense suffering is a form of madness; we are not quite "with it." The torment can be too great.

At times, we may go through periods of fairly peaceful and stable life experiences where the torment is not so great. We may have momentary experiences of happiness and a sense of joy, but even so, according to Buddhism, there is always an underlying sense of dissatisfaction gnawing at us. In order to enhance our lives, we need to deal with the explicit or underlying suffering and torment that arises in many forms. There are varieties of causes of suffering and therefore, it has many forms. We normally do not have the insight to deal with all of the causes of suffering that we experience, but even so, we have the potential to arrive at a place where we can develop these capacities. We can do this through spiritual cultivation, which includes practices such as meditation. According to Buddhism, if we increase our capacities, we can deal with the causes of suffering.

Among the things that cause us suffering are some that we can actually do something about. However, there are many others that come from sources that we have no control over. In other words, we are contingent beings and live in a contingent world; a world that is unpredictable and that operates in a manner that is completely independent of our choices, desires, and aspirations. There are many things that happen in life that go counter to our wishes. There is a vast range of sources of suffering that we have no control over and we respond to these in many ways. Things happen that upset us, that cause us anything from mild irritation to outright panic. We cannot necessarily control what others think of us, how they treat us, or whether they will appreciate the good actions that we have done for them. We cannot bank on any of this. There is a lack of certainty that all of the good things that we do will be reciprocated and so we may feel let down. We may feel all manner of things due to external situations and circumstances and because other beings are individual, independent beings with their own minds and capacity for making their own choices. So what do we have left?

According to Buddhism, what is left is our emotional life. What is left that truly impacts on our well-being or "ill-being" hinges on our emotional life. When we are not faring well with our emotions, we suffer and our life becomes dimmed and diminished. It is said that something like darkness takes over, a great sense of being weighed down. We feel heavy. These are descriptions that are given in traditional literature regarding how we feel when we are emotionally mixed up. When excessive anger, jealousy, or other destructive emotions are churning us up, we feel mixed up and confused. This causes us an incredible amount of unhappiness.

Unlike other causes of unhappiness over which we have no real control, there is something that we can do about our emotional experiences. This is so because in Buddhism, as we have discussed, we do not believe that thoughts and emotions are separate, that thoughts are one thing and emotions are something else. We also do not believe that emotions are more intimately related to our bodily functions or corporeal life experiences while our thoughts relate to our higher mental faculties and functions. Of course, there is a difference in terms of certain extremely refined thoughts and certain base, gross emotions, but Buddhism believes this to be more like a continuum. Therefore, you can have a very emotional state and thoughts that are less tainted by emotional states, but basically, they are not completely separate.

Buddhism also does not believe that on the one hand, emotions cause distortions whereas on the other, thoughts provide us with some possibility for objectivity. The reason for this is that from a Buddhist point of view, as ordinary human beings, even our thoughts are distorted. Our thoughts have the capacity to distort and are biased. This is why, according to Buddhism, they are called obscurations of the mind. We need to make some distinctions with respect to thoughts and emotions in Buddhist terms because the approach is quite unique and distinct. This is where language may sometimes become a barrier.

In Buddhism, what is translated as "emotion" in English relates only to the negative emotions or the destructive emotions. The positive emotions have a different name. As I mentioned at the beginning of section three, the negative or destructive emotions are called "klesha" in Sanskrit. In English, this term is often translated as "conflicting emotions." The conflicting or destructive emotions are tied to distorted thoughts. The combination of the two creates what is known in Buddhism as "the deluded states of ordinary sentient creatures." In other words, we are prone to negative emotions because in a sense, we are born with this variety of disposition. Discursive thoughts and the destructive emotions go together; they are intimately related. In Buddhism, the training relates to correcting that. This is what Buddhist practice involves. What we need to understand is that the destructive emotions and discursive thoughts lead to a state of mind where we are deprived of seeing things clearly. In other words, even when our mind is not so very disturbed, when we feel fairly calm and peaceful, according to Buddhism, we are not free of these negative emotions and distorted thoughts.

How do these negative emotions arise? It is due to our self-perception. Buddhists say that this self-perception has two layers: one is innate in that we are born with a strong sense or feeling of "me-ness" or "I-ness," and the other is acquired. Through life experiences, we learn to define ourselves. We accumulate various ideas about who we are, what we are, our station in life, and so forth. This is how we construct our identities, as discussed in section one.

The negative emotions are then related to this self-perception in that our negative emotions are actually a way of expressing this self-identity.

Of course, we do not always react in the same manner. There are many different modes of expressing anger or jealousy, for example. There is variation between us as individuals in terms of whether we express our anger in a more deliberate, planned, and premeditated fashion or in a very spontaneous outburst of rage such as for example, when engaged in road rage. Sometimes, months of planning can go into strategically working out how to best repel, destroy, or attack the object of our anger. In all of these situations, the fundamental reason for our actions, although often this is not articulated, is that it all relates to our own self. Although it relates to our own self, we are however either unconsciously or only on a minimally conscious level aware that this is happening.

The negative emotions are most definitely, in a sense, a response to solidification of the self, of one's identity. This means that whether we are thinking about these things clearly at the discursive level or thinking about them on a very basic level, in either case, there is appraisal going on in terms of what is occurring or what is happening to us. Without this appraisal, there would not be an emotional response of a negative kind. For example, if we did not believe that someone else was more attractive, wealthier, or healthier than us, there would be no jealousy. However, as human beings, we are peculiar and therefore, sometimes we are jealous for other reasons. For example, we might become jealous of someone who is less fortunate than us due to the attention they receive. We could be healthy and feel that no one is taking any notice of us while someone who is sick is getting all of the attention. We could be asking, "Why not me? Why don't I get any attention?" In all of these situations, appraisal precedes the emotional response. This is why Buddhism says that distorted thinking always goes with the negative emotions.

The destructive emotions are responses to perceived threats or some such related thing. An appraisal has been made and based on that, we have the emotional response. The emotional response is supposed to have a positive effect on us because otherwise, there would be no such response. The idea is to solidify, reestablish, and consolidate the self, to eliminate the perceived threat. However, it fails to do that. According to Buddhism, the result of this is that we suffer. Instead of easing things, it exacerbates them. Our experience of distress and discomfort increases. This is one important point.

The other point involves the nature of the self. The reason that the emotional response fails to bring about the relief that we are seeking is due to the kind of beings that we are in relation to our psychophysical makeup or system. According to Buddhism, as living beings, we are fluid. We do not have fixed identities. This is a very Buddhist concept. For this reason, trying to respond to external environments and situations and deal with other living beings from a fixed vantage point does not work. We are always in a state of transition even if we do not recognize it. This does not mean that we have no identity whatsoever. In spite of the fact that each of us is an individual being with an individual mind, body, personal life experiences, and so forth, nevertheless, we are in constant flux. We are in flux both mentally and physically. Everything that constitutes our notion of the self is in flux. Any attempt to arrest or solidify that will fail. It will not stick because we are always in transition, always moving. This is an extremely important Buddhist insight. Failure to understand this is what causes us to develop various forms of distorted thoughts that then give rise to destructive emotions.

When we operate from this fixed vantage point, we are caught up in an illusion. We are not fully engaging with what is happening.

We are adrift, operating in our own make-believe world. In Buddhism, this is what is meant by the delusional state of the mind. Buddhism is always speaking about "the delusory state of mind" and this is what the delusory state of mind is. It is the mind that keeps us trapped and prevents us from fully engaging with what is occurring. It does so because we are constantly in flux and what is happening is also always in flux. Just because everything is in flux does not mean that there is some variety of discontinuity between one mental process and another. The continuity is there without the fixed vantage point. From the Buddhist perspective, the way to deal with our suffering must begin with this form of understanding. Not appreciating this will keep us trapped in our own make-believe world and our suffering will subsequently continue.

With regard to the relative goal and ultimate goal, the ultimate goal is the attainment of buddhahood, where suffering has ceased and we arrive at the eternal, blissful state of nirvana. The temporary goal is to lessen our suffering. If we understand this interconnectedness between our own self and everything else within which the self is embedded, our suffering will be lessened. That is our immediate goal. Our immediate goal is not necessarily to go beyond suffering altogether, but to make our life more satisfying and meaningful. For this to occur, we need to have some form of appraisal.

In Buddhism, leisure is also an extremely important concept. We do not have leisure because samsara or cyclic existence, the negative emotions, propel us forward. We are constantly caught up in this cycle of self-abuse and self-destructive behavior. Therefore, there is no relief. We find no relief from the samsaric grind, no leisure. We have to find leisure from this grind and this comes from realizing what it is that we are trying to protect or consolidate, meaning our own sense of self. Buddhism says that we only assume that there is something fixed and immutable but when we look into ourselves, we do not find anything that is immutable. When we take that leisure, in spite of the fact that the self is in flux, the self becomes enriched. The poverty of the self lies in its unsatisfied hunger for consolidation and reaffirmation. Buddhism sees this to be at the source of all of our problems. This deep-seated dissatisfaction comes from the hunger of the self and its need to be acknowledged, confirmed, affirmed, and reaffirmed. Buddhism says therefore, that if we think of the self in this way, instead of the self becoming empty, it becomes enriched. This is so because the self is given the opportunity to become that which it can become. Otherwise, the self is prevented from doing this and this occurs due to our excessive fixation on our own distorted perception of what that self is.

Buddhism states that most of this is unarticulated and we have this innate capacity to assume that there is some form of immutable self in our possession. This is sometimes reinforced by all manner of popular notions or theories about the self, philosophical or religious notions of the self, soul, or higher self. Buddhism sees all of these attempts as spurious and that in the end, they will only add to our suffering. There are many conflicting theories of the self. In the end, one cannot truly come to a decisive conclusion based on either experience or reasoning. If this could be settled by reasoning, it would have been settled long ago and the philosophical discussions would no longer continue.

On the other hand, if the self can be experienced, we should subsequently be able to experience it. But it is not experienced directly. Often, it is described in language of transcendence rather than the language of something that we can experience. In Buddhism, direct experience is gained through becoming intimate with our body and mind complex. This is why meditation is encouraged. Then, without theorizing or speculating about what one's self is, what we are experiencing is being paid attention to. What we are experiencing is what we ultimately are and what we are not experiencing is what we are not. If we pay attention through the practice of meditation, even the experiences that we experience but are not fully conscious of can become more conscious. There are many forms of meditation. To deal with the destructive emotions, we need to have a better grasp of our own self. To do this, we need leisure. We have that leisure when we are not in a state of disturbance, worked up, or when our mind is not running all over the place. In this way, even if we are not attempting to attain enlightenment right now, from a Buddhist viewpoint, not only as a spiritual person but also as an ordinary individual, if we want to make our life more meaningful, we have to understand ourselves better. We also have to address our negative emotions. These negative emotions must be addressed because they diminish us and our conduct and they can make us miserable and unpleasant. They make us unhappy.

From the Buddhist perspective, goodness and happiness can coincide. Happiness can mean many different things. Happiness is valued over "goodness" because "goodness" happens to be serviceable to the creation of happiness, not the other way around. This is also a uniquely Buddhist approach. You could even call it "enlightened hedonism." This is an extremely important point. In Buddhism, the good life, the virtuous life, is encouraged because it leads to a state of mind where we find satisfaction instead of being dissatisfied. When we are dissatisfied, all of our hidden and sometimes dormant but most often, awake negative emotions raise their ugly heads and take over. As human beings therefore, to lead a life of satisfaction and fulfillment and not be left wanting, we need self-satisfaction. We have more self-satisfaction if we have a more intimate relationship with ourselves. This intimate relationship has to be such that our fabricated notion of who we think we are has been dispelled, when we have less of an illusion about ourselves.

These destructive emotions may not completely disappear. We have to also distinguish between more reasonable expressions of negative emotions and unreasonable or completely irrational, crazy, and extreme reactions. With regard to anger, we become less spiteful, bitter, and resentful, but this does not mean we will not become angry. If there is a reason to get angry, we may still get angry. It is about our character; we work toward a change in our character. Despite the fact that we are in flux, it is the character that we have that sustains us and helps give shape and form to the kind of person we are and wish to become. When we are less resentful, bitter, consumed by unforgiving vengeful thoughts, and so on, we are subsequently less tormented. This is so despite the fact that we occasionally lose our cool and end up being angry with someone for a good reason or even no reason at all.

This is the general outline of the Buddhist view on destructive emotions, referred to as negative emotions in Buddhism.

Chapter Seventeen

Overcoming Negative Tendencies

To reiterate an important point, in Buddhism, the ultimate aim is to attain buddhahood, enlightenment. This is the state that goes beyond all forms of suffering. This is our ultimate goal and our immediate goal is to reduce suffering in this life and lead a happier life. A satisfying, meaningful, and happy life should be our goal.

In Buddhist thinking, when we want to reach our ultimate goal, there are intermediary goals that we have to attain. These intermediary goals are of more immediate concern. From a Buddhist point of view, while we are still alive, making our life meaningful is not selfish. People often believe that to wish to make one's life meaningful and actually want to cultivate oneself is selfish and means that one is excessively self-obsessed.

Buddhists do not agree with that view. If we cultivate ourselves, we are better able to function as human beings. We are better able to interact and relate with others and are therefore of more help to others. If we are caught up in our own internal dramas, internal emotional turmoil, and as it says in the teachings, knocked about by the upsurge of the waves of emotions, not only are we unable to do anything for others, we also cannot do anything for ourselves. We do not have the leisure that I spoke of in the previous chapter. We can be constantly tormented to a degree and in some state of upset. In that state, we only know suffering, there is no real experience of happiness.

Even if we achieve many things in life materially or by gaining recognition, fame, and so on, if there is a lack of real understanding of our own condition, our own self, the pain and mental torment does not disappear. Famous people are just as likely to be depressed, suffer from self-loathing, and feel unwanted and unloved as ordinary people. From the Buddhist perspective, we have to learn to reduce suffering in our lives because when we suffer, we cannot make our lives into something that is worthwhile. Living without real meaning is difficult. By thinking in this manner, we come to realize that the Buddhist spiritual goal of enlightenment and the more temporary goal of leading a better life coincide.

Our conventional lifestyle does not assist us to function effectively in the world. When we are excessively emotional, we cannot function or operate effectively. When we are too emotional, we are more prone to ill health, being upset or depressed, and getting caught up in negative ways of thinking and negative appraisals of everything. We can find ourselves seeing everything without and within as bad and terrible. From this point of view, addressing our emotional life should be a primary concern. This is the case both as spiritual persons and as human beings with the intention to do something about ourselves.

We should also be concerned with having a real sense of what Buddhism refers to as self-recognition. Self-recognition is a form of self-awareness that is different from being self-conscious. Often, when people make use of methods of self-awareness in Buddhist practice, they slip into the mode of being self-conscious. Becoming self-conscious is different from being self-aware. Having some knowledge of self-awareness, self-recognition, is important and comes from dealing with our emotional life. By dealing with our emotional life, we are dealing with something that we are capable of changing and improving. We may have no control over many of the things that upset us or cause us distress, but when it comes to our emotional life and how we experience our emotions, we can do something. In the Buddhist way of thinking, this means that we have choices in our emotional life.

It may be difficult to overcome certain tendencies within us and also dispositions and propensities toward certain emotional reactions, but nonetheless, they can be modified, contained, and in fact educated through practice. Simply because they are habituated does not mean that we cannot actually choose to respond in one way or another. We have a wide range of choices. It is not simply a matter of responding in either an aggressive or a non-aggressive manner. We can respond with aggression in so many diverse ways. Even when we react with aggression, we do not always react in the same fashion. This suggests that we are making choices. How we respond, how we express our emotions, can be modified and by doing so, we can reduce suffering. His Holiness the Dalai Lama has explained that doing this is like improving our immune system on a physical level. If our immune system has improved, even if there is a cold going around, we may be less likely to catch it and even if we do, we are less likely to experience the same level of physical misery. In a similar fashion, if we have improved our skill in managing our emotional life, even if there is a great deal of tension going around and many upsetting things happening in our environment, we are less likely to be affected by them. If we are affected, the impact will be less than if we had not trained ourselves in emotional management or made the effort to deal with our emotions.

If we look at it in terms of our emotional life, we will see that positive emotions have a positive effect on us. This is wide ranging. They affect us physically and mentally. These emotions come into play even in terms of our spiritual goals and practices. If we get caught up in negative emotions, these can lead us to becoming prone to ill health and feeling upset. This form of mental state is conducive to unhappiness. We then develop negative attitudes toward things and ourselves and this also affects our moods. We become darker in our moods and generally feel more down. If we have positive attitudes and emotions, we subsequently have more positive attitudes toward life and ourselves and we would want to approach others. We would like to approach the world rather than recoil or avoid it. According to Buddhism, there is a greater and more genuine sense of self-esteem and less of the negative self-appraisals that come from self-obsession. Our general mood is also lifted because our attitude has changed and we have a more positive outlook.

From the Buddhist perspective, we try to cultivate positive emotions and avoid negative ones as much as possible, but not because they give rise to sin or are non-spiritual. This is also perhaps true, but it is also the case that negative emotions interfere with living our life fully. Even in our everyday life, if we become exceedingly caught up in our negative emotional states, our life becomes compromised. Our ability to function well becomes compromised. What may happen if we are gripped by jealousy is an example of this. If you have recently broken up with your partner and subsequently found out that they are going with someone else on a holiday, while you are in the office trying to work, suddenly, the thought could come into your mind that everyone is laughing at you. All manner of jealous thoughts may arise and when they do, we cannot function. We cannot eat and we feel sick in the stomach. We are completely affected even physically and our ability to function is compromised.

Many of the other negative emotions also have a similar effect on us. For example, when we are extremely angry, we cannot concentrate. That same feeling of hatred or spite repeatedly returns. We become disengaged from the world and other human beings. Even when we are speaking to someone, we are not truly there or conversing effectively. Our mind is preoccupied, so everything that we do suffers as a consequence.

Buddhism says that we cannot live effectively in this world if we are caught up in our negativities. It is incorrect for people to say that if you follow the spiritual path, you must become otherworldly, that worldly concerns are set aside and you do not have to be effective in the world. What Buddhism suggests, however, is that to be effective, we must be engaged and be able to do everything that we need to do fully and completely. If we are unable to give one hundred percent and are always preoccupied with something else when we are trying to do something in life, we are not effective. We become caught up in a make-believe world that does not relate to what is truly happening. Even though we can speak about appropriate and inappropriate responses to anger and so on, when we are caught up and have developed the tendency to become angry to the extent that it has become a permanent character trait, after a while, we fail to distinguish appropriate responses from the inappropriate ones. Everything subsequently becomes a source of threat. Everything is seen as a source of some variety of harm to us, so we indiscriminately become angry with everyone and everything.

The same applies to the other emotions. For example, jealousy can become ever-present whenever anyone speaks to our partner. Totally inappropriately, anyone going near our partner or speaking to them may bring out jealousy. Despite understanding this and comprehending that if our partner were actually doing something, jealousy can be an appropriate response, when we get so entrenched in our negative emotional responses, the ability to discriminate becomes completely compromised.

I will now briefly discuss the list of negative emotions that I discussed in chapter twelve as it relates to the topic of this chapter. In Buddhism, the list consists of a set of negative emotions and also certain mental states that are not really emotional states but mental states that are conducive to giving rise to negative emotions. These mental states either give rise to negative emotions or encourage and perpetuate them, allowing them to develop and flourish. There are two sets of lists. The first list involves the six primary conflicting mental states: excessive anger, excessive desire, pride, ignorance, doubt, and opinionatedness.

As discussed in chapter twelve, doubt and opinionatedness are not strictly emotions as they are cognitive rather than affective in nature. Doubt, or being two-minded where the restless mind is not able to make up its mind about anything gives rise to all manner of emotional states and causes one to become vulnerable. This relates to being unable to make up one's mind regarding what is beneficial, not beneficial, helpful, and not helpful. Opinionatedness references when one holds on to whatever it is that one believes in as being true, even when contrary evidence may be available. A lack of open-mindedness can subsequently give rise to emotional conflicts of all kinds, such as hatred. These are the six primary emotions. As I mentioned, when we unpack these six, in Abhidharma, there is a subsequent list of twenty mental states, derivatives of the six primary negative emotions. I will briefly summarize them here in the context of our current discussion.

With regard to anger, we have wrath, resentment, spite, envy, jealousy, and cruelty. These are different expressions of anger. Wrath is episodic. This means that when something happens, it triggers the response of getting angry but it then dissipates. Spite and resentment are different in that they are longer lasting. If we are resentful or spiteful, it is more like disposition. From a Buddhist point of view, envy and jealousy are also seen as a byproduct of anger. Jealousy is an emotional response that we have in relation to those that we consider our equals. It may also be confrontational whereas envy is more passive. Being envious of the wealth or beauty of others is different from being jealous but it is also a byproduct of anger. Cruelty is also an expression of anger that manifests in a different manner. This involves genuinely wishing to inflict serious harm on others and deriving sadistic pleasure from causing their pain and suffering.

Excessive desire also has a series of derivative emotions. The first is avarice or greed. Excessive desire gives rise to greed in such a way that instead of thinking about satisfying our needs, we think of satisfying our wants. Our wants are limitless, so we sometimes express rampant greed. The next one is egoism or self-expression. This is a form of attachment to oneself. Next, we have three mental states related to this that are not emotions but create conducive mental states for excessive desire to occur. The first is related to a mental state that is excitable and easily aroused. The next is concealment. According to Buddhism, due to the wish to satisfy our desires, being upfront may not be so effective and therefore, we use dubious means to go about obtaining what we want. We have to be conniving and crafty in how we go about satisfying our desires. We then develop skills in hiding our real motives in order to get what we want. The third mental state that is conducive to this form of emotion arising is dullness. Dullness here means that there is a lack of real mental clarity. If we are not clear in the head, we yield to whatever strong arousal of emotion we experience and simply follow it. As soon as we want something, we think of trying to satisfy that want without thinking about whether it is a good thing to be following or not. We simply follow the impulse.

Ignorance was listed in the list of primary mental disturbances or conflicting states. Here, ignorance is not an emotion but it is seen as causing our emotional conflicts to flourish. This flourishing of emotional conflicts is encouraged by such mental states as blind faith, sloth, forgetfulness, and lack of self-awareness. What is common to all of these mental states is the lack of mental clarity.

Blind faith, whatever is going around, whatever the popular notion is, we latch on to it and simply follow hearsay. We do not bother to analyze or examine it. Sloth basically comes from not training or exercising the mind. If we neglect to do this, the mind becomes dull. Forgetfulness means not having presence of mind. With this, we immediately react to whatever presents to our senses. Lack of self-awareness means that we have little understanding of where we are coming from or what we are experiencing. All of these mental states cause our conflicting emotions to exist and flourish. If we do not do anything about our emotional states and continue to follow them, according to Buddhism, we go on to develop further mental traits that are difficult to overcome.

The first is pretension. This means that far from being spontaneous, emotions are used as tools in an extremely strategic and crafty way, not in a wise fashion. We subsequently develop all manner of personas around our intentions. The next is deception, where we learn how to be deceptive and lure others into our traps. We then become shameless. If we can get what it is that we want, whatever our emotion dictates, even if it is an exceedingly shameful act, we disregard that shame. Next is inconsiderateness, not showing any regard for other people's feelings. If others are hurt, so be it, as long as we are able to satisfy our own needs. We do not believe that it is our problem. We believe that it is the problem of the person who is experiencing that anger. The next one is inattentiveness. We become so habituated to acting in an extremely emotional way that we are not attentive to anything that is happening. Distraction is the final one. With distraction, we have no control over our mind. It is scattered as is said in the teachings, completely scattered. This completes the list of twenty. As we can see, only some of these are truly emotional states. The rest are mental states that are conducive to the negative emotions thriving.

Here, we could ask, "Are all negative emotions destructive or are some of them not as destructive?" I would like to address the issue of whether negative and destructive emotions are the same. With the negative or destructive emotions, instead of lumping them together, can some negative emotions be worse than others? The answer to that question seems to be yes. Certain negative emotions encourage more undesirable mental states. In another context or different situation, the less harmful negative states may in fact have some use or even be necessary. For example, with anger, we have the derivatives of resentment, spite, envy, jealousy, and cruelty. We also have wrath, which is different from resentment, spite, and cruelty. As I mentioned, wrath is more episodic. For example, if you see a farmer flogging their horse mercilessly and you ask them to stop but the farmer does not do so and you get angry and tell them to stop, that is different from sitting at home and being resentful of your spouse, boss, or friend due to their recent indiscretions. From a Buddhist viewpoint, it seems that the expression of wrath can sometimes be an appropriate response under certain circumstances. This is not to say that wrath is a virtue.

We have to be careful here because in Buddhism, we do not have the notion of social indignation even in the face of social injustices. Wrath can never be seen as a virtue, but a certain expression of wrath in the face of social injustice for example, might be an appropriate response. However, being cruel, resentful, and spiteful have no function whatsoever. These only cause negativities, wear us down, and are demeaning. An extremely bitter person is wearied, depressed, and completely beaten. A feeling of powerlessness comes from a strong sense of resentment. The expression of wrath or momentary anger does not have to originate from that place of feeling powerless. When we feel helpless and powerless, resentment may follow.

Desire can also be necessary and is a very important motivator. The aspect of desire that is seen as unhealthy from a Buddhist point of view is that desire is capable of causing obsession. In Buddhism, this is called "fixation." With excessive desire, we become fixated on the object of our desire, blinkered, as the object subsequently becomes everything. The object begins to dominate our lives. In Buddhism, this is referred to as attachment. Attachment in the Buddhist context does not mean having attachment to others. There are many forms of attachment in the Buddhist context that refer to the overwhelming state of attachment that can arise and be directed toward either living beings or inanimate objects. We can be attached in this fashion to our home, our ideas, and so on. For example, attachment to ideas leads to dogmatism related to the opinionatedness that we discussed earlier. When we become obsessive in that manner, it becomes unhealthy.

I will make a few distinctions here with respect to desire. There are desires that we should in fact pursue and cultivate. These desires are not necessarily very harmful. The desires that we should pursue but often do not pursue are related to the desire for improvement in our lives, for self-transformation and greater self-understanding and the desire for more intimate relationships with others and the world. To reiterate, from a Buddhist point of view, desiring self-improvement is not egotistical. It is a must.

Desires that we already pursue and may not be so very harmful are things such as attempting to find a better paying job and trying to find a loving and caring life partner. We have these forms of desires and there is nothing wrong with them. Being a Buddhist does not mean that we should look for the lowest paid job or the most unsuitable partner. If we have the desire to learn to play music, paint, study philosophy, or any number of leisurely activities, we should not think that we should not do it. We should not think that this is all a distraction for a Buddhist. If one is pursuing an interest with a sense of thoughtfulness and greater sense of self-presence, this can coincide with one's spiritual goals. There does not need to be any real conflict.

The desires that we pursue that are very harmful are those that involve becoming so dependent on what we desire that we lose all sense of ourselves. These desires then become unhealthy. Spiritually, they are also destructive. It is like developing a gambling habit where in order to satisfy the addiction, we keep on gambling with no regard for the feelings of others, such as our family members. I mentioned this with the twenty subsidiary mental states where we find lack of shame, lack of conscientiousness, lack of attentiveness, and lack of consideration for the feelings of others. Consideration for the feelings of others flies out of the window and our obsession takes over. For example, this may occur when we desire someone as a partner.

From the Buddhist perspective, we have to look extremely carefully at what is positive, what is negative, what are healthy emotional states, and what are unhealthy emotional states. There are subtle distinctions between these and we cannot put them into clear categories of one or the other. This means that it depends on the type of emotion that we are referring to, in which context, how that emotion is expressed, and so on. This is so even with respect to negative emotions. How negative a particular negative response is also depends on the reasonableness or unreasonableness of that emotional response. Thus, it depends on whether that response is justified or not.

You may ask, "Why are other emotions such as fear and anxiety not on the lists that we have discussed?" Fear can be a negative emotion, but it is not always negative. It depends on the intensity. If we are fearful of everything, that is a problem. Fear, however, makes us more cautious and guarded. If we are fearful, we may avoid quickly jumping into things without testing the water and so fear is capable of saving our lives. Therefore, fear may not always be bad. Anxiety, however, is different. From a Buddhist point of view, anxiety would be seen as one of the mental states that we should attempt to completely overcome. It serves no real purpose. In Buddhism, it is said that fear of not doing something about our emotional states leads us to understand that if we do not do something about it, the fear will only get worse. It is like having a toothache but dreading going to the dentist so much that you allow the tooth to get worse and worse until your whole jaw needs to be reconstructed. We can have fear that says, "I cannot allow this to go on" because we fear the outcome. In terms of actions such as being inconsiderate, obnoxious, and so forth, if we fear the consequences of these actions, it is more likely that we will refrain from doing them, which is in contrast to not fearing them. However, it depends on the context and what it is that we are afraid of. If we are fearful of something that we should be fearful of, that is good. If we are fearful of something that we should not be afraid of, that is not so good. It is important to be able to discern the difference.

This is why, in Buddhism, we are encouraged to become more intimate with our own experiences. Then we can have some form of discernment. This is similar to Aristotle's notion of *phronesis*, meaning "practical wisdom." It basically comes from being attentive, which is something that we learn from meditation. Experiences such as forgetfulness, distraction, and dullness are the kind of mental states that do not allow us to have that, so through meditation, we develop discernment. We cannot have blanket answers to life's specific situations. It says in the teachings that we should think of destructive emotions as being like drowning in turbulent waters or consumed by a raging fire. We should fear these things. In that sense, fear has its use but we may fear all manner of things that may be completely baseless.

It is a matter of how one see these emotions. Whether one sees an emotion as positive or negative depends on the social context and who has prepared the list. For example, in ancient Greek thought, qualities such as pride and anger were seen as good and virtuous. In many societies, revenge is seen as important and acceptable. In Tibetan culture, there is a history of clan warfare that can continue for generations. These examples illustrate how it depends on who prepares the list and the social context of what is seen as acceptable. According to Buddhism, these approaches are not seen as good or ultimately worthwhile. Rather than being about happiness, they are about honor, pride, or other similar issues. This will only increase suffering.

In Buddhism, we should attempt to do whatever lessens our suffering and that of others. With the primary and secondary mental states we reviewed, we can see that when we speak about happiness, it is not simply our own internal happiness that is being referred to. Following this approach allows us to be able to function properly in the world. Thus, there is also an interpersonal, intersubjective dimension to it. It is not advocating some form of solitary cultivation of oneself. Self-cultivation inclusive of consideration for others and the world helps us function better as a human being. Being angry, resentful, and excessively fearful does not assist us in being able to function well.

From the Buddhist point of view therefore, we should attempt to cultivate the positive emotions, the healthy emotions, in relation to our own character traits. We should try to develop healthier attitudes in order to build up our character. If we do this, our self-esteem will rise. If we have better self-esteem, we will have a better view and outlook in relation to ourselves and life, which will also subsequently impact on our moods. In terms of our day-to-day experiences, negative emotions may still arise. Our job, however, is not necessarily to eradicate negative emotions, having the absence of these experiences. Rather, it is to try to manage them better so that their impact is more temporary than lasting. We need to make sure that certain habits that we have developed diminish over time so that we can respond differently with less frequency and intensity when compared to the past.

If we cultivate the positive side of our emotional life, this will gradually overshadow our negative aspects or destructive emotions. They will diminish. This basically means that we do not need to tackle them head on or seek to eradicate them. Instead, by developing the healthy emotions, the unhealthy ones will recede. This is similar to a situation such as when our health picks up and our sickness diminishes. If we focus on developing what we need to develop, we do not have to spend time excessively dwelling on the negativities that we have problems overcoming.

Dwelling on the negative may in fact perpetuate or accentuate the experience. For instance, if we try to become more aware of ourselves and we notice more of these negativities in ourselves, we can easily get too caught up in them. In this way, some negative states of mind can become an obsession. Our fixation on them can make the negative tendency bigger. It can make us feel that we are incapable of overcoming them. In Buddhism, the emphasis is put on developing the positive so that our attention moves away from the negative. By diverting our attention skillfully, the destructive emotions have an opportunity to recede rather than dominate.

We have to notice the destructive emotions, but after noticing the negative emotions, we need to go about developing their positive counterparts. The idea is to realize how the negative emotions are perpetuated and what kind of mental states are conducive to allowing those negativities to continue and flourish. The lists of the primary and secondary emotions et cetera are used to help us with this. Once we develop more insight and recognize what is going on in the mind, we try to address it by counterbalancing. We do this by using the various methods of dealing with our emotional life found in Buddhism. Some techniques will be discussed in the next chapter.

Chapter Eighteen

Varying Approaches to Meditation

In Buddhism, when we refer to overcoming the negative states of mind and negative or disturbing emotions, we are not simply speaking about overcoming them because of their tendency to lead to immoral action. We speak about overcoming them principally because they cause us suffering. In some ways, this is a more persuasive approach in terms of leading us to want to change our attitudes or behavior than saying that we should not be jealous because it is immoral or that we are committing a sin and will be punished if we engage in these forms of activities.

Getting involved in negative states of mind truly removes the quality of life that we could be having. Our quality of life becomes diminished because we are deprived of the opportunity to make something of our lives. The torment and mental distress can be too great. Negative states of mind are not only episodic but the more we indulge in them, the greater their tendency to impact our dispositional tendencies and character traits. We can develop very deep-seated, entrenched habits. These then encourage us to behave in a certain fashion, such as being pretentious, shameless, inconsiderate, distracted, and so on. All of these behaviors are the result of overindulgence in our negative states.

By getting excessively caught up in these mental states, we can end up in our own head, overthinking, and milling over the same obsessive thought processes. Being distracted and self-absorbed in this way means that we are not actually present and interacting with others in a proper fashion. Seeing the harmful outcomes of negativity, according to Buddhism, should persuade us to do something about it. Knowing that by addressing these negative states, our life will be made easier and more fulfilling should also help persuade us. In the teachings, it says that certain negative emotions give rise to other negative emotions. For example, when anger arises, it does not only remain as pure anger. It has a tendency to give rise to other forms of destructive states such as extreme selfishness, jealousy, envy, and so on.

When we are caught up in these destructive states of mind, they do not simply remain mental, but manifest in our behavior. This can occur not only in terms of how we treat or interact with others, but even in terms of our demeanor, our physical expression. We may say terrible things or cause physical harm. If allowed to run rampant, these unchecked mental states can lead to extremely harmful conduct. Emotions have the tendency to become very convoluted and complicated, as the list of secondary disturbing mental states suggests. We develop ways of maneuvering people and situations to satisfy our desires. Such maneuvering can lead us to harness all manner of dubious and devious means in order to secure what we desire. In that way, gradually, all that is decent in us begins to corrode. It gets eaten away like rust. This leads to the lowering of our moods and an increase in such states as depression, despondency, and despair. Our habitual pattern is to believe that by indulging in negative emotions, our sense of self-worth will go up, but in fact, it does not. It goes down.

When we begin to see what is happening in greater detail, it is clear that it is in our own best interests to address the issue of negativity. It is not a question of abstract moral principles but a matter of our fundamental and overall sense of well-being, including psychological and spiritual well-being. If we have that fundamental sense of well-being, more altruistic and caring motives will follow. Based on this form of understanding, we will behave in a more ethical manner. This is the Buddhist view. We cannot say that it is an understanding based on wisdom, but it is something akin to wisdom. We might call it a semblance of wisdom, which in Buddhism, is called *prajna*. This is translated in many different ways, sometimes as "transcendental knowledge." This transcendental knowledge leads to wisdom. Therefore, there is the coming together of wisdom and goodness, which are necessary for us to attain happiness from a Buddhist perspective.

The reason that we do not have happiness is because when we normally pursue happiness, the ingredients for happiness are missing. We may attempt to find happiness through indulging in sensual pleasures, for example, through eating, drinking, shopping, or the pursuit of wealth. It is not to say these things cannot be pursued and enjoyed. However, even from the point of view of modern psychologists, material wealth seems to have little bearing on happiness. This does not mean that poverty is a precondition for happiness. Of course, we do need some form of material comfort, but it is not the most important thing. For happiness to truly flourish, from a Buddhist viewpoint, the right ingredients must be there. Even from a secular perspective, we are actually happier when we have people that we can love, when we have friends and caring, nurturing relations with others. This variety of relationship is more important. Even if we lose all of our wealth, most of us, except for a few, can live through it, but if we lose a dear one, the loss is more greatly felt.

This aligns with the Buddhist notion of happiness insofar as even from that perspective, to truly be happy, we must have good relationships with others, based on an affectionate and loving relationship. This is one of the key ingredients. When we do not feel connected, as is the case when we are completely caught up in our own emotional turmoil, our suffering is increased and our loneliness becomes predominant. It begins to assert itself and take over. From the Buddhist perspective, we need to make sure through our training that this need for close and affectionate relationships is not corrupted by excessive attachment and obsession. Obsession and addiction can interfere with our relationships. Genuine affectionate relationship is not shunned in Buddhism. Many people have the idea that in Buddhism, it is a solitary journey and that to be a Buddhist is a mental trip, that you seek your enlightenment and that is what you do. This is not the case. We seek our enlightenment in relationship to others and with others. It is by dealing with others that we also learn how to deal with our own emotions. Our emotions have objects of focus. They are about someone or other, something or other, other than oneself. When something happens and our joy, love, jealousy, and so on arise, they have an object of focus.

Different Meditative Approaches

We will now discuss how to deal with emotions so that we are able to attain a greater state of happiness. In order to attain happiness, to have the necessary ingredients, we need to look at meditation practices that we can do. Thus far, I have discussed an outline regarding how destructive emotions are understood in Buddhism. There are extremely detailed descriptions of this in some of the works of Buddhist literature. There are also many different methods that are mentioned. In this way, Buddhism is extremely rich.

In Tibetan Buddhism, we try to arrange these methods in an order so that there is some form of structure. Different contexts are used within the different practices to help us deal with our destructive mental states in different ways. If the practices are out of context, it may not make as much sense. Some practices can seem quite foreign to some Western students, particularly when it is viewed from outside of the appropriate context. In Buddhism, we must always place everything that we are doing in context. This is extremely important, especially in Tibetan Buddhism, where we believe in training the mind in order to help free up the mind. This is central to all schools of Tibetan Buddhism. This means that we need to begin at the beginning with the different techniques. What is useful on one level may not be useful to the same extent on other levels. There is a real notion of developmental process and maturing involved.

1. Noticing the destructive mental states

The first step in mind training is to in a sense, notice what is entering into our head before the negative state is manifest. We try to build awareness in this way. As we become more conscious of a particular destructive mental state or emotion, we also need to become conscious of what brings it about. This is fundamental to view and understand. What is feeding our negativity? There are many different kinds of disturbing states listed in Buddhist literature, but in the beginning, we need to simply know how and what is being generated.

2. Noticing what attracts or repels us and what we are indifferent to

In Buddhism, it is said that we should take notice of things that we are attracted to, that repel us, and that are of no interest to us. In other words, all of our mental disturbances are in one way or another related to these three fundamental responses. We want to become more conscious of these. Instead of analyzing and attempting to look at the subtleties of what is happening, we look at whether the emotion or thought that has arisen is in relation to attraction, aversion, or indifference. This is related to the three fundamental disturbed minds: excessive desire, anger, and ignorance.

3. Revealing fixation

After practicing the observation exercises 1 and 2 and having greater recognition of what is occurring when negative emotions arise, we then need to learn how to deal with our different states. We can begin this process through practicing meditation exercises and by also making some adjustments in our life circumstances. I will describe some of the meditation exercises here. Keep in mind the importance of the context.

a. Replacing the object of desire with an opposite object

This is an example of meditations of this type. To overcome excessive desire for example, there is meditation on the repulsiveness of the body. The idea is that whatever is in the mind causing excessive desire, we visualize something that is the opposite of that. If we do this, gradually, we are upsetting the mind's tendency so that the habit will subsequently be disrupted. Instead of mentally habitually and immediately seizing that object, we replace it with another object that is its opposite.

This practice can be taken out of context, which may subsequently make it difficult to relate to. The point of this approach is not that the body is itself repulsive. Buddhism does not say that the body is repulsive. However, as a helpful method, it is used in order to reduce our fixation on beauty and we can instead visualize something repulsive. Therefore, it is done purely for practical purposes. It is not to be carried on and maintained as a fundamental practice of meditation. Its purpose is simply to introduce something new into our mental thought pattern, to create some form of gap and shift our mind's focus. In this fashion, instead of directly thinking that something is beautiful and having all of the associated emotions arise, such as lust and so on, we visualize something repulsive.

In order to understand why this is done, it is necessary to give a brief explanation of Buddhist psychology. According to Buddhism, when we see something such as a person or object, both the sense organs—eyes, ears, nose, et cetera—and sense judgment preferences are involved. First, something is perceived. This is then followed by some form of conceptual judgment that creates a mental image in our mind that corresponds to the object that we have apprehended with our senses. The image in our mind corresponds to the object but due to our mental processes—attraction, aversion, or neutrality—the object has been distorted or personalized to our own preferences. The mental image that we created from experiencing the object with our senses is not the same as the object itself. How it exists before we have perceived it is different to when we have overlaid judgments and prejudices on it. This mental image that supports and reflects our preferences and judgments becomes solidified in our minds. Like a freeze-frame, it gets stuck in our head. Therefore, this mental image that we are carrying around with us serves as the catalyst. Our responses to similar objects can become habitualized. The freeze-frame image, our response to the object, can become fixed, which over time, can become entrenched.

For example, if we see a beautiful car in a display yard, that mental image is created. Our thoughts then return to that mental image over and over again and therefore, the emotions become progressively more riled up. Some form of mental image is created. This mental image does not change. The car that we saw may have been sold and someone else driving it, but in our own mind, it is still there, unchanged. This is why we so often use visualizations in Buddhism, because we are image makers. We always create images. With regard to this exercise, if we are fixated on a beautiful image, we instead create something repulsive, one that can disrupt the mind's tendency to go straight to the freeze-frame mind image and latch on to it.

Visualizing opposing images is one form of exercise. If it is a person that we are fixated on, we try to look at the repulsive aspects. The idea is to go under the skin, which is supposed to put us off or at least bring things into perspective. As it is said, "Beauty is only skin deep," or "Beauty is in the eye of the beholder."

We can also do this practice to help us with other types of things that we may obsessively or excessively desire such as a car, house, or whatever the case may be. Another technique that is discussed is that instead of thinking of the car, house, holiday, et cetera as a whole piece, we can dissect it. Often, we subsequently do not find its constituent parts so attractive.

b. Removing oneself from the situation for a short time

The other technique that is used when doing this meditation, even if it is only for a short period such as a weekend or week, is to remove oneself from the situation that is actually eliciting this form of negative or disturbed state of mind. Separating ourselves, even if it is only for a short period, does have an impact. As Aryadeva says in the *Catuhsataka* or *Four Hundred Stanzas*, we have an innate tendency to react to things with lust, anger, hostility, and so on, but in most cases, we need something to trigger it or set us off. This trigger differs from person to person. If, as an individual, we know that in a particular situation or environment, something always sets off a reaction in us, removing ourselves from that situation, going away, and doing some variety of self-analysis and meditation work also helps. It gives us the opportunity to work on ourselves without the external distraction. Aryadeva, who was an Indian Mahayana teacher, was very insistent on this. He said that it is an extremely good thing to do, even if it is for a short period. One removes oneself from the environment, goes away for a short time, and does some work on oneself. This can provide a new perspective and give space or pause between oneself and the triggers. Such distance can give us the opportunity to feel and respond differently.

c. Analyzing the effect of negative mental states

In Buddhism, to do these practices in a structured way, we move from one practice to the next as we have discussed, and then engage in analysis. In Buddhism, it is called vipashyana or analytical meditation. We analyze in a particular way by asking a series of questions. For example, "Is my anger serving any purpose? What effect does anger have? Even though it is said that anger is not a good thing, is it really a bad thing or is it just said to be bad? What are the consequences of my anger? What impact does my anger have on others?"

We do a thorough analysis in that way. Having developed some understanding of the Buddhist teachings, we then need to test or review it by using this type of analysis. We need to elucidate the Buddhist teachings by performing our own analysis. The teachings may aid us, but ultimately, we ourselves need to be convinced that for example, being angry may not serve any useful purpose and that being angry may interfere with being a good parent and our relationship with our life partners and friends et cetera. This may be true, but we have to come to the conclusion ourselves. This kind of analysis is extremely helpful to this end and is considered important and to be encouraged.

d. Analysis in terms of impermanence

The fourth practice of this type is also in relation to analysis. In our meditation, we analyze the idea of everything being impermanent. This also works in relation to seeing how we create mental images, which I referred to earlier. Everything is subject to change but if, for example, we form an opinion of someone as being good or not good or as attractive or unattractive and so forth, these can become fixed in our head. However, in reality, everything is subject to change. It is impermanent. From a Buddhist perspective, this is a necessary and important insight. Seeing things as permanent and fixed gives rise to our emotionality and our habitual emotional responses. Our experience of emotions, how we respond to the world generally, what we experience, and how the emotions impact on us, are all subject to change. With this perspective, the hold the destructive emotions have on our lives is lessened. If we have a fuller grasp of the fluidity of life, we will see more opportunities for growth, transformation, and release. Importantly, all of these practices need to be combined with the meditation of shamatha, also known as tranquility or calming meditation, or doing some variety of breathing meditation.

4. Inducing positive states of mind

In this form of practice, rather than using the previously mentioned approaches, namely, trying to replace a beautiful image with a repulsive one or removing ourselves from environments that may bring out a particular response in us, instead, we try to cultivate positive mental states. Instead of attempting to deal with the negative and self-destructive states of mind, we directly deal with the positive states of mind. There are many diverse ways of doing this, but the most popular one many people are familiar with is the practice of the "Four Brahmaviharas," "Four Immeasurables," or "Four Infinities." The four are the meditation on love, compassion, joy, and equanimity.

When we meditate on love, we do not have to attempt to remove anger. When we generate love and are in that frame of mind, anger cannot easily arise. Simply becoming familiar with and having more loving thoughts overpowers anger. Rather than attempting to overcome excessive desire, we meditate on compassion. If we develop genuine compassion, we will consequently feel a sense of empathy with and sympathy for others. We will be able to be affectionate, understanding, kind-hearted, and so forth without it leading to its opposite. Instead of trying to overcome excessive jealousy, we meditate on joy. When we are joyous, in a happy frame of mind, it is difficult for jealousy to arise. When we meditate on joy, we attempt to meditate on others being happy, having a good and fulfilled life, and so on. Instead of competing with and trying to outdo them, we rejoice in the good fortune of others. Egoism is trumped by meditation on equanimity. With these practices, we are not attempting to directly overcome the destructive emotions, we are not trying to address them, but by focusing on the positive mental states and cultivating the positive emotions, we will automatically be able to overpower the negative mental states and influences.

In Buddhist moral psychology, the destructive mental states lead to vices and these come about due to ignorance. The more we indulge in negative mental states, the more our ignorance flourishes. Conversely, when we are contemplating on positive mental states and cultivating constructive mental states and constructive emotions, this then allows us to develop first transcendental knowledge and then wisdom.

From a Buddhist viewpoint therefore, the emotions are central to our moral life and ethical behavior. Even when we are progressing on the spiritual path, our emotional life needs to be healthy. Contrary to the belief that the emotional life is what keeps us trapped in the world of contingencies and that spiritual freedom must come from being free of this, instead, it is the positive emotions that tend toward wisdom and goodness. These are two of the central ingredients for attaining happiness. The destructive states of mind and emotions encourage the growth of ignorance and the constructive states of mind and emotions encourage the growth of wisdom.

5. A subtler level of analysis

This is again another meditation exercise based on analysis with subtler levels of sophistication than earlier. Here, we focus on the relative reality of our experience. We look at the destructive emotions and see that they are not real in themselves. Their nature is insubstantial. In other words, from the ultimate point of view, the destructive states of mind do not have a nature of their own. This is seen as an extremely liberating insight to gain. If they had some intrinsic nature, they would be very difficult to overcome. As they do not have any type of intrinsic nature, which is not to say that they completely lack reality, it is easier to overcome them. We come to this conclusion by seeing that our destructive states of mind do not exist in isolation. They are not some kind of self-existing, autonomous mental state but a product of causes and conditions. These causes and conditions, in turn, do not have any fixed nature, but in themselves, are also insubstantial. The various experiences that we have and the consequences of these destructive mental states are also the same in that they only have contingent reality. There is nothing absolute.

In actuality, this line of thinking takes us further than only seeing their relative reality. If we go further, even the destructive state of mind, if we really analyze it by asking questions such as, "What is this mental state?" in the end, we see that it is not something that we can pinpoint; "This is, in itself, what the destructive state of mind is." We can only define it in relation to other things, not in relation to itself. According to Buddhism, we can deduce that the destructive state of mind is not something that has some reality of its own.

To reiterate, Buddhism does not distinguish thoughts from emotions. Therefore, even though this type of analysis may seem excessively intellectual, because thoughts and emotions are so intimately linked, by analyzing in this way, changing our understanding of destructive mental states can lead to a different experience of our destructive mental states. In other words, the more we think of a destructive mental state as being something solid and substantial, the more it keeps us weighed down. They can seem insurmountable. If they are insubstantial, subsequently, everything that is going on in our mind is in movement and transformable. So everything is open to change.

6. Transforming negativity

These methods are found in esoteric Buddhism where deities—gods and goddesses—are visualized. These gods and goddesses are like emotions that we have given form to. All of the emotions are basically played out in an imaginary world. The visualizations are done in a very structured way. Using this method, the destructive emotions are not abandoned or overcome but utilized and transformed. Through the visualization of deities, the five destructive emotions are turned into five wisdoms. This is a very complex process but the principle is quite simple. For example, instead of suppressing anger, one visualizes oneself as a wrathful deity expressing this wrath. That wrath is consequently transformed into its counterpart, something edifying and liberating.[15]

7. Bare awareness and our innate wisdom

What follows is a brief description of another method of meditation that is found in certain schools of Tibetan Buddhism. Here, we deal with the disturbed mind, the destructive emotions and so forth, without the visualization of deities or visualization of any kind by using a simple meditation where we work through different levels of mind. Mind is considered to have many different levels—gross, subtle, and very subtle. Here, "gross" means the mental processes that are completely caught up with the disturbing emotions and thoughts. "Subtle" signifies the normal functioning of our consciousness. "Very subtle" means very basic and untainted bare awareness.

By recognizing this bare awareness, we come to have a realization of our own innate wisdom. Wisdom is not something that we have to acquire, but to realize. This is made possible by maintaining this subtle awareness. We do not have to attempt to remove the disturbing mind, the destructive mental states and emotions, but rather, they begin to subside by themselves through maintaining awareness. This awareness is quite different from our normal practice of awareness in meditation. It is the subtle mental state that is not based on the act of awareness. The act of awareness is one thing that we also practice in meditation but I am referring to a more natural awareness where we are not even attempting to be aware, a subtle awareness. When we have a grasp of that, all of the disturbances begin to subside by themselves.[16]

Conclusion

This is a brief outline of the different types of methods that we use to deal with the destructive mental states and emotions in Tibetan Buddhism. It is very structured in that way, both in terms of presentation and practice. As I mentioned, when we speak about different practices, we have to ask, "In what context?" We should not take the different practices out of context because we may not then be able to find benefit from them.

From the Buddhist point of view, when we are deluded, we are deluded on both the physical and mental levels. When we are not deluded, when we come out of the deluded states, we become both physically and mentally transformed and transfigured. Therefore, we must understand the context of each meditation practice. If we understand the context, we can see how it works. We can see not only how it works, but also how the different methods fit together and complement each other. We can see that they are not in conflict even though in many respects, they are very different approaches.

We use many different methods in order to address our disturbing mental states. Buddhism takes our emotional life extremely seriously both in its disturbed states and more constructive states. Due to this, there is richness in the materials that we can employ. By doing so, we begin to have a better sense of ourselves and can become a better, more responsible agent of our own actions. We also begin to develop understanding, which then leads to wisdom so that our ability to read ourselves and other people is improved. In Buddhism, this is also seen as a very important step in our growth.

In the beginning, Buddhism says that we are strangers to ourselves. Therefore, we have to be introduced to ourselves. By learning how to read ourselves, our own thoughts and emotions, we get to know ourselves better. When we get to know ourselves better, we also become better at reading other people. Even though we know that certain physiological changes are experienced when we have certain emotions, sometimes there is no visible sign at all.

According to Buddhism, this helps us to grow and to be more effective in terms of our dealings with others. By doing so, we will feel richer as a human being and we will experience this because we will have the goodness and wisdom necessary to feel good about ourselves. It is difficult to feel good about ourselves when we find it hard to see ourselves, others, or the world in a positive light. According to Buddhism, our happiness is based on that capability. It is said that one develops or uncovers wisdom in order to help oneself and the goodness is developed in order to help others. The compassion flows from there. If we have these two, our life will become richer and happier.

This does not signify that we are going to immediately attain buddhahood, but if we aim to understand the mind for our own sake and that of others, it will not seem so far away. "Twofold fulfillment" means that ultimately, we can attain buddhahood and in more immediate terms, we can have a happier life. If we believe in rebirth, we will also have a better rebirth. Buddhism says that our future rebirth is determined by our present mental states, so it depends on what kind of being we are. If we are working toward being unselfishly happy, we will also have a happy future life.

In Buddhism, we believe that a homogenous relationship exists between various mental states. There is much emphasis placed on this relationship of homogeneity between mental states and this is because we do not believe in a soul, fixed psychic substance, or permanent self. Due to this, we need to have some notion of how the dispositional properties of the individual become transferred from one state to another and from one lifetime to another. This happens because there is a homogeneous relationship between the mental states. In our future life, we will inherit the propensities that we now possess. Even with the future life in mind, we can look at our present life and make it more meaningful. From every way we may view it, making the most out of our present life is the most important thing, both in terms of attaining eventual enlightenment, attaining a better future rebirth, and attaining a happier, more fulfilling life in this life.

Chapter Nineteen

Developing a Healthier Relationship to Depression

The subject of the next two chapters is meditation and depression. In this context, I am not discussing clinical depression as such but rather, an underlying or overt sadness that befalls us from time to time. It may also be a perpetual experience of varying degrees of intensity.

Depression is something that we all experience. It does not make any distinction in relation to young, old, rich, or poor. It is cross-cultural and cuts across all boundaries. Depression affects both religious minded as well as non-religious people. Practically every one of us, at some point, would have had to deal with it. We experience depression in many ways. Depression may be mild or very intense and debilitating. For some, it lasts for a short period and then disappears. For others, it may persist for many years and possibly, an entire lifetime.

Some psychologists and psychiatrists have made a distinction between "indigenous depression" and "reactive depression." Indigenous depression is treated medically whereas the reactive form of depression is treated with psychotherapy and so on. As I stated at the beginning of the chapter, I will not discuss depression from the medical and therapeutic points of view, but rather, I will discuss it in the context of the practice of meditation and Buddhist spirituality.

Generally, we view depression as a terrible state. It is seen as something that we have to overcome. We may feel self-conscious and seek to hide it from others, which suggests that depression or being perpetually sad has a form of stigma attached to it. This is probably due to the fact that when we suffer from depression, our energy level often reduces sometimes dramatically and we can develop a lack of motivation and become withdrawn, uncommunicative, irritable, resentful, and so on. We may become very difficult to be with, or at least feel that we are some kind of a burden to others.

The state of depression can often include a great deal of anger, jealousy, or envy that can manifest and become mixed with depression. When we are depressed and see someone happy, it can sometimes make us feel worse, self-conscious, or angry. We may not want to go out and meet happy people, as they may seem to cause us to stick out as "a very miserable person," at least in our own mind. When we are depressed, our self-esteem and self-confidence diminishes. We begin to doubt ourselves and think that we have become somehow lessened, a failure, or incompetent, and that we are the worst at everything that we do.

For these reasons, it is also not uncommon for a depressed person to actually suffer from a form of delusion, thinking that others hold an extremely bad opinion of them. When depression becomes very intense, we begin to behave slightly "mad" due to the delusions. We may also suffer from hallucinations. All of this occurs because depression gets mixed up with all manner of other emotions, be it anger, anxiety, guilt, sadness, shame, envy, or jealousy. All of this is going on and churning inside us. Once this pattern begins, it takes on its own momentum; it becomes very difficult to stop it and let go, in a way, a type of blinkered obsession, a state in which we can become trapped. The ancient Greek physician, Hippocrates, referred to depression as "melancholia." From the Latin *deprimere* comes "depression," meaning pressed down, de-pressed, depression.

There are also connotations of lack of courage, being pressed down, feeling as though you are carrying the world on your shoulders.

From the spiritual perspective, we need to realize that we can change our relationship with depression. First, we need to understand or remind ourselves that the depressed state of mind is brought on by how we interpret our experiences. Depression is not something that automatically arises from nowhere, even though it may appear to do so. Certain Western psychotherapists say that if you look into an individual's biographical history, genes, and so forth, one may learn a great deal about the reasons that certain individuals experience depression.

From the Buddhist point of view, the fundamental understanding that we need is that depression is brought on by interpretations, by placing various interpretations on one's mental experiences. Here, I would like to share a story that I read in the book, *Healing Grief* by Victor Parachin:

> As two sisters returned from their mother's funeral, one sister said, "I'm angry with you!"
>
> "Why?" asked her sister.
>
> "Because you didn't act appropriately at the funeral."
>
> "What do you mean?" the sister asked.
>
> "Well, I was having a good time."
>
> "How can you act that way with mother dead only a few days?" the sister almost shouted.
>
> "*I think sorrow and joy run on parallel paths like two horses pulling the same wagon. The important thing is to recognize each in its place and in its time.*"
>
> The sister's wisdom made an impression on the sister who was upset. The upset sister simply responded:
>
> "But you were laughing so much and..."

> "Sure, I found joy in seeing old friends. I loved talking about mother and reliving happy memories. The grieving I do on my own. If I seemed happy, I was—in that moment. And I liked the food that was brought."
>
> "But what about appearance, how all that looked to others?" the sister asked.
>
> "Appearances are your problem, not mine."
>
> Again, the accusing sister softened her words and thought, admitting:
>
> "You are right about the food, though."
>
> "I'm right about the joy too," her sister responded.[17]

You can imagine a scenario like this with two individuals participating in the same event but interpreting it in an opposing manner and feeling differently in terms of moods, feelings, and so forth. This is what we need to understand first and foremost, that depression is based on our interpretations of our life situations, circumstances, self-conceptions, and notions of who we think we are, what we are. We become depressed through not being the person that we want to be and failing to achieve things that we want to achieve in life, thinking that we have not been able to achieve them.

The second important perspective is that depression is not necessarily always a bad state to be in. One can see depression as providing another window on our life. Being in a depressed state can also reveal what in Buddhism is called, "The world of samsara," which is the world of everyday life. Simply because we are in a state of depression does not automatically mean that how we see things must somehow be completely unreal and illusory. When we are depressed, we may be able to see through that which we take to be real and non-illusory in life, the falsity, the deceptive nature of the samsaric world. In other words, we should not think, "When I am not depressed, I am seeing everything clearly and when I am depressed, my mind is distorted, messed up, and I'm seeing everything in a completely lopsided fashion."

In and through depression, we see the world through an alternative window. In that sense, there can be value in the experience of depression. I am not referring to severe or chronic depression or depression that is out of hand. In this case, professional help may be advised. The form of depression that may pervade our life but where we are still able to function can make us stop and think, reevaluate, and see that everything that we thought was valuable, important, significant, and meaningful in life can be seen, all of a sudden, in a different light due to this experience of depression. This form of depression can aid us in terms of spiritual growth because we begin to question ourselves. For many years, we may have been thinking such thoughts as, "I'm this particular kind of person." "I'm a mother." "I'm a father." "I'm an engineer." But suddenly, for one reason or another, one's whole familiar world crumbles. The rug is pulled out from under our feet and we are left dangling.

These experiences can actually be very enriching, mature our spiritual journey, and bring greater and more meaning into our lives. These types of experiences provide us with an understanding of and conviction in the insubstantial nature of the samsaric world, the world of everyday life. We can have a direct experience of insubstantiality. According to Buddhism, the world that we perceive, interact with, and live in is insubstantial. Therefore, through the experience of depression and despair, one can in fact begin to see things more clearly, not less clearly. It is said that we are ordinarily charmed or bedazzled by life particularly when things are going quite well. It is like a spell has been put on us by the allurement of the samsaric comforts, excitements, and entertainments. When we become depressed however, we subsequently begin to see through that, being able to cut through the illusions of samsara.

If we view it in this manner, we can work with depression and this is my third point. We can view our experience of depression as something that is not all "bad." Ordinarily, when we experience depression, we think of the dark, gloom, blackness. The light that allows us to lose our illusions is to experience and understand the notion of insubstantiality, which we can gain from the experience of depression. When we view it in this fashion, instead of seeing it as negative, as something dark, sinister, destructive, and that is going to gobble us up or suck us down into a dark black pit, in fact, there is light in depression. Depression can teach us how to see things more clearly. According to Buddhism, this is the starting point of our spiritual journey. Subsequently, we can see that depression is something that can be worked with.

Depression has many forms and varieties. There are depressions that are liberating and those that may lead to mental breakdown, but there is also a type of depression that is insightful, not at all anathema to creativity, insight, a greater sense of intuition, and gaining non-discursive knowledge of oneself and others. When we work with depression, it can be a signal, something that puts a brake on excesses and reminds us of the banality of the samsaric condition so that we will not be duped into sliding back into old habits. It can constantly remind us of the futility, insignificance, and insubstantiality of the samsaric condition. With a genuine constructive relationship with depression, we can become nakedly in touch with our emotions and feelings. There is the feeling of need for us to make sense of everything. Our efforts do not necessarily bear fruit if we seek meaning in the manner that we are accustomed to. We may need a new approach. This is because making sense of everything from the samsaric point of view does not work. All of the old beliefs, attitudes, and ways of dealing with things, if they have not worked, will most likely continue to not work. Therefore, we need to reevaluate and say, do, and experience things differently. This can come about by using depression in a constructive fashion.

Depression can be used to curb our natural urges to lose control, become distracted, and completely outward directed where one's energy becomes dispersed in all directions and no one is inside maintaining some sense of mindfulness and awareness. The feeling of depression reminds us of ourselves, as opposed to being lost in our activities, our experiences of this and that. A genuine constructive form of depression keeps us vividly in touch with our emotions, feelings, and various aspects of ourselves so that we do not break out. In that sense, a modest form of depression is like a state of mental equilibrium.

Everything that we experience is normally experienced and done with self-indulgence from an egoistic and narcissistic point of view, at least to some degree. However, a constructive form of depression takes away the brashness, security, and illusory forms of self-confidence that we can often display so that we always have the presence of mind to reevaluate and check. Instead of thinking, "I've got it. I know what is going on, how things are," with such confidence, one is constantly reminded to be more observant and question one's assumptions, attitudes, behavior, and also how one is interacting with others and the world at large. Such consideration and awareness must be there if we are to make progress on the spiritual path. The individual is then open to new ways of doing things and thinking in creative, fresh, and novel ways. This is instead of thinking, "I know what I want and how to get it. I've worked it out. This is how to do it."

Buddhist teachings emphasize the importance of learning to ride with life. We need to evolve and be responsive to change. Life itself is a learning process and we can only do that when we are open. We can be more open when we question and we question only when we are aware of our inadequacies as much as our abilities, in balance. Being aware of what we do not know is more important than what we do know. If we concentrate on what we do not know, we will always be inquisitive and want to learn. We will want to learn if there is a slight sense of the experience of depression. This has the connotation of being tired of all that is unreal, a sham, and illusory. The mood of depression can, in fact, propel us forward. Even though many people who experience depression say that they have a feeling of being stuck, in fact, the feeling of depression can be a motivating force to go forward. Christian mystics have referred to "the dark night of the soul." They suggest that you have to experience the dark night of the soul in order to go forward. You cannot simply embark on the mystical journey and subsequently experience light while everything is "hunky-dory." We are sure to experience the carpet being pulled out from under our feet and experience ourselves without ground, dangling and questioning, filled with doubts and uncertainties, not knowing what is going on. In some Taoist texts, it has been said that those who say they know, do not know and those who say they do not know, know. It is similar to the point that the true intuitive knowledge that we must have on the spiritual path comes from doubt, uncertainty, and not knowing. The arrogance of knowing is expiated.

I am attempting to emphasize that depression, in terms of its symptoms and so forth, can be debilitating and paralyzing due to the conflicting emotions associated with the mood of depression, but not all forms of depression are so debilitating. There are types of depression that can actually aid us on the spiritual path. In order to progress on the spiritual path, we must look at depression in a much more positive light than we normally do. This is because depression has the potential to give us insight into ourselves and the world. We are familiar with the world that we simply take for granted. The onset of depression can upset everything and turn it upside down, which subsequently becomes an impetus to want to search and explore, thinking, "There has to be more to life than what I have been doing up until this point."

This is extremely important, according to Buddhism, because if we are not convinced of the illusory nature of the samsaric condition, we will always be two-minded. We will have one foot in the spiritual realm and the other in the samsaric realm, never being fully able to make that extra effort. Shantideva said that this kind of experience can inject a lot of fear and anxiety in us because we feel totally uprooted. When one is feeling uprooted, everything becomes uncertain. However, if one persists with it, the experience of the feeling of "uprootedness" is itself a valuable experience that one needs to have on the spiritual path. In other words, the spiritual path does not consist of everything that massages the ego, making it feel good and comfortable. Rather, the ego has to be challenged continuously and repeatedly for one to be able to grow. One of the first things that the ego needs to learn is to see that nothing in this world is stable or absolutely true.

Chapter Twenty

Depression and Courage

Two symptoms often mentioned in the literature on depression are the loss of concentration and the weakening of one's memory capacity. If that is true, meditation is going to be a useful tool for someone who experiences depression. Meditation is designed in such a way that the individual learns how to concentrate, to not get distracted so easily, or yield to the upsurges of emotions or overwhelming feelings that can befall one, thus being better able to maintain a sense of stability. From a Buddhist perspective, meditation can be very helpful for some depression. There are many different types of meditation; those that involve recitation, visualization, physical postures and yoga, mudra or hand gestures, as well as meditations that focus on contemplations, analysis, or tranquility meditation in order to simply rest the mind. Whichever form of meditation practice we are doing, we need to use the meditation to deal with the varieties of mental states that we find ourselves in. We can very effectively deal with and relate to many forms of depression through meditation.

Even if one is not immediately aware of it or does not realize that one is actually experiencing depression, when we start to practice meditation, one may become aware of an underlying depression. Sometimes, in the beginning or even after some time as meditation practitioners, we may meditate peacefully for a while and then find that our mind becomes agitated, unruly, and restless. Slowly and gradually, we may be able to then relax around such experiences and somewhat stabilize the mind. We may have an experience of tranquility or meditative concentration and subsequently notice ourselves being in a state of depression to some degree. I am attempting to emphasize that when we are meditating, we can discover or experience depression and that it may take on many different forms. The depression may be related to our practice of meditation, for instance, thinking that we are not progressing and are stuck. If we have a pleasant meditative experience, particularly in the beginning, after a period of meditating, instead of things getting better and better, we may believe that things are getting worse. In our meditation, if we do not believe that we are progressing or advancing, we may become depressed about it. These types of experience are common. They are noted and written about by great meditation masters in Buddhist literature on meditation.

In terms of meditation to help deal with depression, in Buddhism, we need to have and cultivate courage. This means that one must have the willingness to allow oneself to be in that state. If it is the state that one finds oneself in, one should not become alarmed and see the depression as signaling something terrible or a sign of something bad. One needs to have the courage not to recoil but instead be able to let it arise and remain with it. This means that when we are courageous, we are not letting our fear or anxiety distract us. When we are anxious and afraid, all manner of other conflicting emotions can arise such as resentment, guilt, self-condemnation, frustration, and so on. This form of courage in meditation is based on a fundamental conviction in oneself that one is able to deal with whatever it is that has arisen in the mind. We do not want to fall into the habit of thinking that meditation will have an adverse effect. When you decide that meditation is going to affect us adversely, fear and anxiety tend to arise. With confidence, when we can say, "Whatever arises is okay," we do not have to be so protective of ourselves. By allowing the depressive mood, if that is what arises, to simply be there, that is showing courage. If one has this form of courage, one is not harmed. Hiding behind the illusions and delusions does more harm; the conflicting emotions become insidious. Therefore, we need to be courageous.

It is due to lack of courage that we may have a pathological need to protect ourselves, thinking, "I won't be able to handle this. I won't be able to cope with that. It will be too much. I will be crushed. I will be destroyed. I will collapse. I will go crazy. It will take over." Indulging in all of these negative monologues is a reason that our minds become disturbed. It is less about our having certain experiences. It is not because of the experiences but due to our reaction to the experiences, whether internal or external, whether we are approaching them with a sense of courage or are feeling timid, shaky, vulnerable, and having the sense of, "I'm going to be overwhelmed and sucked in by the currents."

It is unhelpful to indulge in negative internal dialogue such as, "How long is this depression going to last? Is it going to get worse? How is this going to affect me? How am I going to be able to cope with myself? What will people think of me?" If we approach everything that we experience courageously and fearlessly, the negative dialogue will diminish and have less effect. We can become more empowered. We can forget about ourselves and the constant thought that we are somehow going to be harmed. Rather, we should concentrate more on the mental act itself, the courageous act of being able to accommodate what arises and accept that it has arisen. In that way, we are providing room for the depressive state of mind to be there and not reacting aversely or creating a sense of alarm, realizing that the depressive state is only one aspect that may have arisen in the mind. It is not the whole mind or the sum total of all that we are experiencing at any given time.

Courage and awareness should both be present in meditation

practice. Awareness is *shes bzhin* in Tibetan. This means "aware-ing." "Shes" means "aware" and "bzhin" means "continuous, the continuous act of awareness," or "aware-ing." Awareness in the meditative context means being able to see what is happening in the mind. If we cannot bring courage to our meditation, this will subsequently reduce our awareness and we will automatically or instinctively recoil. Without the support of courage and awareness, when something disturbing or unpleasant arises in the mind during meditation such as a depressive mood, self-criticism, et cetera, one would then recoil. If we show courage, we can exercise awareness more effectively and stay with our experiences with less disturbance. We need to practice awareness not only in relation to things that we believe are harmless or innocuous, but also for those experiences that we find unpleasant. Having shown courage, we can remain aware of what we are experiencing. If we allow ourselves to experience certain things that we would normally shy away and recoil from, then we can pay attention to them and be aware. As well as understanding what is going on in the mind more clearly, the power that these states of mind have to always overwhelm us can be diminished.

Awareness is a process. It is not a state but you could call it "aware-ing." Whatever arises in the mind, the mental states, are also processes. Even if we are in a depressed mood, that mood shifts and changes and we can see that if we remain aware. If we were not aware, we may not see or experience change, transmutation, or movement within our depression or within our minds more generally. If we can remain aware, we can notice change. We can become aware of permutations and see that the depressive moods fluctuate. When we see the fluctuations and changes, it can be experienced as less permanent and more insubstantial, so it can be experienced differently. Due to our habitual tendencies, we automatically assume that the depression is there again and again, manifesting the same way as always. If we become more attuned and in tune with what we are experiencing, we will notice that it is never exactly the same. It is always dissimilar, always presenting itself differently.

This is one of the things that Buddhism encourages us to do through the practice of meditation. This is because not noticing is what encourages us to solidify our experiences, whether it is depression or another mood, feeling, or mental state. When the solidification takes place, our mind becomes fixated on it and when that happens, there is no awareness because one is not in touch with one's own mental state. If we were directly in touch with our mental state, we would see the changes, variations, and nuances. We would see the changing colors and hues of the depressive mood.

To reiterate, the depressive mood is made up of various elements. Sometimes one or two elements will be predominant. We can look at and notice this. Sometimes the element of guilt or self-recrimination may be predominant. At other times, anger and resentment may be stronger, and so on. It is always in transition. This is why awareness is so important. If our depression or other states of mind did not change, what could be learned from being aware? There is no point in being aware of something that is always the same. We attempt to be aware only because our states of mind change. We do this, not by retracing the past or anticipating the future but by paying attention to what is there in the mind at the time, what we are experiencing at that particular moment.

When Buddhists speak about being in the now or the present moment, people may think, "The now must somehow be selected as the focus of one's meditation and it should have no relevance to the past or future." But this is not the case. Instead, it means that we try not to think about what we are experiencing in relation to its past or where it may be going in relation to its future, but rather in terms of the past and the present as human experiences; it is embodied in that experience that we are having. Whatever experience we have, we have it due to the past and/or concern for the future. We cannot have an experience that is completely disconnected from our past. The reason that we have an experience in the first place is due to our past.

That is karma. The present mental state that we are in is the product of previous mental states and previous life situations and life experiences. What we are experiencing now is the fruit of what we have experienced in the past. When we pay attention to what we are experiencing now, through awareness, we are determining our future or how our karmic history may manifest in the future. If we do not pay attention, our karmic history will not be changed or altered, it will stay on course as it were. But, if we pay attention in the present, as our karmic history arises in the mind, we have an opportunity to change its potency and direction. We can take the opportunity to allow ourselves the freedom to take a different course.

Staying in the present is important not because one disconnects oneself from the past and the future that is yet to come and one is then simply in this state of "nowness." In the Buddhist teachings, it is said that there is no such thing as "nowness." It is purely a concept. As soon as you say, "I am in the now," you are in the past. This is not a metaphysical discussion but a genuine one, phenomenologically speaking, in terms of our experience of time, because "nowness" is a concept. In fact, we cannot be other than in the now and the now is not separate from the past. Depending on our relationship with what is going on in the mind, it can govern and impact our future. The point is not that we must be in the now but rather that it is in the importance of paying attention to what is currently happening in the mind and to realizing that it is vital for our spiritual progress to practice awareness.

Often, another sign of a depressed person is the posture. The person may slouch and feel heavy as if loaded up. This weight can affect their whole demeanor. In meditation, we pay attention to our physical posture to help stabilize the mind. We try to not to sit with our shoulders slouched, looking defeated and forlorn. It is said that the shoulders are extended with the chest out, showing some kind of majesty. Some form of royal bearing should be there. This is part of the practice of awareness.

I have spoken about courage and awareness and the third factor that we need to cultivate is joy. We have to realize that "joy" in this context does not mean "elation," that we are elated or on a high. When you are riding high, you subsequently crash and come down extremely hard. Here, "joy" means a sense of physical and mental well-being. This means that if you have some very good experiences in meditation, you do not become so excited and if you have bad meditative experiences, you do not feel down and hopeless. In either state, according to Buddhist teachings, there is no real joy; one is being swept along by whatever is there, by our emotional currents. In such a state, when we are happy, we are so happy and completely overwhelmed by it, and when we are unhappy, our unhappiness is so powerful that we cannot bear it. It is like the up and down of a yo-yo.

"Joy" in the meditative context means being on an even keel, but "being on an even keel" does not mean that we cannot then have experiences of feeling uplifted and joyous and at the same time, sometimes not feeling so great, for example, through experiencing a sense of flatness. Here, "joy" means the underlying mental attitude that one has, developing a joyful disposition. If we have that, when things do not go our way, we do not completely break down. If things are going really well, we also do not "lose it." There is the sense of equilibrium, which is emphasized tremendously in Buddhist teachings.

More than other teachings, Buddhism emphasizes the notion of change and impermanence. Therefore, we do not know what to expect. Sometimes things will be wonderful and at other times, they will be terrible. However, having practiced meditation and dealt with the depressive mood and other states of mind, we should have an underlying sense of joy. To reiterate, it is a general mental attitude. Therefore, it is different from other varieties of feelings of joy because there is no one particular reason that one is joyous. It has nothing to do with what one has been able to attain, acquire, or experience but it is generally having a cheerful disposition, a general sense of not going up and down. If we learn how to deal with whatever arises in the mind in the present, the underlying joy can be there, but if we are always thinking that things should be better, always fighting against what we have and are experiencing, we cannot subsequently experience joy.

I think this particular story from the book, *Heart of the Enlightened: A Book of Story Meditations* by Anthony De Mello illustrates it:

> A man grew up with the conviction that he would be satisfied with nothing but the very best. This conviction helped him to become very successful and very rich so he now had the means with which to provide himself with nothing but the best.
>
> Now it happened that he was suffering from a severe attack of tonsillitis, a condition that could have been dealt with effectively by any qualified surgeon in the land. But impressed as he was with the sense of his own importance, and goaded by his obsession to provide himself with the very best that the medical world had to offer, he began to move from one town to another, one country to another, in search of the best man for the job.
>
> Each time some particularly competent surgeon was recommended to him, he began to fear that there might just

> possibly be someone who was even more competent.
>
> One day his condition became so bad and his throat so infected that an operation had to performed immediately, for his life was in danger. But the man was in a semicomatose state in a godforsaken village where the only person who had used a knife on a living creature was the village butcher.[18]

According to Buddhism, dealing with one's own present situation is the most important thing, not always thinking that it should be different, that something else should be happening based on our own wishes. That is joy.

Another important point is that we should have love and compassion. In ourselves, we need to have courage, awareness, and be joyous in order to deal with not only a depressive mood, but also all manner of other things during meditation. We need to have love and compassion in relation to others. In Tibetan Buddhism, love means wishing that other beings have happiness and the cause of happiness, and compassion is wishing that others be free of suffering and the cause of suffering. This is how love and compassion are defined.

When we become depressed, it is an extremely lonely and private world that we enter into. We feel cut off, disconnected, and the suffering is internalized. It is important for us to feel connected to ourselves. Not only that, we also need to feel connected to others. Meditation is not only about developing certain attributes or virtuous qualities through this form of personal journey, meditation is also about developing certain qualities in relation to others by interacting with them. Enriched interaction comes about only through love and compassion.

In Buddhism, love and compassion are cultivated not purely for the sake of others, but for the sake of both oneself and others. As it is said in the teachings, we cannot grow without others. A truly spiritual person can only grow in relation to others. This kind of individual is called a "bodhisattva." Both love and compassion are not seen as based only on feelings and emotions but are also related to how one views oneself and others. For example, when we are depressed, we do not feel worthy of receiving love, let alone giving it. We do not feel worthy of receiving or giving a gift of compassion. However, through the practice of meditation on love and compassion, collectively known as "mind training" in Buddhism, we begin to realize that we have something to give. We can give. When that feeling returns, we then feel more connected to other beings. Love, according to Buddhism, is something that we have to give freely. Love does not have to be reciprocated and we cannot give it and then receive it on demand. This is repeatedly emphasized, that we should not expect something in return, whether it is acknowledged or not. That is not the point. Simply being able to give enriches us.

Here are two stories from the book, *Taking Flight: A Book of Story Meditations* by Anthony De Mello,

The first story:

> Friedrich Wilhelm, who ruled Prussia early in the eighteenth century, was known to be a short-tempered man. He also detested ceremony. He would walk the streets of Berlin unaccompanied and if anyone happened to displease him—a not infrequent occurrence—he would not hesitate to use his walking stick on the hapless victim. Not surprisingly, when people saw him at a distance they would quietly leave the vicinity. Once Friedrich came pounding down a street when a Berliner caught sight of him—but, too late, so his attempt to withdraw into a doorway was foiled.
>
> "You there!" said Friedrich "Where are you going?"

The man began to shake. "Into this house, Your Majesty."

"Is it your house?"

"No, Your Majesty."

"A friend's house?"

"No, Your Majesty."

"Then why are you entering it?"

The man now began to fear that he would be taken for a burglar. So he blurted out the truth.

"To avoid Your Majesty."

"Why would you wish to avoid me?"

"Because I'm afraid of Your Majesty."

At this, Friedrich Wilhelm became livid with rage. Seizing the poor man by the shoulders, he shook him violently, crying,

"How dare you fear me! I am your ruler. You are supposed to love me! Love me, wretch! Love me!"

The second story:

A massively built woman strode into the registrar's office, slamming the door shut behind her.

"Did you or did you not issue the license for me to marry Jacob Jacobson?" she said, slamming the document on the table. The registrar inspected the document closely through his thick glasses.

"Yes, ma'am, I believe I did. Why?"

"Because," said the woman, "he's escaped. What are you going to do about it?"[19]

In the teachings, it is said that the gift of love or compassion is in the act itself, in the act of giving. It is not that we have to receive something in return that shows acknowledgement or that it must be reciprocated. This is because without others, we would be solitary, lonely, cut-off, and very likely miserable. Life would be far less rich than it is due to others. As it is said in the teachings, even with those who give us difficulties, problems, and provoke all manner of negativities in us, if we are able to deal with them properly, they cause us to grow. How much more so when one is able to connect with others in varieties of ways?

In Buddhism, there are many different levels of friendship and connection that are spoken of, including karmic connections. Sometimes, we are karmically connected with someone—just by seeing that person, one feels connected. With others, even after twenty years of living together, we may not feel connected. Many different forms of connections are spoken of and they are all important for each of us. In the West, individualism is valued and seen as very important. At the same time, we also need to have feelings of connectedness and belonging. It is difficult to be just going through life adrift, not connected to anything or anyone. There needs to be a larger context within which we, as human beings, live, interact, and grow.

According to Buddhism, although the concepts of justice, rights, and so forth are extremely important in themselves for social harmony, love and compassion are even more precious in terms of the concept of community. This applies both on the secular as well as spiritual levels. Practicing love and compassion and the other virtues that I have spoken about, according to Buddhism, will then keep Churchill's "black dog" at bay.[20] This does not mean that we will rid ourselves of depression overnight but we do not need to attempt to get rid of it overnight.

The negative effects of depression can decrease and our ability to make use of depression in a constructive fashion can increase over time. If we are able to meditate and learn to develop courage, awareness, joy, love, and compassion, we will grow and depression will dissipate. We do not need to get rid of it. Depression will wear out by itself when managed and approached skillfully. This is important. Thinking of depression as an enemy and trying to conquer or overcome it, from the Buddhist point of view, is a self-defeating task. Our task in meditation is not to do that but to learn the skills that are necessary to deal with whatever it is that we are experiencing presently and to do so as skillfully as we can.

Section Four

Happiness

Chapter Twenty-one

Theories of Happiness—East and West

The topic of section four is the concept of happiness. If we look at His Holiness the Dalai Lama's teachings, the notion of happiness is taken almost as seriously as the Buddhist concept of suffering and the Four Noble Truths.[21] Therefore, whenever we speak about suffering, we inevitably speak about happiness.

The goal of Buddhism is to attain happiness and even the notion of familiarizing oneself with the concept of suffering in relation to the Four Noble Truths is related to the attainment of happiness. This is because if we understand suffering better, we will have a greater chance of understanding what happiness is. If we do not bother with what makes us suffer, how we suffer, the nature of suffering, or where that suffering is coming from, we will be less equipped to produce happiness. Whether we experience happiness or not originates from how we cope with suffering and deal with it. In other words, the notion of suffering and the notion of happiness are not unrelated, at least from a Buddhist perspective. In fact, they are intimately related. It is extremely important for us to have a comprehensive idea regarding what Buddhists mean by happiness and this is what I will attempt to do throughout this section. In this chapter, I will give a very broad outline of theories about happiness in various Western and Eastern traditions.

What is normally meant by happiness? Happiness is often seen as a state that does not allow any form of pain, suffering, or dissatisfaction to be present. This type of belief in happiness means that individuals may not expect to experience any pain at all in the midst of happiness but instead only expect to experience pleasure. Importantly, sometimes happiness and pleasure become conflated. For many people, happiness means pleasure because happiness must come from satisfying one's desires. In the minds of many throughout history, there has been some form of link established between desires and the object of desires. The reason for this is that if one is able to obtain the object of one's desire, pleasure then arises. When one is deprived of or denied the object of one's desires, pain arises. Therefore, in order to minimize or reduce pain, as a human being along with other living creatures, in life, one believes that they need to pursue pleasure. Here, one has desire for a life that must be filled with pleasure where one is not wanting because one has the things that one desires.

The object can be varied and plural. The plurality of objects that one may wish for ranges from something within oneself to something that one owns or obtains. Even in terms of one's possessions, it can be inanimate objects or other living beings, including non-human living beings. Whatever we believe is going to satisfy our desires, will bring about more pleasure and a life filled with pleasure rather than pain is what we are, more often than not, searching for. This is one of the ideas regarding happiness that has persisted throughout history. In the minds of many people in contemporary times, in order to attain happiness, many of us attempt to satisfy as many of our desires as possible, so we need to try to find the objects of our desire. If we have that object, we will subsequently have happiness. To reiterate, this object does not have to be an inanimate object like a mansion, fast car, or a well paying job. It could be something about oneself. For example, one could think, "If I get smarter and do a particular course and transform my body, I will then get what I want," whether it be better mental capacities or physical looks et cetera. We will supposedly then have a pleasurable life because our desires are being fulfilled. This form of idea is common.

The object of one's desires can also be seen in terms of goals that we set for ourselves. Some people may wish to extend the idea of the object of desires a little further because satisfying desires in the manner that we have described might mean that we are looking at everything from a short-term perspective. As human beings, we need to have long-term goals. Satisfying an immediate desire or finding the object of satisfaction, in itself, is not sufficient. This is because as human beings, we do not have to immediately satisfy all of our desires, but we do need to develop an overall perspective in life—to set a goal for ourselves and then evaluate how well we are doing in life in relation to that particular goal.

Happiness therefore, is not to be thought of purely in terms of whether we have a great deal of pleasure or hardly any pleasure in life. To determine whether we are experiencing happiness or not, we should instead measure whether we are experiencing happiness in relation to our objectives. Are we getting any closer to attaining the fundamental goals that we have set for ourselves? Here, the emphasis or focus has shifted from simply wanting to fill one's life with all of the objects of one's desire, which may not be possible. It is important to see that in life, there are more desires than objects that we can possibly obtain. Even if we are blessed with propitious circumstances and situations, our desires are too numerous to be fulfilled so easily.

Therefore, as human beings, we need to have a purpose in life. We need a goal in life and whatever the goal, we should look at everything from that perspective. This is another way in which people have thought about happiness. Happiness is not about trying to locate all of the objects of one's desire and attempting to bring as many of them into life, trying to satisfy each desire singularly in succession. Rather, it is about attempting to have some form of goal in life and then trying to find the objects that we think we require. It is trying to create a hierarchical position of things that are important to us, things that are not, things that are significant, not so significant, et cetera.

Instead of attempting to find every object of desire, we try to impose some order in terms of what we desire. This means curbing certain aspects of our desires, exercising some restraint, while not showing restraint in other areas due to the choices that we have made. This comes into the picture based on the basic goal that one has set for oneself. Ordering things in this manner, one says, "This is important to me, so I have to pursue more of it. These things are important to me, but they shouldn't be so important when I look at it from the overall perspective. I should let go of this and I should not spend too much time, energy, money, et cetera on that, pursuing the other things that I also find very desirable and pleasurable. By doing so, I will also be able to achieve the goal that I have set for myself in terms of my life's orientation. All of these things fit very nicely."

This is another way that many people think about happiness. The proponents of this view argue that after reflecting on these matters, one realizes that there are many different varieties of desires and objects of desire and that we need to pursue all of these things. This is true whether thinking purely in immediate terms, being a hedonist of some kind, a person who simply pursues pleasure for its own sake and not seeing anything beyond pleasure, or alternatively, someone who wishes to use some form of discrimination or judgment and say, "Some objects of desire are worthy of pursuit and should be pursued. Some are desirable and some are less worthy of being pursued and therefore, I should learn to curb my desires as far as these things are concerned." However, even when we think about desires in relation to setting one particular goal that orients our life, such as a major life goal where we try to direct everything that we are doing for the sake of attaining that objective, there is still going to be conflict. Even when we are well directed toward our major goals, many different kinds of desires will arise and we often believe that we need to fulfill and satisfy them.

The other question that those who have thought about happiness have tried to address is the harmonization of the conflicting interests that an individual may have. We have varieties of desires in relation to other people, objects, religious and political ideals, and so on. Sometimes, we cannot pursue all of them and even though we may want to do them, we attempt to eliminate as many desirable things from our list. We say, "I want those things, but I should not spend too much energy in satisfying these kinds of desires. I should focus on the ones that I really need to focus on." Even then, one is left with many choices, things that one still feels a need to satisfy.

Therefore, some thinkers have said that for many reasons, happiness is very difficult to attain and one cannot truly attain happiness because it is extremely difficult to create harmony among and between the warring factions within one's being. They believe this mainly because they see too many desires within one individual to be able to arrive at a consensus or agreement among these conflicting voices. Therefore, many conclude that happiness is just a dream and not something that can be practically realized. Some people have attributed this idea to Friedrich Nietzsche. Whether that was his view or not is another matter. This is a brief summary of some ideas expressed by different philosophers and thinkers regarding the pursuit of happiness.

Another view is that harmony is something that we must achieve, so there is agreement between these two camps. One camp says that we have many diverse voices and so the voices cannot be silenced and we therefore have to live with that cacophony of sound. The other group says, "No, we have to find one voice. After consideration, we should arrive at an agreement and say, 'This is the direction that I am going to go in.' Just like in a public situation with diverse individuals discussing various issues, we should do the same with ourselves and try to find a predominant voice that will give us clear direction and purpose."

The two positions have been seen as extremely different. There are those who say that as long as there is conflict within the individual, there cannot be happiness, and people who say that conflict exists, but happiness can be attained because the conflict can be brought to an end. These two groups agree on one point, which is that if conflict is there, there cannot be happiness. However, as I will illustrate, the Buddhist view does not go along with either of these views. It says that it is possible to have harmony and conflict in one individual and still attain happiness.

Some thinkers have said that happiness is not something that we can attain. They say that even if it is possible, it should not be the goal that we set because as human beings, we should not be thinking about satisfying our desires. These thinkers have argued that people belonging to the whole spectrum of this discussion on happiness have all said that happiness and desires are linked. Buddhists would also agree on that point, that there is a link between desires and happiness. This being the case, the point has been argued that happiness should not be the sole pursuit of human beings because happiness and morality conflict or happiness and ethics conflict and satisfying desires has nothing to do with morality.

One thing that can sometimes be highlighted in theories on happiness is what is seen as distinguishing humans from non-humans, that is, discussions around the concept of morality and ethics. Unlike animals, it is believed that we think in terms of what is fair, good, worthy, et cetera. In doing so, we need to do things that do not bring about pleasure and we have to do things that actually go against our desires but we force ourselves to do them anyway. We may not like doing these things and in doing them, we do not feel pleasure. They may not bring about any satisfaction, but nonetheless, there is a moral reason for behaving in the way that we ought to behave. If we do this, they believe that we are showing our real human ethical and moral qualities. If we fail to do so, we are not truly living up to our ideals. Therefore, happiness should not be a concern for humans.

In Buddhism, it does not have to be an either/or situation. It is true that we frequently have to make sacrifices and behave in ways that go against what we immediately desire, want, or wish. However, this does not mean that we are not going to experience happiness if we engage in certain moral or ethical behaviors. This is because as human beings, what we desire and do not desire is fluid and does not need to be so entrenched. What we desire or do not desire changes from moment to moment and day to day.

One may say, "I desire to eat this chocolate cake and not share it with anyone." Morally, it would be better to share it and not eat it all, but it is possible to teach ourselves to have desires, such as wanting to share and be generous. Buddhists think of human nature as being more flexible than we may often believe. Although human beings do have a nature, and this is recognized in Buddhism, at the same time, human nature is not so fixed. We can teach ourselves new tricks. Our nature is not so hardwired that we just have certain sets of desires, wishes, and inklings that are preprogrammed and inbuilt, as if we were incapable of having other forms of desires. We are capable of gradually allowing some desires to simply live out their useful date and let more compelling ones take over. In Buddhism, there is the concept of sharing in other people's happiness. We get to share in the happiness of others only if we think of others. If we think of others, we can share in their happiness. If we do not think of others, there is no sharing and of course, morality or ethics inevitably involves others. Whenever we are not only thinking about ourselves and are thinking of others, the notion of morality or ethics is present.

Therefore, in Buddhism, we need to discuss desires and objects of desires, our goals, how we satisfy our desires, the link between dissatisfaction and pain, whether the experience of happiness must truly come from the harmonization of conflicting tendencies or not, and morality. Can we truly pursue moral goals and objectives and still think of happiness as being important? These are matters that we must attempt to deal with. We can do this and in Buddhism, there is no problem with the notion that there can be conflict and harmony existing in one individual. Morality and happiness actually follow from that. Because conflicting tendencies exist within us, the notion of moral obligation is used in order to overcome the conflicting voice. However, I wish to emphasize that the conflicting voices are never completely overcome until one attains enlightenment. We often get hung up on the idea that happiness means that there is no trouble whatsoever, no sense of disquiet, and everything is therefore completely peaceful. This is not something that we can realistically attain.

An important point is that what is meant to be understood in the context of Buddhist meditation and what is meant to be understood in relation to one's everyday life experience are often not clearly spelled out. Therefore, people may think, "What I am experiencing in meditation is exactly how I should experience everything in life," but Buddhism has never stated that what one experiences in meditation will be what one experiences in daily life. However, this should not then mean that one is incapable of experiencing happiness. In fact, happiness can actually arise directly from a sense of struggle or pain, which is something that Buddhism speaks about. Not all forms of struggle and pain lead to real pain.

In Buddhism, words like "pain" are quite elastic in that "pain" means different things in different contexts and not all forms of pain are painful, in the true sense, like something that incapacitates you and does not allow you to do anything. Some forms of pain can wake us up and teach us certain things about life. Certain forms of struggle are good, but all of this is related to what in Buddhism is referred to as *skillful means*. "How?" is the question, not "what?" What we are dealing with is secondary to how we are dealing with what we are experiencing and going through.

Happiness needs to be understood in that context. Happiness should not be thought of purely in terms of satisfying all of our desires or attaining a state of harmony where there is no sign of conflict, a total state of peace and quietude. Instead, in Buddhism, there is an emphasis on the notion of change. Trials and tribulations in life will be there, but it is how we deal with these that will determine whether we end up being happy or unhappy. It is not about not having them. Unless we are not truly facing up to reality, we will experience upheavals as part of living. It has to do with how we deal with whatever arises.

In Buddhism, this relates to what kind of person one believes oneself to be, the Buddhist notion of the self; what form of "self" can withstand certain things and what form of "self" cannot cope or deal with various aspects and vicissitudes of existence that arise as one lives one's life? We have to look into change and consistency. How the individual deals with all of this is another aspect of happiness. Change and consistency are both necessary. It does not need to be one or the other, having a dependable, reliable nature versus being fickle and constantly changing one's mind about everything. We do not need to change our mind constantly or remain completely rock solid. We can invite, incorporate, and make use of changing circumstances that may be forcefully introduced into life, many of which will enter our lives without having pursued them.

In Buddhism therefore, in the end, it is the individual who deals with whatever manifests in our lives in terms of desire, objects of desires, and goals. It is a question of how to satisfy our desires, how to harmonize conflicting desires, how to bring about a reconciliation between happiness and our moral objectives, how to go through life with all manner of struggles and painful experiences, yet still experience happiness, and how a certain amount of pain does not then lead to being totally or even partially incapacitated. The person in search of happiness, from the Buddhist point of view, must be one who has some ingenuity in terms of how to play the many roles in life. It is knowing that as an individual, one must play many roles and that this is not a terrible thing. These roles are not only aspects of oneself, but each of these roles is oneself; being one way in one context and being another in a different context. One is then able to enrich oneself through all of the experiences involved in playing varieties of roles, as we must do in life.

This comes from the Buddhist concept of self-perception or self-understanding. It is important to keep in mind all of the different views on happiness that I have briefly presented here because Buddhism says something unique and different that contrasts with the other theories on how to be happy. Buddhism believes that we can be happy even while recognizing that there are problems and obstacles. The fact that obstacles are present does not then mean that we are incapable of being happy.

Further, the conditions for happiness do not need to be as

stringent or perfect as is asserted by some of the others who claim to promote the notion of happiness. Plato, for example, was very keen on the idea that diverse elements in the individual must find some form of harmony in order for the individual to be able to experience happiness; happiness must come from harmony within the individual, just like in relation to the state. In the state, diverse elements in a society must approach some form of unity and there is then peace. Similarly, the diverse elements within the individual, the warring factions, should lay down their arms or at least, stop shouting at each other and the person will then enjoy quietude, peace, and felicity. There are many points that Buddhism would agree with in relation to some other theories of happiness, but unless we have become a buddha, fully enlightened, there will be some inner conflict—different voices, aspects, or elements within ourselves. However, though reflection and understanding, we can achieve a modicum of harmony within ourselves. This is what we can aim for in the immediate sense.

These conflicts, if handled properly, can lead to some exciting new things. They can lead to new realizations and understandings about ourselves, which may propel us forward instead of always needing to lead a predictable and restricted life. Sometimes, people may believe that Buddhists are just a peaceful, boring lot and do not participate in many exciting things; they are simply happy being peaceful. To have conflict and struggles within oneself could be a bad thing, but it could be good if related to in the right manner. These times can lead us to breakthroughs. When we emerge from difficulty, we can be far more advanced as a human being than we were before.

Therefore, in Buddhism, there is a constant reminder for Buddhist practitioners to learn to deal with the sense of stillness that we are aiming toward in meditation and the dynamic nature of our involvement with the world. We cannot emphasize one or the other too much, either in relation to oneself and one's own embodiment, or in relation to our involvement with the world. In Buddhism, this idea comes up in terms of meditation, in terms of meditative equipoise and post-meditation experiences, and the Buddhist notions of relative truth and absolute truth. On the relative level, we need to have a certain form of understanding and on the absolute level, we need to have another kind of understanding. This is something of which we need to develop an understanding.

Chapter Twenty-two

Happiness and its Relationship to Suffering

Happiness is seen as an extremely important concept in Buddhism. Throughout the ages, Buddhists and those that came after the Buddha have thought about happiness in relation to suffering. That is the predominant thing as far as Buddhists are concerned. It is not about going to heaven, being united with God, or creating a utopian society on Earth. Often, people may believe that Buddhist teachings tend to be utopian, that they want heaven on Earth. This is a very good ideal and Buddhism also has ideals like that, not only for this world but also for other worlds known as "buddha fields," paradisiacal forms of realms. In certain aspects of Mahayana Buddhism, we also overdo the whole notion of utopianism in the sense that utopianism is not only for human beings on this planet, but it is also for other realms, planets, and galaxies; they can also have their own utopianism. In Mahayana Buddhist history, this notion begins to take hold and becomes very important in a particular way that concerns the laity and the masses. To be clear, I am not saying that there is anything wrong with incorporating notions about what the masses want. There is literature that supports the notion that utopianism should be taken to all manner of places and times, not only to this place called the Earth—we should take it to all of the other places known as "buddha fields." If you deeply think about it, it logically follows. The notion of happiness has been extremely important in all areas of the Buddhist way of thinking. This is so not only in terms of Buddhist practice or meditation, sitting on a cushion and finding your own happiness, but happiness is also seen as truly having a far ranging notion that permeates all aspects of human life. This is how a Buddhist sees it.

I spoke about desires, objects of desire, and goals in the previous chapter and I will briefly recapitulate before we move on with the discussion. Thus far, with regard to desires, objects, and goals, I mentioned that many people have said that pleasure is the greatest thing; as long as we can have pleasure, we will have happiness. Life without pleasure signifies that we do not have any form of the experience of happiness. Some alternative theories have stated that this is too shortsighted; we need to have and set goals for our lives. These goals will then bring about satisfaction because the satisfaction of specific pleasures is not the only thing that we should aim for. We also need to calculate what our lives add up to in the end; "Will the interests I pursue give my life richness and meaning? When I die, will I be able to die peacefully?" People who subscribe to this idea believe that we must set goals for ourselves and make assessments and summation of our activities, interests, and goals so that there will be no discrepancies when we audit our value and existence.

There are also proponents who argue that in order to have this lack of discrepancy, there must be harmony. They say that conflicting tendencies and propensities within oneself must come to a point where they end up agreeing with each other rather than disagreeing and fighting—unity and pursuing goals while sacrificing happiness overcomes inner conflict. They see the best way to deal with happiness is to recognize that it cannot be experienced and that this is not necessarily bad; life is full of conflicts without and within. Such theories conclude that there is no real happiness. The other view mentioned was in relation to morality and happiness and the belief that we cannot be happy and moral at the same time. They argue that there is no happiness because morality is more binding than one's own pursuit of happiness.

Thus far, we have discussed that desires, objects of desire, and goals are interconnected. In Buddhism, goals are treated as being very important. Objects of desires, in accordance with some other theories of happiness, should be treated differently to goals. Therefore, trying to satisfy our immediate desires will not bring lasting happiness. It is far more important to have a goal in life. Objects of desires are many but we can deal with it by having one goal in life. In Buddhism, we have that understanding; we have one goal and many objects of desires.

Proponents of theories about the notion of happiness often see a conflict between satisfying all of the desires that we have, in terms of objects of desires—material things such as a bigger car, more spacious living environment, unpolluted air, et cetera—and wanting a life that is not purely directed toward amassing wealth, such as having a spiritual goal or a goal in life that says, "The fact the I have lived on this Earth would mean something if I did something that I could be proud of in terms of my spiritual vision." However, Buddhism says that there does not need to be any real conflict between the two. People believe that there is a conflict but I will explain why no real conflict exists.

There is no real conflict between the Buddhist notion of renunciation and the promotion of ideals of monasticism, aspiration to have a good family life, a prosperous living situation, a workable environment, et cetera. This is because in Buddhism, it is about emphasis. It depends on what aspect of our lives we choose to emphasize and this varies from individual to individual. Buddhism discusses this idea in terms of a person's capability, capacity, inclination, and aptitude. It is possible therefore, to set oneself a goal in life that incorporates many of our desires so that we still desire, but we desire in a different manner and go about satisfying those desires differently. In other words, we can have an ultimate goal of reaching fulfillment in terms of the embodiment of wisdom and compassion, the goal of Buddhist practice, in concert with our everyday life goals and pursuits.

In Buddhism, it is said that whatever social position that we may occupy, doing it to the best of our ability is what counts. In terms of being a parent, businessperson, government official, and treating people fairly if one is in a situation of power, all of these things can be done dharmically or undharmically, dharmically meaning following the Buddhist ethics of non-harming and studying the dharmic teachings. One could go about things in a totally different manner, in an undharmic way, and this will only bring suffering for oneself and others.

I wish to emphasize that the Buddhist notion of renunciation should not be seen to mean that the individual is in a complete state of dispassion without desiring anything. For example, the interaction between the lay and ordained members of the sangha in Buddhism has always been intimate and based on a sense of community. Monastics often live within a monastic community and serve the lay community in many ways.

Many people mistakenly believe in the notion that Buddhists wish to escape from the world and want nothing to do with it. Buddhism has always emphasized the interpersonal dimension of human experiences and our pursuit of happiness. We do not become happy in isolation, we become happy in relation to others. Therefore, setting certain goals for our lives is important for our enrichment. If one is an ordained person, one may say, "I want to be a good monastic," and then live one's life according to that aspiration. If one is a layperson, one may aspire to all of that which a monastic aspires to in terms of attaining happiness but approach the attainment of the goal differently. In both early and later Buddhism, Mahayana in particular, there is an emphasis on the notion that as Buddhists, we can attain ultimate happiness regardless of how we go about achieving that end, be it as a monastic or as laity.

Is it possible to think that one can attain real happiness and try to satisfy all of the other desires in life? We cannot satisfy all of the other desires, but as a Buddhist, one could have one objective, which is to attain enlightenment, nirvana, liberation, and at the same time, try to satisfy as many of the desires that we have in life to the best of our ability and do so in an intelligent fashion by discerning which desires are worth satisfying and which are not. Of course, we have to learn some of these things from living. Buddhism also emphasizes that we learn from living, so there is no real contradiction in saying that Buddhism instructs us to orient our lives toward attaining nirvana and also go about leading a normal life and satisfying all of our desires, as a normal, responsible, ethical, and moral person. It is possible in life to aim toward that. It is possible to satisfy our normal desires that human beings have for varieties of things. As we know, human beings have physical, psychological, and social needs in terms of wanting friends and a supportive social environment. We also have a desire for a political climate that helps us grow and does not inhibit our liberty and aspirations. These are not in conflict. The bodhisattva ideal demands it.

The other point that I mentioned earlier is the harmony and conflict aspect, how the Buddhist path and stages are full of struggle and striving. This may seem in direct contrast to the idea of self-acceptance. It is okay to accept ourselves as we are, but other people may not support that. The idea that you do not have to do anything and simply accept yourself with all your faults and everything will be fine does not seem true in reality. When we say that we need to work with our shortcomings and defects, we do not need to feel that we are condemning ourselves. This should not automatically make us think, "I am the worst person on the planet. I am despicable." This should not follow. Certain aspects within us may need some work, but this does not make us a bad person. Not having the confidence that we can deal with our weaknesses and faults is more the issue. When Buddhism says that we should accommodate certain aspects of ourselves, it is saying that we should accept that we have shortcomings and that we have the capacity to deal with our shortcomings and weaknesses in order to overcome them.

In Buddhism, it says that we are prone to exaggeration and can make a big deal out of different things. If we exaggerate the seriousness of our shortcomings, they can become like a mountain instead of a molehill, as they say. If we have a negative tendency and try to accept it as if it were a positive tendency, it is unlikely to work in reality. It is important to recognize our negative tendencies but at the same time, we should avoid becoming negative about our negative tendencies, as this compounds the issue. There is a huge difference between recognizing negative tendencies and becoming negative about them. To some degree, becoming negative about our negativities produces a negative person trapped in their self-loathing.

From a Buddhist perspective, we do have the capacity to manage or overcome all of the things that life throws at us. We can handle them. This is what Buddhism teaches and that is how we can live a happy life. We can have pain, struggle, and go through all of the ups and downs of life, but overall, we can have a sense that we can be happy. We do not need to become bogged down by life circumstances through compounding negative states of mind. Buddhism's notion of impermanence and the changing self believes that we are capable of dealing with what arises. We can be empowered and not be afraid to play any role, whatever is necessary to deal with situations as they arise and in that way, we can retain our integrity. Whatever kind of person we need to be within a given situation, we can rise to the occasion to our greatest capacity. We do not have to resist being malleable due to some fixed notion of ourselves or our identity. We can be one hundred percent who and what we need to be in any given circumstance.

In Buddhism, it is said that we should learn to truly understand suffering in order to appreciate life and understand happiness. Understanding happiness comes from understanding unhappiness or suffering. To reiterate, suffering and unhappiness are related, but they are not the same. Pain can be distinguished from suffering, as pain is not as dimensional. Much of the pain that we experience comes from physical and mental depravation. With some degree of contrast, suffering and unhappiness can come from being deprived of higher needs. We may have many things, companionship, being able to socially interact with other human beings, having many of our physical needs satisfied, or being surrounded by material goods and comfort, et cetera. All of these may be present, but there may still be a form of lack, a vacuum that one feels within oneself in spite of all that one has.

Suffering is experienced as a sense of dissatisfaction that is nefarious and enigmatic. It can sometimes be difficult to pinpoint where that variety of experience is coming from. Unhappiness is an accentuated sense of suffering and being unfulfilled. It can be accompanied by a feeling that one has not led one's life as one wished. Even if one does not have a clear idea of what that life was to be, the feeling that one has missed something or messed up can pervade everything else; "I am not living in the manner that I wished."

Therefore, suffering and unhappiness have many dimensions to it that are not there in relation to pain. In Buddhism, we do not spend too much time speaking about how to overcome pain because it is much clearer how to do that. We can often find the objects of pain and to some degree relieve, remove, reduce, or fix it. If it cannot be fixed, at least it can often be understood. But with suffering and unhappiness, we need to do something much more significant and enduring. It is different to relieving discomfort in one's life, and we often mistake or do not distinguish between pain, suffering, and unhappiness. When we feel unhappy or we suffer, we still think of it as some variety of pain. We subsequently attempt to go about addressing it in that manner, thinking that the solution to our suffering or unhappiness is finding a solution to dealing with the pain.

Mahayana Buddhism says that we must understand suffering, as does Tsongkhapa in the *Lamrim Chenmo* text or *Great Paths and Stages* in English. First, we should think about the value of suffering and make distinctions between suffering and pain; suffering is more complicated and amorphous than pain, as we have been discussing. It is not at all like experiencing discomfort and then going about easing or fixing it. Understanding suffering will wake us up and so it is said that we should contemplate Tsongkhapa's teachings. Other Mahayana teachers have said that we should contemplate on four points that will help us regarding suffering:

1. The first point references "the good qualities of suffering in terms of its ability to spur us on to liberation." In other words, if we obtained everything that we wished for in life such as a romantic partner, job, wealth, et cetera and we did not experience any real pain, there would still be suffering. Experiencing suffering is what makes us human. Despite having all of the things we need, we may still seek to be free of samsara; "I have to liberate myself from this state," instead of thinking that it is something fantastic. We may think, "I need to go deeper into myself. I need to look deeper into what it is all about; what reality is, what life is, what ethics are, a

good way to live and a bad way to live." This impulse can arise from suffering but not necessarily from pain. Many people experience pain and they are not necessarily woken up by it. Experiences of meaninglessness that occur after reflection may be born from some experience of pain but being troubled by the fundamental notion of life is very mysterious and inexplicable. In this way therefore, we should think of suffering not as something completely useless but as good and helpful. This is because if we felt contented and became complacent, there would be no impulse for us to inquire and be inquisitive about life. We would take life for granted or continue to take it for granted, as many of us already do.

2. The second good quality that Mahayanists recognize regarding suffering is related to the dispelling of arrogance. The point is that when we suffer, we become equal. It is very humbling that regardless of what we believe we have achieved, we may have the feeling of some form of gnawing, something eating inside us, corroding away. We then feel humbled because we realize that we are the same. All of the human beings that we know are in the same boat because ultimately, whether they recognize it or not, they are suffering in one way or another. They are experiencing a sense of meaninglessness, void, and emptiness.

3. The third good quality is that suffering teaches us to shun a bad attitude or bad behaviors. This means that we begin to make a link between what we do, what we think, and what we are experiencing as a human being. If we are feeling empty, it is inevitably related to not having the right attitude or not dealing with things in the right manner. This is not referencing "right" in a moralistic fashion but instead in relation to what Buddhists would regard a wholesome and constructive manner. Therefore, it is not truly benefitting oneself or others in terms of how one is going about trying to reduce suffering. We may attempt all kinds of things but nothing may be working out to our satisfaction. This may then

point to where we are in terms of our own mental space. Making the connection between suffering and our mental attitude is the third good quality that is associated with the experience of suffering.

4. Following from the third, the fourth is the good quality of producing compassion. When we suffer, automatically, through empathy and sympathy, we understand what suffering is so we therefore have some feeling for others. If one had never suffered, even if the pain is great but one had not suffered in the way that we are speaking about, one may not have woken up. One would not understand that other people also have feelings and go through the same things that we do. The experience of suffering can make us feel connected to others and less isolated and confined to our own egoic preoccupations and self-possessive ways of thinking and behaving et cetera. So we feel connected or interconnected.

In this way, in Buddhism, we attempt to think of the experience of suffering not as a good thing in itself but recognizing that it has a useful purpose. We can put it to good use if we have the right attitude. To do so, we have to deal with the desires, objects of desires, goals, satisfaction, dissatisfaction, harmony, conflict, morality, happiness, struggle, pain and happiness, change and consistency, and so on.

Chapter Twenty-three

Happiness and the Distance Between How Things are and How They Appear

When we speak about human happiness, the issue of money, wealth, and possession will always come up. What we do with it and how we deal with these issues is very important and in Buddhism, it has been spoken about a great deal. Buddhism does not say only one thing about how we should deal with our material possessions or what we should do in terms of how we lead our lives. Should we simply give everything up and spend the rest of our lives in a cave? Would that be the solution to all of life's problems? Or is there a way in which we can still continue to work with material conditions in such a manner that one can, for example, still have a career, be married with children, and run a business?

We have a whole gamut of possibilities available to us and Buddhism addresses all of it. Buddhism says, "Yes, if one feels so terrible about having to deal with people and living in a very stressful environment, escaping into a cave may be an option for a few." This is an option and it is a good one if you have had enough or too much of life. A person may have been unfortunate in their life, with tragedy after tragedy for example, one disaster and failure after another. A person may have experienced everything as a failure so they then say, "I've had enough. This is not working for me so I'll spend the rest of my life, not idling away in a drunken stupor, injecting myself with drugs, or wasting my life, but I'll go into a cave and spend the rest of my days doing something else. That would be a good thing to do, and why not?" In the East, some people practice departing for a solitary life such as living in a cave. All over the world, many decide at one time or another to escape or at least find a quieter existence. There is not only one way to lead one's life.

In Buddhism, surprisingly, people who do this often come out of the caves totally transformed and begin to have students. They begin to socialize and have somehow become rehabilitated back into society. They are not only rehabilitated but also in fact, admired for what they have achieved. Such practitioners who go into isolation form an important part of Buddhist history: being completely involved in society, doing everything that is expected of them and taking opportunities as they arise, becoming disappointed and disillusioned, and "leaving home." They go into total isolation, become a recluse, and then reemerge and socialize again but as an admired person this time instead of a failure. With regard to many of the hagiographies of great Buddhist masters, if we read them, we may become dazzled by the notion that they could leave everything behind. But often, we may not understand the process that one individual has gone through in terms of the process of disappointment, seclusion, and then reemergence and the resumption of a social existence. Even with people who have had enough of society, often, in the story as it is told in traditional Buddhist literature, they return as a transformed individual and no longer shun social situations or responsibilities. Many of these great masters in Japan, China, and Tibet became advisors to emperors, kings, and ministers. An interesting development took place between these individuals and people who were living in the center of political, economic, and social power.

Buddhism believes that happiness is something that we have to earn. If we have not earned our happiness or do not merit it, even if we think we are happy, we may not be. The process that occurs with the people who were part of society and had social demands that became so much that they cracked and gave it all up, went off into wilderness, found something different, and returned, is part of that whole idea of attaining happiness with struggle. This includes how we may want to lead our lives as a Buddhist. Even without thinking about leaving everything behind and not cracking under the burden of social demands, the struggle is still there. We still find life difficult. This is true even if we have not been driven to the point that some Buddhist masters have, where they had to give everything up and go into seclusion in order to acquire happiness. These individuals could then be with others and feel comfortable about it without problems, no longer seeing others as the enemy. Why would one want to leave everything behind if one did not believe that others are to be blamed for all of their problems? The impetus to want to leave everything is the thought, "I've had a series of bad luck caused by others, or at least, the facilitators in bringing my bad luck to fruition in a more efficacious fashion."

We cherish the Buddhist concept of happiness and think that happiness is something that we all must aspire to precisely because it is hard to get. It is not because it is easily attained as if we just change our perspective on life and then suddenly happiness is there or we look at our lives differently and happiness is there. This can help, but it may not be enough. Buddhism says that we should change our perspective on life in order to experience happiness but changing our perspective is not the only thing. This is why the notion of striving or struggling, aspiration, and mind training come up again and again in Buddhism. This then suggests that we have to make ourselves become happy, we have to go about things in such a way that we can create happiness for ourselves. Happiness is not something that will necessarily just come by itself. It will not simply arise; we need to work at it for it to arise.

In Buddhism, two different approaches are mentioned in terms of how we can do that. One relates to how we deal with our emotions, feelings, attitudes, body, and our senses. The other way comes from contemplating on transcendental matters. Basically, happiness is something that we should attempt to attain by contemplating on and working with experiences, empirical things, and at the same time, contemplating the transcendental. In this way, we can secure happiness for ourselves. Being lopsided in our approach to attaining happiness means that something will be ignored. Sometimes, the world may become too much and we want to ignore all worldly concerns and focus our mind on higher things, on high ideals, abstract things. In Buddhism, we need to combine the two contemplations. We cannot separate dealing with the empirical world on a practical level and approaching more spiritual contemplations.

From a Buddhist point of view, the notion of happiness and liberation go together. A truly happy person or individual is one who is liberated, in other words, someone who enjoys total freedom. The person who enjoys total freedom is not someone who does not have to abide by certain external demands or situations, but more importantly, someone who has liberated themselves from inner constraints. With regard to a liberated individual in Buddhism, we would not call them a "liberated soul," but rather, a person who has freed themselves from all forms of suffering.

As I stated, the notion of suffering is related to pain but suffering is much greater because we suffer not just because we are experiencing pain right now, but because we can imagine ourselves experiencing all manner of horrible things in the future; we spend much time on the past thinking about past difficulties and unpleasant memories. We then begin to experience suffering and all of the painful things that we think happened to us can reemerge. What happened to us is dependent in part on our perception. Our memories may be distorted and at least partly unreliable. It is more than very possible that not everything that happened to us that we believe was painful happened as we recall it. It may have become truly painful only in retrospect. Sometimes the pain can grow the more we ruminate over a memory and as many Western psychologists would also suggest, our memory does not serve us as well as we often believe.

In that way, suffering is something that human beings experience, much more so than other living creatures. Even though we share the pain and suffering of other creatures, our form of suffering and unhappiness is quite unique to our humanity. Therefore, in Buddhism, we are instructed to look at ourselves, pay attention to our own mind, see how we think, and see what impact our thought processes have on us. Almost always, if we become reflective, we will detect a distinction between how things appear to us and how things actually are. We will develop an understanding that not everything that we believe is happening is actually happening as we think it is, and whatever we believe to be true or truly existing is not truly existing as we believe it to be. It does not require a great deal of reflection to come to that realization. We come to see that, "Whatever I thought was happening, did not actually happen like that. Whatever I think reality is, is not what reality is." This pertains both to how we perceive things and how we interact with other beings. In Buddhism, there is the perceptual element, which includes the cognitive activities of the mind. In Buddhism, this is an extremely important point. As human beings, how our senses operate is an important part of understanding what is going on, which kind of sensory stimuli are inciting what type responses within us. Unless we have knowledge and understanding of this in terms of empirical things, of the objects of sight, smell, and taste, and so on, we remain bewildered to the many influences within our lives. In Buddhism, this is referred to as ignorance, being ignorant of the human condition.

As soon as we begin to contemplate and consider in this way, we will come closer to and understand more fully what Buddhism says about how suffering arises. We begin to understand the sensory apparatus and that there is never a complete match between the stimuli and the response, the sensory stimuli that incite the responses within us, be they pleasurable or non-pleasurable. We always assume, in our ignorance, that there is a complete match, that whatever the stimuli is, it will always bring about the complete and correct response in terms of one's experience of pleasure or pain. But that is not the case. Something else is at work in between these two, the stimuli and response. This conditionality comes in and interferes with the stimuli and the corresponding experience of pleasure or pain. In other words, different individuals placed in the same environment who are all subjected to the same sensory stimuli will have different experiences in terms of their pain or pleasure responses. It is the same with an individual over a period of time; if the person is subjected to the same stimuli over a period of time, the response is not going to stay exactly the same. It will change. In fact, even whether it is experienced as pain or pleasure can change. Therefore, from the Buddhist perspective, something else is there. The Buddhist view is that we always believe that our level of happiness is contingent on what we experience through our sensory apparatus. Therefore, we believe that, "If I can only see things that are beautiful and am attracted to, hear things that are always pleasant, have people always saying nice things about me, and taste food that is always nice, if I have this all of the time or as often as I can, I will then be happy."

However, in order to have some appreciation for the Buddhist notion of happiness, we need to understand the idea that there is an absence of a complete match between sensory stimuli and our sensory or psychological response. Our own mind is there, assessing everything. As human beings, we cannot help but do this, so we assess whether something is painful or pleasurable. We are not in touch with reality to begin with and we misapprehend the world through our senses. We are normally confident that we know what is happening because we are experiencing it; "Because I experience it, it is real, because it comes from my senses, because I've heard and seen it. I have smelled it and touched it." Buddhism asks us to create a pause or some spaciousness around our judgments and to not judge our experiences too quickly. As long as we continue to habitually respond to the world without any freshness, consideration, or pause, we create limits on experiencing happiness.

Therefore, we need to learn to distance ourselves from our own immediate experiences, to truly see what is happening on the empirical level. Buddhism says that if we do this, we can see that not only one or two things are happening in terms of what we are experiencing at any given moment, both externally and internally, but so many things. It is mind-boggling in terms of the varieties of things that are happening. Because the mind does not have the capacity to comprehend everything that is happening all of the time, all at once, the mind has to then become selective. It conducts an editing process so that certain things are eliminated out of the purview of one's consciousness, other things are suppressed or thrown to the side, some other information is selected, and one's mind then becomes focused on these. What the mind chooses to focus on is somewhat random except that it is the habit of the mind that really determines what it is that one chooses to focus on.

From the Buddhist point of view, if we want to experience real happiness, we have to understand and appreciate this notion that there is no commensurability between the sensory stimuli and the psychological responses that one has in terms of one's own experience of pain or pleasure. This is because we will continue to believe in our own stories and then not be able to have any effect on our inner environment. Even though we may believe that we can impact on our personal environment, the neat world we have created for ourselves where experience and everything is slotted into different pigeonholes and is extremely organized, it does not correspond with the reality. When we begin to question and understand this discrepancy properly, which is helped through the practice of meditation, we see that there is a discrepancy, a gap, that it is filled by our subjective interpretations foisted on sensory stimuli, we can then pause and reassess what we see as true and real.

One of the objectives of learning to be happy is to learn to be more in touch with reality and to move away from not being in touch with reality. The Buddha and many other Buddhist masters have stated that the degree of our estrangement from reality is a measure of our ability to be happy. As samsaric beings, we believe that whatever we experience reflects or mirrors reality. We experience total conviction in how we interpret our experience and our delusional thoughts normally arise in our minds as real without doubt, pause, or reflection. In other words, whenever we experience certain things, we take them as being real.

The many factors involved in our own experiences are never simple, even if some may seem straightforward to us. If our mind becomes extremely narrow in focus, it latches on to specific things. It zooms in and selects a very small portion of the myriad of potential experiences that we may be having. This then becomes concretized or reified, to use Buddhist language. We become fixated on that and it subsequently produces definite or strong emotions. Unhappiness therefore, comes from the tendency to be so judgmental and monofocal in our view that we automatically grasp on to things; "This is the reality. This is how it is." In fact, we could have very easily settled our mind and intention on something else and responded to that instead but within the same habitual repertoire.

This does not mean, however, that in Buddhism, we should then end up with some notion of relativism, that everything is the same. In order to open up the mind, to truly overcome suffering, these are the fundamental steps that we needs to take. Our mind is so habituated to always go in one direction. It is monodirectional, focusing and settling on one thing and not only that, it then reinforces it, supplying that fixation with all of the emotional energy, the investment of the extraordinary feelings and emotions that we experience. This makes that whole experience become even more burdensome for the individual. In Buddhism therefore, it is said that as we go through our life, we are getting burdened, we are carrying such big loads. These are metaphors that are repeatedly used in Buddhism. This is how it happens, our mind goes in one direction and it latches on to things. We become burdened because there is so much investment put into our delusional thoughts and intense emotions, which run contrary to reality. Unhappiness is the result of this fixated pursuit.

In order to attain happiness, we need to open up our mind, unburden ourselves, and not carry such a load. This is sometimes called "samsaric baggage." We need to not carry this and instead, travel through life lightly, because otherwise, we become bogged down, weary, and tired. These are also metaphors used repeatedly in Buddhism; the weariness of travelling through samsara is emphasized again and again. We become tired and bogged down. Where does the weariness come from? It comes from doing the same thing again and again, not getting the results that we expect, and never learning from our mistakes. Samsara, in itself, also has that connotation, the repetitive nature of what we do, how we see things and go about trying to solve our life problems. Life can begin to lack newness and freshness. When we become monofocal in this fashion, we do not necessarily see the opportunities that life can offer because we have blocked them out. Having banked everything on our view of the world, when lacking skillful means and insight, we can believe, "If I do this or if I do that, my life will be meaningful and bear fruit." We can put everything into it and things can go amiss and astray.

Seeing how we see and hear things with our own eyes and ears is emphasized because our thoughts follow our sensory impressions. They go together. Opening up our mind is one of the most fundamental ways to learn to experience more happiness rather than suffering and unhappiness. This directly relates to what Buddhists mean by the non-substantial or insubstantial self. Among our many fixations is the belief in having a fixed and solid sense of identity or self. This is because one's own notion, the fixation on the self, is so strong that whatever is perceived through the senses is also related to how we see ourselves, our identity. This is also monofocal. Even if the things that we experience do not produce happiness, fulfillment, or satisfaction, we continue with how we wish to see things because our fixed notion of the self only allows us to perceive things in a particular fashion. From the Buddhist perspective therefore, we are unable to appreciate the interconnecting influences within the human experience in relation to social interactions between individual and society or the individual and nature. The samsaric mind thinks in very linear terms but things are not simple in this way. The complexity that Buddhism focuses on in terms of how we apprehend the world, in the end, is supposed to bring about simplicity. If we simplify everything by improving our relationship with reality, life becomes less complicated. From the Buddhist point of view, when we become fixated and grasp this and cling to that, life brings more complications and we become burdened by it. Our life would be simpler if we did not shy away from or deny the myriad of factors and the complexity of experience. Rather than persisting with a monofocal, fixated approach, we can seek to understand the different factors that are at work within the inner and outer environment. Such a relationship then becomes less delusional and distorted and more freed-up, open, and clear.

Chapter Twenty-four

Happiness and Our Sensory Experience

In many ways, happiness is a very complex subject. Buddhism has said much about it precisely because it takes the notion of suffering seriously. Suffering is important to understanding because we cannot understand what happiness is without understanding suffering. Suffering should not be understood purely in negative terms. There can be many beneficial outcomes from understanding suffering, unhappiness, and so on. It is vital to take into account the important role that the senses play in our lives, what we see, smell, hear, taste, and touch. As part of Buddhist meditational practices, we need to contemplate and reflect on the impact that our sensory impressions have on us.

Sensory pleasures are not to be discarded but instead, they should be understood. Sensory pleasures have many sources, not only a single source. There are many varieties of sensory pleasures arising from many different sources within the individual. Buddhism emphasizes the pleasure that we derive from the five senses. These are significant because they have an enduring psychological effect and over time, largely determine what kind of human being we become. Through paying attention to what we see, hear, smell, taste, and touch, in the present moment, we have some sense of our past, how we have come to be where we are. We can look at, "why I prefer this to that, why I choose to focus on one thing rather than something else, and why I find this smell or that smell to be significant." If one has noticed something to be significant in terms of one's cognition, apprehending something in one's visual or auditory field, the judgment that one has performed speaks to one's psychic history. How we automatically respond with pleasure or displeasure regarding different stimuli points to our past experiences such as finding a smell pleasant, aromatic, or soothing and another as being revolting, vile, and disgusting.

One begins to see how the role of the self is played out in one's sensory experience. The individual, the self, is ever-present. It is not only when one is conscious and deliberately behaving in particular ways that one has some cognizance of one's personal notion of self or agency; the self or agency is involved in everything that one is experiencing. It could not be otherwise. Therefore, the involvement of one's own self in everything that we experience determines whether one is experiencing happiness or unhappiness. This is because self does not remain aloof. The agent is not like a pilot in a cockpit or driver in a car; a driver is separate from the car. The car is only to be utilized in order to get from point A to point B. In Buddhism, the self is part of the mechanism that allows us to travel from one place to the other. There is no separation. The agent is not necessarily, in a detached manner, directing the course of the path that one is going to take in life, using emotions, sense impressions, memory, psychic history, et cetera. It is not the self being driven by these things as if they stand apart from the self. In reality, there is some kind of center point that we may refer to as the "self" in terms of denotation and connotation of what we might mean by "self." However, it is very difficult to describe what that self is apart from its involvement with the fields of one's own experiences and embodiment as a living, conscious being who also has intentions, dreams, aspirations, memories, and so on.

In Buddhism, if we wish to speak about self-mastery, we have to think about self-mastery in this manner. I discussed how to reconcile the notion of harmony and conflict and how conflict and harmony must be seen as totally separate. According to Buddhism, we can seriously think about that. Whenever we speak about agency and self struggles involved with different aspects of one's self, we want to attribute some autonomy to one aspect of the self and deny that autonomy to other aspects of one's self because these aspects may be thought of as superfluous, on the fringe, marginal, to be discarded, ignored, and not important. In Buddhism, we do not have this singular concept of the self because one is all of these things when the notion of the self is present. Often, there is no difference between what is being transformed and the agent who is trying to transform certain things. They are the one and the same, just like water turning into ice.

It is possible to bring about fundamental changes within oneself without trying to disown or distance oneself from certain aspects of one's own experiences, thinking, "This is not 'me.' This is not really 'me.' The real 'me' is something different to what I just did and said." In Buddhism, such a notion will only lead to more of a sense of self-dividedness in terms of genuine self and false self, superior self and lower self, or real self versus unreal self. Who decides which set of attributes or qualities belong to the real self and which belong to the lower, marginal, or disowned self? Instead of getting bogged down by such matters, attributing certain behaviors and opinions to the lower, marginal, or denied self, we can own up to all of this and see that all these things are aspects of ourselves. We can acknowledge that "whatever I am expressing, all of it, has to do with the kind of person that I am." When one begins to look at oneself like this, in Buddhism, it is believed that we can address the issue of being self-divided. All of our different aspects can be included in our spiritual path and addressed in a serious manner. Otherwise, knowledge of the self will remain superficial. We would know that there are aspects of a hidden self that we have not yet discovered, addressed, or understood. With regard to whatever work we may think we need from a spiritual perspective, our approach will lack seriousness and be incomplete.

To allow all that we are now to be included on the spiritual path allows us to become transformed. When we look at the sensory impressions and how we accumulate and store the information that we gain through our sensory inputs, we will see more clearly the role that the mind plays in how and what we experience. We will see that there is a tremendous amount of thought going into our experiences. We are not only experiencing many feelings and emotions in concert with our sense of a self or individual, but we are thinking and conceptualizing our way through our experiences in an excessive manner. Even the notion of wishing to disown certain aspects of ourselves or wanting to say, "That is not really 'me,'" or "That is really 'me,'" are all based on what Buddhism calls the "proliferation of discursive thoughts." This means the proliferation of thoughts or conceptualizing excessively. This is what we do. We constantly conceptualize without having any form of philosophical training or being aware of any philosophical notions about these things. We conceptualize all of the time; what we perceive through the senses, what we make of the experience of pain or pleasure, and how these experiences of pain and pleasure are appropriated by that individual self.

Buddhism says that one of the biggest misconceptions that we have is that there is a unitary self standing apart from one's experiences; "I am the master of all my experiences and everything else revolves around how I organize my own experiences and my experience of things in the world." Buddhism however, says that this is not the case. If we reflect on how we think, we can see that this is not the case. When we have the experience of the self and we engage in thinking, if we are really aware and attentive, we do not see a self that is separate from whatever it is that we are experiencing.

Believing that there is such a self subsequently gives rise to the proliferation of discursive thoughts or conceptualizations. We are constantly assessing and thinking, "This is good. This is bad. This is good for me and this is bad for me." Thinking in these terms incapacitates the self. When we believe that there is an agent that is doing all of this thinking and that doing all of this thinking is somehow good for us because everything is then ordered, labeled appropriately, and organized into categories and we believe that there is a self standing apart from this, according to Buddhism, this is a form of imprisonment that one has not yet realized. This imprisonment, although not recognized, is due to resistance on the part of that fictitious self or ego that says that all of these things are true; "What I determine to be true, is true, because I think it is. I think in this fashion so therefore that is how the world is, the world out there and there is 'me' and I know what is going on and I am in a relationship with that world." However, Buddhism wants us to review and deconstruct that idea in order to look at this approach with more clarity. We want to see both the potency in this approach as well as the devastating effect that thought can have on us. This is something important to be explored.

In what the Buddhists call a "deluded state," we can produce all manner of thoughts that are untrue. We need to contend with the notion that we are thinking beings. This thinking human being is subject to all manner of illusions. One of the biggest illusions is to think that to be oneself, to be "me" or "I" must signify that "I" have to stand apart from everything else. Much of the confusion with regard to this notion has not necessarily come about due to the conflict between oneself in terms of sensory stimuli and our psychological responses. Rather, the process has been disrupted due to excessive thinking and conceptual elaborations. Therefore, in almost all circumstances, it is very difficult for us to think without there being some degree of distortion and illusion.

To be happy, we must let go of the notion that the agency or agent has to be something that stands apart from everything that it experiences. Like everything else that we perceive and experience about the world, both within and without, the self is also capable of executing all of its desires and intentions without having to think of itself as being totally in charge. In Buddhism, we need to understand that we are part of the fabric of experience. This is what the five *skandhas*, the five collections or aggregates that formulate our individual personality truly represent in terms of the self. I will briefly discuss the skandhas in more detail in the next chapter. In Buddhism, we are taught to understand ourselves as five skandhas and these constitute all of the things that we have discussed so far, including the physical embodiment of oneself, being situated in a particular environment, having a certain racial background, being of a certain age, having been born in a particular place, and so on. All of these go toward contributing to one's notion of one's own self. To be clear, there is nothing wrong with that.

From the Buddhist perspective, if we recognize all of this, we have a better chance of finding happiness than if we did not recognize it. In other words, if we do not believe that our involvement with our senses, physical experiences, memory, and perceptual experiences matters in relation to our sense of well-being, we can limit our access to happiness. To be a part of life, we cannot work against our surroundings or operate apart from it. The Buddhist notion of the five skandhas as a description of the individual in terms of a self suggests that whatever sense of self that we have and believe we are is embedded in our own environment. This is the fundamental Buddhist insight because the whole notion of the mastery of self that Buddhism promotes is extremely important. It cannot come from denying any or all of these aspects. The concept of progress and self-cultivation on the spiritual path will not manifest from a self-styled amorphous or nebulous concept of the self that is divided from the world and separate to one's experiences.

In Buddhism, we wish to cultivate certain traits and predispositions. These are important as they become constituents of the self, which is even more reason to think about self-cultivation. In order to be truly happy according to Buddhism, many Buddhist texts such as the works of Abhidharma literature speak about cultivating qualities or attributes within oneself. This makes sense because without these attributes, there would be a diminished self. From the Buddhist point of view therefore, all of the qualities and attributes that we are instructed to develop are seen as a way to construct our own sense of self in a manner that is more enriching. Even though the construction of the self is seen as relative, it is still absolutely worthwhile.

According to Buddhism, since we were born, we are constantly constructing our own notion of the self. We may not be able to determine the direction that we go in life most of the time, but nevertheless, we are always in the process of constructing our own notion of the self. Therefore, when we come to the Dharma, we try to review how we have been going about developing ourselves and our sense of self. In terms of constructing who we think we should become, in order to be happy, it is dependent on the individual who has put effort into building themselves up.

Constructing a self is not an issue, it is important to have a strong sense of self. When we put effort into ourselves, we can move forward. That is the Buddhist view. If we do this, we can potentially, in a real sense, be completely transformed. Striving and wanting to attain higher and higher levels of being is something that is emphasized in Buddhism. This means that "being the self" is not something fixed. We construct and reconstruct our notions of who we are or what we wish to be and our notion of self or identity changes.

This corresponds to the Buddhist notion of paths and stages where one is unfolding as an individual, overcoming certain cumbersome or degrading aspects of oneself as one grows, and acquiring new capabilities, capacities, powers, insights, and directions in life. Buddhism emphasizes that this is how we increasingly find happiness. It does not arise from thinking that happiness must come from denying everything that we experience, finding a fixed core inner self. We cannot suddenly, and for no apparent reason, be liberated or freed of all sorrow, anguish, and suffering. If there were something in us which went beyond what we have described thus far in terms of our qualities and attributes and these went beyond the human capacity to articulate and express, even then, the sense of one's own "beingness" can only find expression through the qualities and attributes that one has been able to develop.

So far in section four, I have spoken about happiness in terms of how Buddhism and also other thinkers see it. I have not spoken about Christianity because in Buddhism, we do not have the concept of God. The notion of happiness as discussed in Buddhism does not have much to do with a concept of a divine being. I spoke about Plato's view of harmony, how all of the diverse elements in the human being should come together in order to have the experience of happiness. Plato thought that one should do this by exercising reason or rationality. Plato valued reason above everything else and therefore, there was the downplaying of the senses. There was also the belief that senses lead to deception and are unreal.

In Buddhism, there is the recognition that senses are deceptive, that they deceive us, but on the other hand, senses are not to be ignored. Our sensory impressions are not to be downplayed. In tantric Buddhism, there is the concept of "pure perception" where whatever we see, hear, smell, taste, and touch becomes self-liberated. The concepts would not make any sense if we did not pay attention. The Buddha himself spoke about the importance of paying attention to the senses and through doing so, developing a sense of our "self." Realization of the deceptive nature of the senses reveals both their deceptive nature but also something about oneself and how inevitable it is to have to deal with the senses. Even an enlightened being would still have to see, hear, smell, taste, and touch. Therefore, it is about understanding the senses and doing so in relation to oneself so that it leads to freedom and consequently, an experience of happiness.

I have also discussed the notion of struggle and wanting to achieve in life. Simply remaining content with whatever we are or have is not the Buddhist view. Nietzsche said that struggle is a necessity in terms of injecting meaning into life. However, the injection of meaning in life and the attainment of happiness should not be equated. One could be totally unhappy and still lead a meaningful life. Even if one's life is full of misery but has been worthwhile, what is wrong with that? From the Buddhist viewpoint, we struggle, life is full of strife, we do our best, and still, there can be some form of harmony with the conflict, the resolution of various elements within oneself. We may still fight with disharmonies, but that is no cause for despair or for thinking that happiness is out of reach simply because life is full of struggle, strife, and pain.

Chapter Twenty-five

Happiness and Our Karmic Disposition

Thus far, I have stated that happiness is important in Buddhism because suffering is taken seriously. If we did not take suffering seriously, happiness would not be an issue. Unlike many other religious traditions, in Buddhism, the concept of happiness arises even in terms of afterlife experiences or the attainment of buddhahood or enlightenment. In order to attain enlightenment, one must also attain happiness. One aspires toward having a good rebirth, which means a rebirth that is filled with happiness rather than sorrow, misery, and suffering. For example, the Buddhist notion of heaven is also related to the experience of happiness in the afterlife. If one goes to Buddhist heaven, one also experiences happiness there. In other words, all of the things that we are supposed to be experiencing in all of these contexts have come from our understanding of suffering as a human being.

Buddhism says that all different forms of pain are experienced by varieties of sentient creatures, meaning animals and humans alike. However, only human beings have the opportunity to understand suffering. This is why, in Buddhism, we say that human beings are gifted with an opportunity that is unique. Animals experience suffering in the sense of experiencing a tremendous amount of pain in varieties of ways, both physical and mental. In Buddhism, it is said that animals also experience mental pain apart from physical pain, unlike the view of Descartes. Descartes said that animals do not experience pain and some scientists have also argued that the pain animals experience is different from that of human beings. Nevertheless, from the Buddhist perspective, they do experience both physical and mental pain but they do not know what happiness is or have the opportunity to deal with their pain and suffering in the way that human beings are capable of doing. This is because through the understanding of suffering, human beings can understand how to attain happiness.

I stated that in Buddhism, happiness is seen as a goal and it is something that we aim toward. It need not be seen purely in terms of what we are expected to experience right now, but something that we aim for and that we need to work toward. This is because according to Buddhism, if we did not have to work for happiness, it would not be considered happiness. This is because elation and pleasure are not happiness. This is a fundamental Buddhist point of view that we need to recognize.

Therefore, happiness is something that we have to aim toward and cultivate. Pleasure and elation are experienced, but happiness is something that we can cultivate and can become accustomed to over a period of time. In order to experience happiness, we need to have many different ingredients. Happiness does not come from one single thing, whether it is drugs, a certain experience, or having performed a particular action. Happiness comes from having the wisdom, having developed self-understanding, developing comprehension of how one is related to the world that one lives in, and the responsibility that one has as a living human being to the world and each other in terms of our dealings with other human beings and other sentient beings. The cultivation of happiness comes from this understanding.

I mentioned in the previous chapter that in Buddhism, as a way to attain happiness, we have to understand who one is, who the individual is that is trying to have the experience of happiness. This is extremely important because we usually believe that the experience of pleasure is happiness and that pain is unhappiness. We ordinarily think, "If I have a good experience, it will lead to happiness." Most of the time, we have this notion about happiness. This is what we associate with happiness even in the context of Buddhist meditation practice because we expect that meditation will make us feel good; "If my meditation makes me feel good and produces certain experiences of euphoria or pleasure, this is a good thing and means that my meditation is working. If my meditation does not produce an immediate feeling of bliss, euphoria, or pleasure, my meditation is not working. The meditation is not delivering what I am expecting. I am trying to have pleasure the natural way, by doing meditation but I am not getting the high that I expected. In the beginning, I thought there was a hint of that, but it vanished very quickly. Now all I experience is discomfort in my joints, a sore neck, and a very disturbed mind." According to Buddhism, it is extremely important that we pay attention to our responses in meditation. Paying attention to our sensory experiences hinges on that and provides us valuable insight into the interconnection of the senses and our mind and psychophysical states.

It is explained in an extremely comprehensive manner by Professor Peter Harvey in the book, *The Selfless Mind: Personality, Consciousness and Nirvana in Early Buddhism.* In Buddhism, the notion of selflessness is connected to this idea, that the sensory object or the sense stimuli, the sense organs, and the mind are interconnected. The sense consciousness, sense organ, and sense object, are all interconnected. Due to this interconnection, our notion of our own sense of self is contingent on the kind of experiences that we have. This means that we cannot have an experience that is unmediated by consciousness coming into contact with sense objects, conscious and non-conscious physical objects that then produce certain experiences of pain, pleasure, and so on. The complexity of the physical and mental factors involved means that there is complexity involved in how we experience things. One of the first steps that we can take, according to Buddhist teachings, is to understand that there is complexity involved and to recognize that our tendencies are not simply a result of a linear process but a complex one. We cannot definitively say that "a particular kind of experience" produces "a particular kind of resultant experience," in terms of our senses. If we pause to think about it, we will see that it is not as simple as that.

Considering this further, we begin to see that our own identity and sense of self is shaped, not entirely, but to a large extent, by how we relate to our sensory experiences. For this reason, in Buddhism, this is seen as the first step toward understanding how pain, pleasure, suffering, and happiness arise in human beings. This is the reason that the individual human being in terms of their own perception of themselves as an individual is then contingent on their sensory experiences. They cannot be seen as separate. We do not have a preexisting self somehow thrown into the world who subsequently has no choice but to deal with the world that is also there as definitive. Rather, the self and the world are mutually transforming. This is the Buddhist view, and it is through developing this understanding that we can be freed-up to attain greater and greater unconditional happiness.

Even though we believe in life before the present incarnation, nevertheless, we do not think that the self that we are born with is something fixed and unattached to all of its experiences. The moment we are born, the moment our sense organs begin to mature, as the Buddhists would describe it, we become part of the world in which we have taken birth. In Buddhism, we do not think of the self as somehow preexisting in a fixed state. Dispositionally, there is a sense of karmic inheritance from a former existence but this is also mutable.

To reiterate, whether we are describing the individual in terms of having a self or as part of the world that the individual inhabits, it is spoken of in terms of factors or dharmas, as I have discussed throughout this book. There are many physical factors, lateral factors, and mental factors. Everything that we see is made up of these physical and mental factors or elements. These elements that go into constituting or forming our body/mind complex are not different from the elements that go into giving the form or appearance of the phenomena that the material world assumes. This is seen as being a very important step in our understanding because it actually goes toward cultivating what in Buddhism is called wisdom. As I mentioned, this is an extremely important aspect to consider as part of our ability to attain a more abiding sense of happiness.

From this point of view, there are dispositional factors or elements that we have brought into this world from before we were born. Even our innate tendencies are made up of the factors and elements. As soon as we are born, the innate tendencies may remain in place but this does not signify that the innate tendencies would be immune to outside influences. The innate tendencies are elements just like the elements that one comes into contact with post-birth, after taking incarnation, assuming a physical body, and developing the sensory organs, et cetera. As soon as we come in contact with the outside world, become engaged with it, and begin to replenish ourselves with varieties of sensual experiences, these innate tendencies then become intermingled. The outside influences and innate tendencies do not operate independently of each other but rather, in unison.

According to Buddhism, the innate tendencies or "karmic imprints," should not be seen as completely separate to the external environment. We cannot say that due to our nature, we cannot change, that there are certain things about human beings that make any form or reform impossible. Otherwise, as Buddhists, we would not be able to aspire toward enlightenment or buddhahood. With the recognition that we have innate tendencies, we realize change is possible, we can transform and develop, but nevertheless, it is not something that we can do overnight or so easily. Therefore, from a Buddhist perspective, effort is required. We need to train ourselves and build insight and understanding.

When we are aspiring to greater happiness, from a Buddhist perspective, we acknowledge that we have things working against us both externally, situationally, and in relation to our own nature, both physically and mentally. These can act as barriers to attaining some pleasures and a more abiding happiness. With regard to normal pleasures, we are being thwarted much of the time due to external situations or the internal constitution of our physical and mental capacity. In other words, we desire far more than we are able to satisfy. It can be extremely difficult for us to attain abiding or pervasive happiness because there are personal tendencies that can get in the way of fulfilling even some attainable desires. It is a misconception to believe that Buddhism teaches the idea of not desiring. Rather, it says that we should be careful about what and how we desire. The desire to attain an abiding pervasive happiness can be difficult from a Buddhist perspective because it requires a depth of insight and reflection, without which, obstacles within and without will thwart our attempts, at least to some degree. Buddhism does acknowledge that struggle is part of human life and many of our problems come from having to struggle. We struggle because there are things that are outside of us and inside us that clash.

Sometimes, we wish for something within ourselves and that which we desire is unavailable or alternatively, it is present but we are unable to obtain it. This is one simple example of a conflict.

Alternatively, there may be many different things in the external world and we want to achieve them all so we are thrown into a state of confusion. We may not know what to pursue, what actions to perform, what we need to experience in pursuit of happiness and in order to lead a fulfilling life. The lack of availability to satisfy some of our desires can also cause conflict. According to Buddhism, we do not have two selves, a higher self and a lower self, or a good self and a bad self. From a Buddhist perspective, even when we believe that we have a good side and a bad side, when we believe that we have this dual nature, the good side and bad side are single distinct sides or entities. There can be many different conflicting voices happening within oneself. There is a cacophony of sounds form both "sides." Whatever bad side we believe in, it will have many faces, personas, and identities. With the so-called good side, the various aspects are also clamoring for attention, saying, "You must hear me. You have to pay attention to what I have to say." As I have discussed, there are many factors, elements, or dharmas. We are not as simple as two sides of a coin.

It is inevitable that as human beings, we are going to experience conflict because life has complexity. Even our conscious states, physical embodiment, and experience of the material world are made up of so many elements. We may ordinarily have the idea that we are some form of machine, an input/output machine or a pain/pleasure machine; if we simply work out how the machine works, subsequently, we would have pleasure all of the time and not worry about pain or suffering. From a Buddhist point of view, it cannot be like that because of the complexity of so many elements being involved.

From a Buddhist perspective, knowing that we are multidimensional human beings and that the world is also complex will bring some form of simplicity and clarity to our lives. We have many kinds of desires. An essential feature of desire is that when we desire things from a samsaric perspective, we become monofocal and zoom in. Almost everything else fades into the background and the object of desire begins to assume center stage and becomes the object of our focus. In light of our discussion thus far, this automatically points to the idea that we are seeing the world differently to how it actually exists. In Buddhism, when we say we have to think in terms of elements or factors, this is also referred to as "arising phenomena." "Arising phenomena" means that all of the elements are not fixed within themselves and are mutually interacting, influencing each other, and so on. When we desire, we grasp and fixate on the object, be it animate or inanimate, and that becomes our personal, less dimensional, and potentially more distorted reality.

According to the Buddhist way of thinking, this encourages ignorance or bewilderment. Developing this kind of understanding builds wisdom into the nature of reality and affects our ability to experience happiness. When we pay attention to our sensory stimuli, we can see how our mind simply chooses to pursue certain things at the exclusion of others. While being selective and discerning is important, it is also important to pay attention to the effect that blocking experience can have on our well-being. In Buddhism, it is said that we would not be able to function if we were open to everything, all of the stimuli. How we seek to apprehend our desires can bring up our strong feelings, emotions, and judgments. It is not only the emotions that come in its wake but also the judgmentalism that goes with it, which then causes the proliferation of conceptual proliferation and conceptual elaboration, discursive thoughts. The mind becomes very disturbed.

However, if we learn to experience and deal with pain/pleasure on the sensory levels, we will then be in a better position to know how to overcome suffering and cultivate happiness. Even on the very basic level, the experience of pain and pleasure through our senses as experienced through our desires is something that we can work with. We are not condemned to experience life in relation to our human nature, that of invariably experiencing endless pain and pleasure. By developing some insight into how we can experience sensory input without desire, we can see our many desires more clearly.

Though there are many kinds of desires, broadly speaking, we can put them into two categories. If you keep the notion of the factors or elements in mind, we have good desires and bad desires and by cultivating the good desires, we learn to overcome the bad ones, those that diminish us. By overcoming the bad desires, we experience greater pleasure with that which we do not normally find pleasure in experiencing. Through developing awareness, we can wean ourselves off pursuing pleasure from the things that endlessly result in our frustration. Buddhism teaches that many of the things that we think are pleasurable do not lead to pleasure; there is no real causal or strict causal relationship in terms of our desire for a specific pleasure and the object that is desired to satisfy that pleasure. An object can be unobtainable and if obtained, may not create pleasure or it may be less pleasurable than we expected, it may create aversion, or we may become immune to the stimulation so that the intensity of the pleasure has to be increased through overindulgence, et cetera. Desires can create new problems that did not exist before the desire was ignited. For example, overindulgence and insatiability can be very hurtful for ourselves and others who may be hurt through our own reckless behavior and so on. If there were a real causal relationship between our desire for an object and the object itself, we should then feel satisfied and we would be satisfied in the same manner each time. As we know, we are not. Therefore, unchecked and misdirected desire leaves us open to such experiences as disappointment, insatiable hunger, frustration, resentment, anger, and so on.

When we pay attention to the senses and our desires, we begin to realize that it is possible to learn to desire things in an intelligent manner rather than simply leaving everything to our own instincts and simply pursuing our innate tendencies. Even though these innate tendencies and our habitual modes of operation are well entrenched, they can be dealt with and managed. In order to make worthwhile change, we need to develop our understanding of desires that uplift us and desires that demean us. We can use good desires in order to overcome bad desires so that we can have good forms of pleasure and less of the bad experiences of pleasure. We would then desire the things that are more enriching and fulfilling more than those that create frustration.

Buddhism believes in a changing self, thus, it is seen as very possible to educate or teach the self to learn to be happier and to reach greater potential. Change or transformation of the self is more obtainable through learning how to experience effectively through our sensory fields and how to conduct ourselves well through our actions and interactions with others. The senses influence us so much. They can distract us and lead us astray. This is the Buddhist view because we usually fall victim to our own pursuit of pleasures and simply seek some kind of release, temporary relief, or a feeling of pleasure. Sometimes, when we are doing meditation, this is what we expect. Instead, it is better to think of Buddhism as a method or way of life that teaches us how to be a better human being so that we will experience a sense of pervasive happiness and an overall sense of well-being and satisfaction with life.

We ordinarily believe that if something makes us feel good, it must be good. If something makes us feel bad, even slightly, then it is bad. If we have this attitude, we are doing the opposite of what we need to do in order to attain happiness. Happiness does not come through avoidance or aversion and attraction or excessive desire. Buddhism emphasizes that all pleasures are ephemeral. It is going to change. However, life with some discomfort or experience of pain does not necessarily mean that the individual does not then have the experience of happiness.

From the Buddhist point of view therefore, the ultimate happiness is the aim, but we can learn to have an experience of happiness by learning how to deal with our day-to-day experiences of pain and pleasure through our senses. We do meditation in order to help us with that idea, helping us to see that our own immediate experience is not actually as immediate as we think. Rather, we are seeing and experiencing things in certain ways because of past experiences; we have taught ourselves that particular scents, flavors, and people are enjoyable and others are despicable and revolting. If there were some link between the object of enjoyment and our own desire for these things, a causal relationship, then one should be able to enjoy all of these things in the same manner. However, it does not happen this way because there is a gap between our sensory experience and our own feeling of satisfaction or dissatisfaction of having that sensory experience.

Our thoughts give shape to how much we are going to find something unbelievably enticing and irresistible or how averse and unbearable we find it. The same object can be revolting and enticing at the same time. It is because there is thought that steps in. This is also why in Buddhism, when we speak about the desires, sensory experiences, and so on, we are referring to the self, the person, because our responses are personalized. Even if our preferences are in accordance with society, fashion trends, et cetera, they are supported and perpetuated by the self.

In Buddhism, the self or the person is mentally and physically constituted through the five skandhas or aggregates, as mentioned in the previous chapter. The first skandha is *rupa* in Sanskrit, meaning form. This includes the body, the one that has senses, has eyes, nose, ears, and so on. It describes sensory experience and what we are or become as a result of that. The second is feeling or sensation, *vedana* in Sanskrit, which refers to all physical sensations of pleasure, pain, and neutral sensations that we feel. The third is perception, *samjna* in Sanskrit, the perception and discernment aspect that comes from the thought process that ensues from the sensory experience—the sense organ and its corresponding sense object. The fourth is disposition or mental formation, *samskara* in Sanskrit, which are mental dispositions meaning all our concepts and thoughts from the mundane to the sublime. These mental tendencies can also be the cause for volitional actions to occur. The fifth is consciousness, *vjinana* in Sanskrit, which refers to being conscious of or having awareness of the first four skandhas. That is, it refers to consciousness in relation to what we encounter through the sense objects such as the experience of sights, sounds, et cetera and also what arises or what we encounter via our mental objects and events such as concepts and thoughts.

As I mentioned, in Buddhism, the self is described in this fashion; the desiring person is five skandhas, an aggregate that has mental and physical consciousness and is aware in terms of what has been experienced. The experiences that we have through the senses are not pure sensory experiences because they are vitiated by our own samskaras, the innate tendencies, our human nature. Different people have different personalities, habits, and so on. We are born with some of these dispositionally and physically, according to Buddhism, and they then become reinforced in relation to our sensory and other experiences and the element of judgment that we perform. The combination of these aggregates brings about the sense of self and how we place ourselves in the world. The types of desires that we have and our level of need to satisfy them are related to our skandhas.

From the Buddhist point of view therefore, we are trying to

reeducate the five skandhas, reconstructing the five skandhas in order to attain happiness. There are many different types of desires to be aware of. We desire certain things in themselves; we do not desire certain things because having them would then lead to the satisfaction of some other forms of desires. Some thinkers have spoken about terminal desires and instrumental forms of desires. Having terminal desires means that you do not desire the object because having it will then lead you to find satisfaction in something else. Rather, that object itself is what is desired. With regard to instrumental forms of desire on the other hand, we desire one thing because if we obtain it, we will then get something else. A great deal of our pleasure seeking behavior is geared toward satisfying instrumental forms of desires because we believe that if we do certain things, our life will be complete and full. An example is material pursuit; "If I have a million dollars, my life with be complete," or "If I live in a big mansion, my life would be total." Finding the mansion is not the real objective. The real objective is that life will be full and complete. Other terminal types of desires include, desiring nirvana, liberation, or enlightenment. We desire buddhahood for its own sake because attaining it is fulfillment itself. It personifies the very embodiment of all that is good and sublime. There is nothing else that we believe we are going to get from attaining that state. There are also pleasure producing or inducing desires and non-pleasure producing or inducing desires, hedonistic and non-hedonistic forms of desires.

We do not always desire things that are pleasurable. Sometimes, we desire those that are not pleasurable, even in normal circumstances. Some people have high ideals. Many people sacrifice happiness and pursue moral excellence and some may even sacrifice their lives, even without desiring eternal life in heaven. We desire different things and not all forms of desires bring pleasure. There are people who sacrifice their own lives for the sake of others, with no feeling of gaining any benefit. A parent sacrificing their own life to protect their infant is very likely not thinking about glory. The desire to want to protect the child is just that, it does not lead to anything else.

In Buddhism, it is not said that we must pursue only one or two of these different types of desires at the expense of pursuing the others. Buddhism says that we can pursue all of these kinds of desires but we have to be intelligent about it. Our only problem is that we have often not approached desire intelligently. Wisdom comes from learning how to balance the diversity of our inner elements and tendencies. Learning how to balance these is the aim or goal and this will bring happiness. However, we cannot simply attempt to uproot certain aspects of ourselves in a drastic manner because they may be deep-seated. In Buddhism, our human nature is not considered fixed or unchanging but nonetheless, it is deep-seated. Even though we have aspects and elements that are very much rooted in our biological makeup, these are not completely beyond reconditioning. Also, with regard to our psychological and spiritual aspects and elements, they too can transform and change.

Nevertheless, some of these elements are part of our own makeup or personality and therefore, they are part of our own nature. There is no real conflict in saying that there are certain things that are innate and part of our own nature and saying that we are expected to work with them and overcome the limitations within us. This is what we aim for in Buddhism. We do this through managing our senses, learning about how our senses operate, how our desires arise, and the complex relationship that exists between our multifarious desires and the sensory experiences and the element of our thoughts—the samjna conception or how we judge, assert, and evaluate things.

In Buddhism, it is not only the sensory aspects and the desire element that we have to think about when we speak about pain, pleasure, suffering, and happiness in the "self" equation, but we should also clearly look into the role that our thoughts play in how we go about experiencing in life. From the Buddhist point of view, as human beings, our desires are not completely thoughtless and neither are our sensory experiences. Our emotions arise at the juncture of the sensory experiences, desires, and thoughts. When they all come together, emotions arise, and we have the emotion of joy, love, anger, and so on. We desire different things related to what we experience through our sensory pleasures and these come about when of all these different elements come together.

Chapter Twenty-six

Happiness: a Comprehensive Perspective on Fulfillment

Buddhists have specific interests in knowing what happiness is all about. "Happiness" in Buddhism is not the same as what many people mean by happiness, such as the simple pursuit of pleasure. I have thus far been attempting to present the Buddhist concept of happiness in a manner that spells out what "happiness" means and puts it into context. I have briefly presented some Western alternative and similar views of happiness to help compare and contrast the different philosophies and to understand what Buddhists mean by happiness.

The Buddhist notion of happiness is very distinct from the other theories that I have alluded to. It is unique because in Buddhism, there is a comprehensive approach to dealing with this idea of happiness from perceptual, ethical, and transcendental perspectives. We have been focusing on the perceptual aspect developed through the senses—seeing, hearing, smelling, et cetera. Understanding this allows us to develop self-knowledge.

Buddhism does not believe in somewhat obsessively narrowly focusing on one thing when it comes to the pursuit of happiness. As we know, as human beings, we always attempt to find something or one particular thing that will make us happy; "If I have this particular experience that I am yet to experience, I will be happy," or "If I can just have some real understanding of what it is that I need to understand, I will be happy." It could be something material, empirical, transcendental, et cetera, that will supposedly make us feel good, liberate us, or allow us to have an overwhelming, perfect sense of self-fulfillment and happiness. From a Buddhist perspective, this is not the way to go about pursuing happiness. This is our usual approach, believing that there is one single thing that will fix everything. As I have discussed, Buddhism recommends that we pay attention to our sensory field, sensory stimuli, sensory responses, pain/pleasure responses, and thought processes in order to understand how we currently experience things, giving us the insight into how to experience happiness.

To reiterate, the "self" according to Buddhism, is not something fixed, but nevertheless, it has innate tendencies, capacities, and abilities. From the Buddhist point of view, not everything that is innate is bad or a distraction to our spiritual path. Whatever is in our nature is part of our often deep-seated tendencies. We find that some are good and some are not so good. We have different forms of desires and have experiences of pain and pleasure, all of which need to be discerned and managed. We can learn and encourage some types of pleasures, those that are self-enhancing and wean ourselves from other kinds that are disturbing or demeaning.

There needs to be a notion of agency in order for us to access our capacity to manage our desires and increase our happiness. Without the notion of agency, we would not have any idea of how to go about approaching this. The self has many elements that run extremely deeply into one's own psyche and being. Some of the tendencies may be biologically rooted and others have a more psychic orientation. The self is not unitary but nevertheless, it sustains uniformity in the way in which it perceives and executes things and through engagement with various physical, verbal, and mental activities. Buddhism emphasizes all "three gates" of body, speech, and mind. We have the tendency to exaggerate the importance of one of the three gates. Some believe that the physical aspect is paramount and that it defines us as human beings, our achievements, the difference that we make to the world through our physical actions. Others concentrate on the verbal. Everything that we express linguistically can be seen as a text, the reading or misreading of the text. Others believe that "everything is in the mind—everything."

From the Buddhist viewpoint, human beings take action physically, verbally, and mentally. To put it simply, we are acting beings. Even when our body is not moving, our lips are moving. If our lips are not moving, our mind is moving, et cetera. Every time an action happens, from the Buddhist point of view, some form of imprint is created. When we say an imprint is created we might automatically think about karma and we could come to the conclusion that all karma is somehow mental. But Buddhism speaks about physical, verbal, and mental karmic imprints. Therefore, the physical karmic imprint is physically imprinted, a verbal karmic imprint is verbally imprinted, and a mental karmic imprint is mentally imprinted, all karmically. Combined, these may go into creating certain preconditions for the next incarnation to develop certain tendencies from the moment of birth. Therefore, in Buddhism, we do not automatically assume that all karmic imprints are mental. We speak about physical, verbal, and mental karma and their respective karmic imprints.

There is a comprehensive way to look at how this works in Buddhism. Understanding the dharmas, factors, or elements allows us to think of ourselves and our behavior in multidimensional terms. Buddhist ethics are contingent on these three aspects of our behavior; physical, verbal, and mental, how we use our body, what we do with it, how we experience things through the body, what we say, how we say certain things, verbal acts, and what we think about and how we conceptualize about certain things. The three are types of actions according to Buddhism, because they are actions that create karma. Therefore, the notion of morality or ethics and happiness or lack of happiness become intertwined and are relevant to the discussion on the Buddhist notion of morality and ethics and the notion of morality and happiness. Some may believe that morality and happiness have no relationship with each other and that happiness involves desire. Some say that even to have desire is immoral. However, in Buddhism, it is not seen in this way. In our effort to reach the optimum level of what a human being is able to achieve, our aspiration to lead a fulfilling life through our moral endeavors and aspirations to have a happy life must coincide. They will coincide if we think about the three aspects, what we do physically, verbally, mentally, in other words, how we engage with others.

I have already said that in Buddhism, we do not think of the self or ego as a free-floating, disconnected, discrete, or atomic entity. Rather, we see ego as embedded in its own environment and surroundings. Therefore, it is inevitable that the agent has to interact with others through these three gates of body, speech, and mind. This is how we engage with others and without them, there would be no sense of agency and no sense of self. Therefore, the self has to have physical, verbal, and mental engagement with the outside world, other human beings, sentient creatures, and so on. When we are interacting with others, we allow ourselves to be deceived and to personalize our experiences through the senses, personalizing our reactions to everything that we experience verbally, mentally, and physically. Based on our discussion in terms of our senses, the Buddhist understanding of ethics or morality is based on what we experience through our senses, not purely in terms of our karmic baggage.

There is a popular but incorrect notion that Buddhists believe that as human beings, we come into this world and have a certain karmic load that we carry with us and everything that we experience or do is based on that. Rather, it is believed that what we experience is based on how we experience through our senses. Further, what we experience through our senses is colored by the karmic baggage. So the karmic baggage interferes but it is not the sole reason for how we experience things. Therefore, in Buddhism, we take very seriously what we are experiencing through our senses and how we react. Our behavior is based on pursuing what we think is pleasurable and fleeing from that which we believe is painful. This is how we normally physically behave. For example, if we believe that we are unable to avoid certain painful things, we may respond with different forms of resistance such as seeking retaliation, having fear, behaving in an aggressive fashion, or having other types of responses.

In Buddhism, every act can be seen as fresh or in some way new, different to past experiences. Nonetheless, there are a variety of influences coming from one's own innate tendencies, with karmic baggage intermingled within the freshness contained within an experience. We should not downplay the role of newness and freshness in an experience. In Buddhism, morality is not seen as purely based on the idea of our action being brought about by a single dominant factor, such as our reasoning capacity or our emotions. In Buddhism, it is always seen as a mixture. How we act is not purely based on our emotions, sensory experiences, or thoughts, but a combination of all of them. When the different elements and influences all come together, we act. They may come together in perfect proportion. At other times, one element may predominate. Sometimes, we may be thinking and conceptualizing more than feeling and at other times, the senses may be predominant. Buddhism says that all of these experiences can be integrated and harmonious. Sometimes we will be thinking more clearly than at other times and sometimes we may not be thinking so very clearly. Sometimes our thinking, emotions, and feelings that arise from our sensory experiences may be in conflict. They may not gel and this may create inner tension. Conflict can arise when our thinking mind is saying one thing and our sensory experiences are saying something else. This type of discordance can generate emotional conflict due to the clash between the thoughts that are going through our mind and the strong feelings that are based on our experiences.

The Buddhist notion of morality or ethics is based on learning to harmonize elements that have become disparate. It is important to look at all aspects of our human experience in order to encourage more cohesiveness between the various elements so that they are working together instead of working against each other. This applies to Buddhist morality or ethics because whatever deeds we perform would need to be accompanied by the relevant emotions, feelings, and appropriate thought all coming together. This includes our underlying intention and motivation. With such harmony and integration, it would be a more moral action. This is why in Buddhism, morality, ethics, and happiness go together.

We can make a distinction between morality and ethics. In Buddhism, we do believe in moral education in relation to the attainment of happiness. It is believed that first we have to be educated in moral sensitivity. We have to sensitize ourselves in terms of moral sensibility and then we can develop and embody ethical goodness. In relation to morality, Buddhism says that we do not have to first be ethical, exude ethical goodness, and have all of the virtuous qualities to begin with. We can learn to be morally sensitive and attempt to do the right thing, such as not taking life unnecessarily, not cheating or lying, and doing this without compunction. In this way, over time, we can exude the ethical goodness that comes less and less from trying and more from simply being.

I spoke about the concept of striving, struggle, various elements, and a sense of goodness all residing within and also the idea of our different sides internally fighting with each other. Both the good sides and the bad sides can be fighting amongst themselves. Morality relates to attempting to work with the inner conflict and lack of balance between the many elements. Working with our situation allows us to learn how to behave physically, verbally, and mentally so that one aspect is not emphasized too much. For example, by refraining oneself, one can avoid physically harming or taking life from another sentient being. In the pursuit of not taking life, we may not have done anything physically, but we may have threatened it verbally. According to Buddhism, one must take note of this. Of course, a verbal threat is not the same as taking of life but it still all goes toward creating one's character and the person that one becomes. By taking note of all the elements, we can work toward a more harmonious approach that can build our character and develop a more inclusive ethic.

Buddhism does not believe in a soul, inner essence, or substantive ego. We think of the self in relation to the variety of attributes, qualities, and the quality of our character. On the spiritual path, all of these aspects become increasingly important as they combine to make us the individual that we are and the individual that we become. From a Buddhist point of view, this is essential work for an ordinary person in order to become a *mahasattva*, meaning, "great being." "Maha" means "great" and "sattva" means "being." The concept of bodhisattva is also similar.

The reason that these qualities and attributes are emphasized so much in Buddhism is that they are what make us great or not great. This is the Buddhist view and Buddhist ethics are based on this notion because through ethics, we become better human beings. Further, we become not only better human beings, but also happier human beings because we can practice morality and ethics in many different ways. We can practice morality and ethics without consideration for one's own happiness or we can practice it with the aspiration to attain happiness. In Buddhism, we should do the latter. Some people may believe that because one still has the desire to be happy, this is an inferior approach to morality. Some may see morality as being about duty, obligation, respect for others, and self-sacrifice and happiness is not something that one should be thinking about. However, in Buddhism, we believe that we can do both; truly great human beings who care for others can also think of themselves. This is the bodhisattva ideal in Mahayana Buddhism and that notion of the concurrence of virtue and happiness is also present in early Buddhism.

The idea that real virtue leads to happiness is extremely important in Buddhist thought. Virtue brings happiness and vice only brings misery and harm to others. Hurting others physically, verbally, and mentally only brings us misery. As it has been explained in Buddhist literature, we may bring misery to someone physically, verbally, or mentally for a period of time but particularly if we get into the habit of doing this, we bring misery to ourselves for the duration of our life, perhaps even into the next life. In modern terminology, we need to think in terms of who the victim is. Is it the person that I am shouting and screaming at and trying to harm? Or am I the victim when I become obsessed with this approach? Here, I am not referring to occasionally losing one's temper. When we become obsessive and it becomes part of our character and natural for us to wish to do harm, hurt, and torment, one should subsequently ask, "Is this making me happy? Is this happiness? Who is suffering, the person I am attempting to hurt, me, or both?"

I have already discussed that according to Buddhism, our thinking and emotions do not operate in two separate regions of the mind. It is often argued that emotions take place separately to thinking and rationality and that they do not meet. As I have discussed, it is the contrary. From a Buddhist point of view, they do meet and are generated by one another. They are different but cannot be totally separated. When we look at the human condition, we can see that we are the victims of our own actions—physical, verbal, and mental. This is extremely important to note. For example, when it comes to seeking to hurt or torment others, we may succeed in creating trauma for them but we cannot do this in isolation and remain personally unaffected by it. It will also be our trauma and the damage that we do to ourselves will cause a great deal of torment.

This is related to fixation. When we experience things through the senses, we automatically become drawn to certain things more than others, be they animate or inanimate. They can become an obsessive concern and almost everything else can be pushed into the background. When we become emotional and self-righteous, for example, this is exactly what is happening. When one is consumed with anger and jealousy, all of the other fantastic opportunities and possibilities that could have been present for one to enjoy have been removed. They have not only been taken away from oneself but also from the others that we are involved with. This can be all due to our tenacity and unwillingness to let go of our obsessions and desired outcomes. Through hanging on to things, obsessing and grasping, one small thing can take over and become a major preoccupation. It occupies the center stage and one's physical, verbal, and mental actions become centered on that. Whatever an individual does directly or indirectly may all be centered around one's main obsession. Verbally, one cannot stop speaking about it to one's friends, others, and even to oneself. One thinks about it all of the time, tormenting oneself, even though one may not wish to admit it to oneself or others.

From a Buddhist perspective therefore, when we reflect in this manner, we can see that it is not good or helpful to ourselves to be too obsessed and fixated. According to Buddhism, graspingness, obsession, and fixation are all anathema to happiness. Learning how not to be "graspy" and behave differently physically, verbally, and mentally, is to lead a more moral life. We are aiming toward the ethical qualities or virtues, the *paramitas* in Sanskrit, of generosity, discipline, patience, vigor, meditative concentration, and wisdom. In order to acquire these virtues, we first need to understand that we have to be moral, not because we actually have a choice. Perhaps it is not a true paradox, but it is somewhat paradoxical that we have no choice but to behave in this fashion. Behaving in a manner that is disruptive both to oneself and others and one that is hostile, angry, and vile either toward oneself or others, does not bring happiness. This is the case even though it may bring some relief, release, or exaltation in the immediate short-term but it is not a policy for generating happiness.

According to Buddhism, the personal benefit one might gain from behaving in a moral fashion does not take anything away from the integrity of the action that one has performed. This is because it still maintains its moral value. From the Buddhist point of view, it is more honest and better to think about morality in this fashion as opposed to how many people often view morality. For example, one may speak about altruism, helping others, and self-sacrifice but may be indulging in one's own neurosis, self-pity, and unhappiness. This does little or nothing to help anyone. One may speak about self-sacrifice but end up indulging in one's own sense of lack of self-trust; lack of trust in others and in everything else, even that which one should have trust in, such as one's own true nature.

Buddhism says that we can lead a moral life by facing up to ourselves in terms of our body, speech, and mind. We are inextricably linked to our own environment and do not operate outside of it. Something to remember is that our notion of individualism is tied to the values that our society promotes. In societies where that notion is promoted, people believe it. Where it is not promoted, people do not believe it. Buddhists also believe in individual salvation instead of collective salvation. We attain enlightenment at our own pace, individually, and therefore, what we do with our lives is based on that. We will be happy if we do not excessively obsess about things, while at the same time, genuinely care about ourselves and others, pay attention, and cultivate awareness.

In terms of what Buddhists mean by happiness and how we should lead our lives in order to gain happiness, we should be morally and ethically involved. We should be involved with everything, other human beings, the world, and do our best to excel ourselves. We should not be thinking that striving is bad or egoistic. Some have argued that if we strive, it is egotistical. Striving and self-obsession are very different and produce very different results. For example, self-obsessing while not striving, being unmotivated, and only thinking about oneself is a recipe for perpetuating unhappiness. It is important to contemplate and experience the value of morality and become morally sensitive and attuned. Morality should be based on the feeling of sensitivity and being attuned to others and the world. It is not about being inculcated with a set of rules. However, for the purpose of guidance, thought guidelines such as not lying, cheating, taking advantage of others, and learning certain moral maxims is very helpful and important.

Providing moral guidelines rather than rigid rules is ultimately about sensitizing ourselves to the notion that morality is good and not being moralistic is also good. There is a big difference between a moral person and a moralistic person and Buddhism emphasizes this point. It is like the difference between a smart person and a "smart alec." Being a moral person is very important but a moral person does not have to be moralistic, rigid, and judgmental, thinking, "I know how everybody should act under all circumstances. I can tell who is wrong and who is following the wrong path." From a Buddhist perspective, a moral person is someone who takes on responsibilities, cares, seeks to help, and believes that helping others is worthwhile not only for the other person but also for oneself. From a Buddhist perspective, it is believed that if we gain satisfaction from having helped others, the feeling of satisfaction, the sense that "I have done a good thing" goes toward our self-esteem. When we feel our self-esteem enriched, it is completely different from the sense of self-esteem that we may feel from having done harm to others, for example in terms of how we may have outwitted, outmaneuvered, or taken advantage of them. The boost that we gain from this kind of elation is nothing compared to the good feeling that we gain when have done something worthwhile in a true sense. These feelings will stay with us for a long time deep down and can deepen our conviction and belief in behaving in a way that matters and makes a positive difference. In contrast, if we have done something atrocious and we feel good, this does not go too deep, because there will be self-denial, justifications, rationalization, and all manner of psychological defensive movements in order to not admit to what we have done. Deep down, the sense of emptiness and insecurity will still be there.

From the Buddhist point of view, if we want to be happy, we need to feel a sense of richness in ourselves. This richness will come from leading a moral life because that morality does not have to be one that is based on something burdensome, such as something that we feel we must do but we do not like doing; "I don't want to be like this, but I have to. It's my moral duty." Buddhism says that we can learn to feel differently. There are many things that we dislike doing but we can learn to like doing them when we recognize their benefits. Also, there are many things that we like doing, but that we wish we did not like. Through Buddhist practice, we can educate ourselves about shortcomings and shortsightedness, what motivates us, and what causes inner conflict, et cetera. By doing so, we can build a new self. We can be reborn, in a manner of speaking, and behave in different ways that lead us to experience more and more happiness.

If real and ultimate happiness is our goal, discomforts or pain that we may feel at different stages of our lives can be better accommodated. They are often something that we cannot avoid but they do not need to derail our ultimate goals. Such accommodation increases our capability for experiencing happiness. We will experience more happiness because there is a real, more genuine sense of self-acceptance or self-accommodation. Thinking that we have to accept ourselves as we are is not what is meant by "self-acceptance" in Buddhism. In Buddhism, we speak about self-acceptance but it is self-acceptance that is inclusive of all our elements and factors, as we have discussed. It is not saying, "I have to accept myself the way I am," meaning, "I don't need to do anything. Either people can take me the way I am or they can lump it." According to Buddhism, this is not self-acceptance because it is superficial. We do not accept ourselves in that way. If we did accept ourselves in this way, we would reduce our awareness of how to approach self-improvement. Saying to ourselves, "I have to accept myself the way I am," is not going to make our issues go away. We accept ourselves in relation to taking the notion of *shila* or morality seriously. This, in itself, is contingent on our experiences of life through our senses and what is meant by "self" in terms of the five skandhas, et cetera. This type of desire for holistic self-improvement helps create opportunities for us to be truly generous and to become more and more able to be of genuine help to others.

Chapter Twenty-seven

Happiness, Morality, and Fulfilling Our Desires

In Buddhism, happiness has always been a major consideration and an integral part of the Buddhist tradition of how to conduct one's life, manage one's mind, and approach one's meditation practice. We know that happiness is what we desire and from the Buddhist point of view, the fact that we desire happiness is not something bad. According to Buddhism, happiness is important and beneficial when pursued in the most appropriate fashion. Earlier, I introduced the notions of terminal, instrumental, hedonistic, and non-hedonistic forms of desire. The different types of desire are satisfied in different ways and are not always associated with pleasure or a specific type of pleasure, such as physical or sensual desires.

These different desires are linked to different forms of pleasure. We do not have to think that it is only the terminal form of desire, such as seeking enlightenment, that we must seek or that only non-hedonistic or non-pleasure producing desires need to be satisfied. This is not the Buddhist view. We can attempt to satisfy all of the different kinds of desires in the pursuit of pleasure. We need to manage our pursuit of pleasure, if pleasure is sought in the right places and in the right manner by managing our desires in an appropriate fashion and by learning to balance these different forms of desires. Happiness relates to being intelligent about what we desire and using positive forms of desires to overcome negative forms of desires. Through this type of management, we can experience contentment and satisfaction.

We need to comprehend how to genuinely understand the Buddhist notion of happiness in order to satisfy and work with our desires. Perceptually, the pain/pleasure/neutrality experience is something that we need to pay attention to because this relates to our physical, verbal, and mental responses and behavior and sense of well-being. How do we respond to our experiences, be they painful, pleasurable, or neutral? On the sensory level, we try to notice things that we may not normally notice. By noticing more of what we are seeing, hearing, et cetera, we can build mindfulness and awareness of how we respond and experience things. In Buddhism, not noticing at the sensory level is known as the experience of non-experience. It is an experience of not having noticed even though the sound or object was present. All of our experiences bring about painful, pleasurable, and neutral feelings and experiences. Emotions arise based on the juncture of the sensory experiences, the thought processes that run through our mind, and our physical embodiment.

Our behavior is a part of what it means to be a human being, to be in this world. Therefore, the notion of morality is inevitable. It is not something that is imposed on us simply because we have a notion of society, culture, religion, or even the concept of spirituality. Rather, it is because we experience pain and pleasure. We experience joy and misery. Due to these experiences, we conceptualize about what is good and what is not good. These thought processes are constantly occurring. This is the unique Buddhist view.

Buddhism says that human beings are born innately moral; we have the innate capacity to do good or evil in terms of our karmic propensities and what is in our nature. Apart from this, the experience of pain and pleasure and seeing pain as bad and pleasure as good automatically impacts on our behavior. We normally think about pain and pleasure within our own experience of pain and pleasure and in terms of the pain and pleasure of others. Most human beings soon realize that constantly causing pain to others does not ultimately bring pleasure to oneself. There is an almost implicit recognition that doing helpful things for others is also helpful to oneself. In Buddhism, the idea that morality is inevitable is the accepted view. If we wish to live as a real human being, morality comes into it whether we like it or not. There is hardly any choice in terms of whether we should be moral or not. It is important to emphasize that morality should not be seen as solid or fixed. We need to develop a personal morality that is responsive to the unique circumstances that we are constantly presented with. In Buddhism, morality is seen as something that is open to each individual.

There is something compelling about the concept of morality and there is no contradiction in the idea that moral choices have to be made. Having choices is not in contradiction with morality. Even though it is almost in our nature to be moral or to behave in a considered manner, this does not mean that we do not have any choices. In order to establish the notion of morality, we need to understand that we have choice. We do not have to say that morality is irrelevant or that human beings are not moral by nature or that morality is something that has to be imposed by society. It would be more difficult to prove the relevance of morality by taking that path rather than saying that simply by being a human being in terms of our constitution and experience, biologically, psychologically, perceptually, and so on, the kind of person who experiences things in that fashion makes morality inevitable.

As Buddhism sees it, morality has to do with thinking about welfare. Morality is contingent on the notion of well-being; "Am I experiencing a sense of well-being? Am I able to bring well-being to others?" There is the understanding that bringing well-being to others also brings well-being to oneself. In other words, treating others fairly is self-enriching. There is the additional understanding that it is more likely that others will reciprocate such behavior. Further, if we treat people poorly, we are less inclined to expect them to treat us nicely in return. When we begin to think in terms of what brings pain and pleasure, we know that when we are able to communicate and connect with others in different ways, it brings a greater sense of well-being. When we feel devalued in different ways, this can develop feelings of lack of well-being. In other words, there is a chasm, gap, and separation. Separation or feeling separate from others can create and produce pain. All forms of suffering and unhappiness are contingent on the experience of pain.

Earlier, I discussed that we often do not consider the distinction between pain, suffering, and unhappiness. Separation and all of these forms of feelings produce a sense of not feeling well. According to Buddhism, when we see this, we realize that the only way that we can feel connected to others and gain this sense of well-being is to learn to be nice to others, to make an effort and take the initiative to approach rather than wait for others to be the initiators. If we take the initiative to make things better instead of waiting for others to do so, while there may always be some critics, we are likely to be verbally, physically, and mentally rewarded by others.

If we look at it in this manner, we can see how in Buddhism, we can link the notion of morality to the concept of happiness. This connection between morality and a sense of well-being, happiness, and pleasure is something that we have to relate to from a Buddhist point of view. Life is like a fabric with different strands of fibers woven together. They are all interconnected. We cannot have a moral life divorced from our pursuit of pleasure, satisfaction, and efforts to find that which we desire and desire very strongly.

Buddhism says that we can have all of these desires and even seek pleasure but we need to avoid approaching fulfilling our desires in a way that will make us feel worse than we did beforehand. We can learn to realize that if we take some initiative in life and not wait for others to do something for us, there is an immediate and long-term benefit that we can attain. We can perform physical gestures such as a handshake, gift, verbal compliments, and saying "thank you," as well as making people feel acknowledged and cared for. We can leave a good impression, with people feeling, "What a nice person." From the Buddhist point of view, thinking, "If I do this and that, people might then treat me in the same way" is not seen as immoral but rather a considered approach that promotes a sense of interconnection.

Therefore, it is in our best interests to be moral. If we behave in that fashion, we become ethical. To reiterate, the difference between being moral and ethical in this context is that with morality, we are striving and attempting to do what we believe is beneficial, wholesome, and conducive to our own well-being and that of others. In behaving with such consideration for others, we can develop natural ethics that spontaneously arise. The ethical notion is something that we embody; we come to embody this type of goodness.

In Buddhism, when we do things in a moral fashion, we are relating to our own mind. As I covered throughout section three, according to Buddhism, we have mental factors—positive mental factors and negative mental factors or mental events and these directly relate to our discussion of morality; the positive mental factors and the negative mental factors are something that we need to relate to when we are learning to be a moral agent. We should endeavor to cultivate the positive mental factors and learn to overcome negative mental factors. Positive mental factors and negative mental factors constitute various aspects within us. As I mentioned, there is a cacophony of sounds coming from both sides, the positive and the negative sides. In Buddhism, we attempt to learn to cultivate those that we need to cultivate in an effective manner and try to overcome the negative states of mind, negative tendencies, and negative predilections by working with the negative factors of the mind.

This is how we transform ourselves and learn to become an effective moral agent. We do not become an effective moral agent by being rigidly moralistic but rather by learning to work with the negative and positive states of mind and cultivating certain positive states of mind to overcome and diminish the negative. As we have discussed, by cultivating positive factors directly, one is also indirectly working with the negative states of mind or mental factors, the dharmas. It is extremely important to understand this notion of dharmas because it comes up again and again in Buddhist philosophy. To become a moral agent, we have to understand, apart from everything else, that there are the positive mental factors and the negative mental factors within us. By working with them in relation to our perceptual experiences and through our verbal and physical behavioral interactions, we transform ourselves. We naturally begin to develop virtuous qualities in ourselves.

In Buddhism, when virtues are spoken about, it has more of a similarity to the Greek notion of virtue than to the monotheistic concept of virtue because virtue is something that one cultivates within oneself. In almost all of the theistic religious traditions as I understand them, virtue is traced back to God. In Buddhism, it is traced back to human nature. In Greek philosophy and Buddhism, the source of virtue is within human beings rather than gods. There is also a notion in Buddhism that a moral person is not necessarily a virtuous one but a moral person can become a virtuous individual because one can become transformed over a period of time. Happiness is something that we can cultivate over a period of time as well through living a moral life. We should not become frightened by the word "morality." Being moralistic, judgmental, and critical is not being moral in the Buddhist sense. In Buddhism, it is important to acknowledge our shortcomings and to maintain a sense of flexibility and appropriateness in relation to our mental, verbal, and physical conduct. According to Buddhism, it is vital to treat other human beings properly in terms of the Buddhist notion of ethics.

Chapter Twenty-eight

Happiness, Appreciation, and Intentionality

Buddhism has something to offer people living in the twenty-first century. We live in a postmodern world and have to deal with our world as it presents itself. Particularly in the developed world, every day, we face conflicting claims of truth. It is very difficult to know and choose what to believe. That which Buddhism speaks about can be seen as one of these claimants to truth. If we believe in what Buddhism says about happiness and a meaningful and good life and it makes sense to us, this does not mean that we need to believe that everybody else is wrong. Furthermore, it does not mean that we should not have any confidence in believing that a good life is the form of life we should have. There is no contradiction in thinking that many different people can claim to have the truth.

As Buddhists, we attempt to live a life that is helpful to others, helpful to ourselves, and maintains respect for other traditions and ways of thinking. We do not believe that we should convert or try to convince everyone to become a Buddhist. Buddhism has always adopted the notion that being tolerant of other people's views and ways of thinking is important, even from a political point of view. In Buddhism, there is the notion that some relationships exist between the personal life and the public life. If we are in power, in a governing position, or an ordinary person, we should tolerate different human beings and their belief systems. In other words, we should not attempt to silence people for voicing different opinions.

This is because even on an individual level, from the moral point of view, to have a good life, doing that which brings about harmony amongst different groups and creates a sense of community is what brings happiness on a temporary level. In Buddhism, what is private and what is public are seen as separate in many respects. On the other hand, there is interrelationship in terms of civil societies and the state and what the state does. How we operate as an individual, as a citizen, should be in concordance with the kind of society that we want. In other words, it comes back to the individual, their own responsibility. It is not only about what the state does and how the civil society is presenting.

As Buddhists, making changes in life both for oneself and others must always come from first making the changes in oneself. I am not speaking about this in temporary terms, meaning first we become like a buddha and then bring about changes. Rather, one should be thinking about oneself in terms of, "What am I like as a person? What am I doing? How am I conducting myself with others and in society? What are my roles and how am I fulfilling my responsibilities within these roles?" All of these considerations are important according to Buddhism. If we pay attention to all of these aspects, we will become happier. It is not helpful to always be thinking in terms of what other people need changing instead of what we need to change, looking at everything and always thinking, "It is all imperfect and lacking and I need to change it," but not seeing that one needs changing within oneself. We need to find enough courage to face up to ourselves and not fall into the habit of always blaming others for everything that happens to "me." Even just an attitude will hamper our progress and diminish our happiness. No matter the social condition in which we live, whatever level of civil liberties that are afforded us, we can find appreciation. Sometimes, in the best of circumstances, particularly when we look at many societies around the world, we can see that we have a great deal. We can acknowledge what we do have rather than only focusing on what we believe we do not have. We do not always have to have a hunger and craving where we always want more.

It is one thing to demand all manner of things from others but it is another to demand things from oneself. The notion that we should not demand things from ourselves, as if having to do anything difficult is too much, can result in traumatic and harmful outcomes. From a Buddhist viewpoint, this way of thinking is incorrect and will not bring happiness. Believing, "If we can just change this or change that, if we can have more of this or more of that, better social conditions, better working conditions, then I'll be happy." It is important to strive for the betterment of oneself and one's circumstances. From a Buddhist perspective, there is a positive and moral way to deal with a desire for things to improve.

A Buddhist way of living does not exclude having a successful business, a well paid job, having certain desires and fulfilling many pleasures, and leading a moral life. This moral life does not deprive us of pleasure or signify that we need not have varieties of desires, such as terminal, instrumental, hedonistic, and non-hedonistic desires. We can combine all of these desires in life and have pursuits that are pleasurable and good, and avoid those that are not so good, even though we find some of them pleasurable. Many of the pleasures that we find immediately pleasurable are not so very good for us in the long run. In moderation, they are less harmful. It is important to make this form of judgment about what to pursue and what not to pursue. Even pleasures that human beings find very pleasurable on the physical level such as sensual pleasure, in moderation, are not to be avoided simply because an individual is a Buddhist. In other words, we do not need to believe that we should not eat good food and enjoy it. As a Buddhist, it is never said we should not enjoy life in general. In Buddhism, moderation refers to reducing our tendencies to become obsessed over certain pleasures such as food, wealth, sex, alcohol, and so on. Of course, these things can bring pleasure but we can learn to exercise some form of control and continence in order to enhance our experience. We need to be realistic and our expectations grounded. Some desires we are working for are going to take time and we may not be able to satisfy them immediately. We do not need to frustrate ourselves. We can learn to postpone our desire for satisfaction.

However, obsession is a part of the samsaric mindset. Some people will be more obsessed than others. According to Buddhism, the samsaric mind becomes monofocal such as obsession with food, drink, or whatever it might be. Even on that higher level of abstraction in terms of our desires, our mind latches on and becomes obsessed and monofocal; "I need this or I won't be happy," when all that one can think of is having it, the mansion or new car. From the Buddhist point of view, when obsession takes over, we can learn to dislike our obsession or obsessiveness. We can think about things that we desire in other ways and still gain pleasure. We can still get pleasure from eating, having a nice home, a supportive family, bringing up our children properly and caring for them, and gaining pleasure from our friendships with others and feeling satisfied. We can appreciate wonderful times with family and loved ones keeping in mind that all experiences are fleeting and impermanent and should be appreciated and understood as precious.

We should know that there is another kind of happiness to be pursued. Buddhism believes that we can learn to enjoy sensory pleasures, lead a moral life, cultivate wisdom, and liberate ourselves to attain total happiness. When we have learned to modify and moderate our sensory pleasures and when we are courageously and openly observing and understanding how our pain and pleasure responses arise and affect us, we can build a better relationship with ourselves, others, and the world. From a Buddhist point of view, looking at happiness in this fashion allows us to have a positive attitude toward our own lives and see that we can learn to liberate ourselves from our own shackles. In the end, nobody is imprisoning us. No one has put us in shackles. It is our own resentment, anger, and non-forgivingness of ourselves and others that have put us in the samsaric prison in which we live. Ultimately, if we can free ourselves from our excessive obsessions and judgments, we can have a greater sense of freedom and have true happiness. True and total happiness is something that we aim toward. It is the distant goal. In the immediacy, what we aim for is to experience more temporary happiness. Every day, we should attempt to have some experience of temporary happiness, which comes from learning how to balance the different desires and the different pleasures that we experience, developing the wisdom to do that. According to Buddhism, such awareness can be built through the practice of meditation.

When we do meditation, we may be seeking to go deeper into ourselves and find a transcendental aspect to our own being. This is important. However, in order to increase our happiness, we need to see how our senses and the thought processes and emotions that ensue impact us and how we experience ourselves in the world. What kind of world do we create in response to our own sensory input? How we see ourselves can be largely based on our senses and the thought processes fuelling and cementing our assumptions, seeing that we ordinarily support the notion of our own sense of self and it is experienced as solid, definite, and in a concrete form. We see the "self" as if standing apart from and separate to all the things that we are experiencing, as if to say, "I am different from my experiences. I am the experiencer—the experiencer and the experiences are separate. They stand apart." We ordinarily believe that the agency is separate from the experiences, that all of the objects of the experiences in particular are far removed, that they stand at a distance to the subject, to the experiencer. Therefore, there is a tremendous misunderstanding that develops from this. This misunderstanding leads to an experience of pain, which then leads to the experience of suffering and unhappiness.

Meditation allows us to become closer to our own experiences, at the juncture of the sensory experiences, the senses, the object of senses, and the thoughts and emotions that arise as a response. In order to understand all of this, we need meditation. As far as Buddhism is concerned, in order to become a truly moral or ethical person, we need to acquire insight into the relationship that we have with ourselves and how we interpret our experiences. A Buddhist can be a meditator and an activist. Whatever we may be passionate about—ending child labor, environmental issues, and the many other important issues to be concerned about—we can better serve these causes if we understand our true motives and intentions and truly take responsibility for who and what we are. Meditation and activism are not mutually exclusive.

We should never lose sight of the long-term ultimate goal of total transformation and this comes from wisdom, gained through meditation. Shamatha or tranquility meditation, calming our mind, is a very important practice but alone, it is not sufficient to build a true understanding of the human condition. To build wisdom, we also need to practice meditation of reflection, analytical or vipashyana meditation. In vipashyana meditation, we use our critical mind in a particular way.

From the Buddhist point of view, we need to rest our mind in tranquility and then once the mind is focused and relaxed, we analyze our mind and the nature of reality—a combination of these two meditative practices, the meditative practice of shamatha to focus and relax the mind and analysis to determine what is real, what is not real, what is true, and what is not true. These might not deliver us the absolute answer because in Buddhism, this is neither expected nor desired, but we can gain a semblance of how things are, how things exist when free of embellishment. Buddhism acknowledges that the true reality has no form so it cannot be formulated in words.

Vipashyana is different from reading critical theory, such as reviewing literature, culture, religion, and state politics and attempting to find something wrong in every theory. If we use our critical mind appropriately in meditation, we are aiming for a different result. In part, we are testing a theory. In order to do this, we should look into our experiences and responses slowly, look at things thoroughly, and try to absorb our insights. We are often taught not to absorb anything but to remain objective and analyze but in vipashyana, we want to review how we experience and seek to see what is real, what is not real, review permanence and impermanence, and so on.

We may find that things that we believe are true are not true and things that we think are not true are true. The Buddhist notion that there is no unchanging permanent self is a case in point. Buddhism says that there is no permanent self in an absolute fashion. In Buddhism, it is said that much of our experience is relative to something else; either to our own experience or to something else in terms of causality, time, and spatial location. Therefore, our experience is interdependent and so not absolutely true, definitive, or solid. However, there are truths and from a spiritual perspective, this is what we need to find. If we come to understand causality, insubstantiality, and interdependence, life will take on a different perspective. It can be transformative and through proper understanding, we can live our life better and as a result, experience more happiness.

Through understanding, through the use of wisdom in this way, we can understand the desires and different types of pleasures. We will become better as human beings and go through the paths and stages of individual development. In Buddhism, this notion of "paths and stages" on the Buddhist path is not about metaphysics, although metaphysics has a place in it in terms of its description. "Paths and stages" serves a practical purpose and this is the most important point. We go through stages of life, whether we like it or not, so why not also travel similarly on the spiritual path? Spiritually, we are hopefully going through the process of progressing in normal life from the time of birth to the time of death. If we are serious about our spiritual practice, we must progress. In this way, the same thing occurs with our meditation practice as with our life. If our ordinary life becomes more and more enriched and we become increasingly mature, this should also be the case in our spiritual journey.

Buddha compared us to ordinary children playing on a beach. This is a recurring metaphor that is used in Buddhist sutras. We mature and then we become elevated beings, beings that still feel some pain, discomfort, and unhappiness but the feeling of happiness or satisfaction is more predominant or obvious. This is what one is attempting to attain. With the notion of the self and the many different factors and aspects, the positive and the negative aspect, the positive factors, negative factors, and so on, how these things work together, according to Buddhism, is how we mature. This is because we learn to completely jettison some of these things. We are instructed to think of ourselves as being in a boat and we throw all of the things that we do not need overboard. All of the things that we do need, we take them on board. As we are travelling and go along, we begin to gain more of the riches that we are seeking. We unload the boat of all the unnecessary junk that we carry. This is a metaphor used because in India, the metaphor of a boat was taken seriously. It was an experience that was very common to people. They went out to the sea in search of great treasures. As they found more and more treasures, they had to get rid of things on the boat that were less essential so that the boat would not sink and would be able to carry the new treasures. Similarly, we have to do the same thing. Certain undesirable, harmful, and unethical traits, in many ways, may have sustained us but are no longer useful. So we acquire new qualities, new understandings. In that way, the undesirable qualities become benign or even disappear as the desirable qualities rise. Over time, we can become totally transformed and liberated. We can become fully liberated through the effective practice of meditation and through leading an ethical life.

Happiness, as Buddhists understand it, is not simple. It does not mean that one must totally deny oneself pleasure. It does not necessarily mean that one has to overcome desire completely. It has more to do with what we desire and how we desire these things. Through the practice of meditation, we will be able to better distinguish the differences. Apart from what Buddhism itself says, through our own experience, by paying attention and being mindful, we will see which aspects and attitudes let us down and which do not let us down. We should learn from this discernment and awareness. We should not let our habitual tendencies stop us from progressing and recognizing how things within us are manifesting and happening. We need to use our initiative and vigorous persistence to progress our understanding of how the mind's many factors work and behave. If we are lazy and do not seek to truly improve and progress our understanding, our samsaric condition will not go away. It may worsen. If we pay attention, we will see that a lot of the time, what we are doing is applying a temporary patch to the problem without mustering the courage or the drive to persist in understanding how we can improve our own condition.

If we have the patience to attempt to understand what Buddhism says about happiness, we can gain more happiness in the immediate sense and this is accumulative and progressive toward the ultimate and distant goal of enlightenment. We might be thinking that everything that we have is the worst, most despicable and atrocious. No matter what we think we are or what we have, we may always believe that we are not good enough. Instead, we could see things differently and recognize that there is so much that is good and still believe that things can improve. One can decide to work toward that, seeking betterment for oneself and the benefit of everybody in society. Similarly, with regard to personal pleasures, we can enjoy them and refresh our minds. With a fresh view, we can learn not to take anything within ourselves and in life for granted. We can reflect on and consider all the fortunate circumstances that surround us and appreciate all that we have.

Notes

1. Ground of Being is also referred to as *self-existing wisdom* and *mind in itself*. The ground of being refers to the way in which things actually exist or the reality of things. Everything that exists is dependent on something else, which is emptiness, emptiness in the objective sense and the original state of the mind in the subjective sense. The primordial authentic original state is non-fabricated and has been pure from the beginning. One does not need to search for this by putting body, speech, and mind to use. One does not need to create a special state of mind.

2. In classical political economy, "use value" also known as "value in use" refers to the features of an object that can satisfy a human requirement or desire or has a purpose that is useful.

3. Shantideva (695-743) was an Indian Buddhist scholar at Nalanda University and an adherent of the Madhyamaka philosophy. He is renowned for his Bodhicharyavatara, a text about the Mahayana Buddhist path to enlightenment.

4. A buddha is a being who has eliminated emotional and cognitive obscurations and achieved full enlightenment. A bodhisattva literally means "awakening being." One can be an *ideal bodhisattva* such as a deity, for example Chenrezig, or a person who has reached buddhahood through following the path of the bodhisattva. Then there is the *aspiring bodhisattva*, a being who has committed themselves to the path of compassion and the practice of the six paramitas or six perfections while dedicating their actions to the welfare of all beings. Kyabgon, Traleg. *The Essence of Buddhism*, Shambhala Publications, 2001.

5. Lojong literally means "training the mind." An important part of Lojong practice is a series of slogans used for contemplation designed to redirect how we normally think, moving away from an egocentric perspective and toward generating bodhicitta or enlightened heart for all sentient beings. The Lojong teachings were developed from the principal Kadampa master Atisha Dipamkara Shrijnana (982- 1054). Kyabgon, Traleg. *The Practice of Lojong*, Shambhala Publications, 2007.

6. Mahayana Buddhism is often described as a later form of Buddhism. The Mahayana perspective is not determined by doctrine, school, or belief but by the internal attitude of the practitioner. The Mahayanist's attitude does not only seek enlightenment for oneself but for all sentient beings. Kyabgon, Traleg. *The Essence of Buddhism*, Shambhala Publications, 2001,

7. Shamatha meditation, also known as tranquility meditation, is a fundamental meditation practice common to most schools of Buddhism, the aim of which is to tame and stabilize the mind in order to practice vipashyana or insight meditation.

8. Vipashyana meditation is also known as insight meditation or analytical meditation. The main goal of vipashyana meditation is the cultivation of wisdom through analysis. Analysis is performed to discover how things exist in reality. Through practicing vipashyana meditation, one is seeking to gain insight into how the mind substantializes everything through distorted thinking and imputing fictitious characteristics and attributes to things.

9. Longchen Rabjampa, Drimé Özer (1308–1364), known more widely as Longchenpa, the shortened version of his name, was one of most revered scholars in the Nyingma school of Tibetan Buddhism elucidating teachings on Dzogchen. Longchenpa

authored the famous, *Seven Treasuries*.

10. Jean-Paul Charles Aymard Sartre (1905—1980) was a major French philosopher, literary critic, political activist, and novelist. He was one of the major thinkers in the areas of existentialism and phenomenology.

11. Patrul Rinpoche (1808–1887) spent much of his life as a wandering yogi. He wrote many profound treatises and works of poetry. His most famous work is known as *The Words of My Perfect Teacher*, a text on the preliminary practices of the Nyingma tradition. He became one of the most revered teachers from the Nyingma school of Tibetan Buddhism.

12. Intersubjectivity has varying definitions in anthropology, religion, psychology, philosophy, and sociology. The sociologist, Thomas Scheff defines it as "the sharing of subjective states by two or more individuals." Olen Gunnlaugson, Heesoon Bai, Edward W. Sarath, Charles Scott (Eds.), *Catalyzing the Field: Second-Person Approaches to Contemplative Learning and Inquiry*. State University of New York Press, 2019. In the context of this book, intersubjectivity is referring to a personally formulated view of oneself, one's ego or identity that one relates to as being permanent or fixed, to have its own reality, and one's perceptional commitment to the idea that their view of their fixed identity—who one believes oneself to be—is a view or perception that is shared by others.

13. It is believed that some of our desires can serve to motivate and uplift us and other forms of desire can become insatiable and diminish us if not managed well, transformed, or overcome. The management of desire is seen as crucial on the Buddhist journey to aid progress on the spiritual path. For a comprehensive presentation of desire, see Kyabgon, Traleg. *Desire: Why It Matters*, Shogam Publications, 2019.

14. Lojong practices are meditation practices and contemplations designed to train the mind to be compassionate under all circumstances to others and to oneself, no matter what internal or external circumstances or upheavals are present. In this traditional mind training, one contemplates a series of slogans to train the mind toward compassion. We often do not appreciate something or someone until they are gone. The development of true compassion also leads to a natural arising of a more panoramic and inclusive sense of appreciation. Note 5 also provides a brief description of Lojong. For a comprehensive presentation of Lojong or mind training teachings, see Kyabgon, Traleg. *The Practice of Lojong*, Shambhala Publications, 2007.

15. Tantric or Vajrayana practices are also known as esoteric in Buddhism. There are many approaches and methods used in Buddhist practices to help us progress on the spiritual path to reach our greater potentials. Esoteric practices are interpretative and contain different levels of meaning contained within ritualized practices. Such associations of activity and meaning are designed to help us transform negative states into positive states of being. For a full explanation of esoteric Buddhism, see Kyabgon, Traleg. Vajrayana: An Essential Guide to Practice, Shogam Publications, 2020.

16. For a full explanation of this approach, see the books by Kyabgon, Traleg. *Moonbeams of Mahamudra: the Classic Meditation Manual*; *Song of Karmapa: The Aspiration of the Mahamudra of True Meaning by Lord Rangjung Dorje*; *King Doha: Saraha's Advice to a King*; and *Actuality of Being: Dzogchen and Tantric Perspectives.*

17. Parachin, Victor, M. *Healing Grief*, Chalice Press, 2001.

18. De Mello, Anthony. *Heart of the Enlightened: A Book of Story Meditations*, Crown Publishing Group, 2012.
19. De Mello, Anthony. *Taking Flight: A Book of Story Meditations*, Crown Publishing Group, 2012.
20. Winston Churchill referred to his depression as his "black dog."
21. The Four Noble Truths in brief are: 1. "the truth of suffering," the pervasive nature of suffering stems from a belief in an unchanging permanent self and phenomena; 2. "the truth of the origin or cause of suffering," the main suffering that afflicts us originates from within ourselves and is caused by some type of craving or obsession often referred to as *grasping* and *fixation* being the primary cause of our dissatisfaction and discontent; 3. "the truth or the goal is the cessation of suffering," we can reach nirvana by overcoming the pendulous reactions that we create through our response to external circumstances and internal stimuli, the three root delusions—attraction, aversion, and ignorance or bewilderment, often referred to as the 3 poisons; 4. "the truth of path is the way out of suffering," known as the "Eight Fold Noble Path" this is a prescribed approach to end suffering oriented toward developing within the individual, moral or ethical sensitivity to develop great compassion and empathy, meditation or a concentrated mind to develop a focused and resilient mind, and wisdom into the nature of phenomena and the human and more broadly the sentient condition.

Index

www.ingramcontent.com/pod-product-compliance
Lightning Source LLC
LaVergne TN
LVHW020526100826
845148LV00010B/1359

9780648686347